CHINESE BUDDHISM:
Aspects of Interaction and Reinterpretation

W. Pachow

University Press of America™

Copyright © 1980 by

W. Pachow

University Press of America, Inc.
4720 Boston Way, Lanham, MD 20801

ISBN: 0-8191-1090-6 (Case)

0-8191-1091-4 (Perfect)

Library of Congress Catalog Card Number: 80-5432

May peace, compassion, and righteousness

prevail among mankind

Grateful acknowledgment is made to the following
for permission to reprint copyrighted material:

INDIAN HISTORICAL QUARTERLY for the essay "Zen
  Buddhism and Bodhidharma," originally published
  in Indian Historical Quarterly (June & September
  1956), used here by permission; reprinted in
  the Encyclopaedia of Buddhism (Sri Lanka, 1972).

CEYLON DAILY NEWS VESAK ANNUAL for the essay
  "The Spirit of Zen Buddhism," originally
  published in Ceylon Daily News Vesak Annual
  (1958), used here by permission.

AMERICAN ORIENTAL SOCIETY for the essay "A Study
  of the Dotted Record," originally published in
  the Journal of the American Oriental Society,
  85/3 (September 1965), used here by permission.

JOURNAL OF THE GANGANATHA JHA RESEARCH INSTITUTE
  for the essay "Buddhism and Its Relations
  to Chinese Religions," originally published
  in the Journal of the Ganganatha Jha Research
  Institute (January-April 1972), used here
  by permission.

THE CENTRE OF ASIAN STUDIES and THE HONG KONG
  UNIVERSITY PRESS for the essay "The Controversy
  Over the Immortality of the Soul in Chinese
  Buddhism," originally published in the Journal
  of Oriental Studies (September 1979), used
  here by permission.

TABLE OF CONTENTS

FOREWORD

It is a great pleasure for me to accede
to the request of my old friend, W. Pachow, for
an introduction to his book of collected essays.
I first met him more than twenty years ago when
I was chairman of a Ceylonese Government Commission
on the development of the University at Peradeniya
and Colombo. He was then Professor of Chinese
and Mahāyāna Buddhist thought at the former campus.
Although I had many great friends in Sri Lanka,
it was a particular pleasure to meet a Chinese
there, someone from my own "adopted country," as
it were.

Now, in later years, as an ornament of learning
at the University of Iowa, my friend is publishing
a dozen or so of his writings. Ever since I
first got to know Chinese culture, I have myself
been more sympathetic to Taoism than Buddhism but
that does not prevent me in the least from admiring
Pachow's learning. Naturally, therefore, I had
particular interest in reading what he had to
say about the Lao Tzu Hua Hu Ching, that fascinating
but fictitious text which commemorates the great
struggles between Taoists and Buddhists. The
title means "The Conversion of Barbarians by
Lao Tzu," and it was intended to show that Buddhism
was only an emanation of Taoism and that Lao Tzu
had travelled abroad to operate the conversions
which founded the opposition religion. The whole
story is now little more than a joke, but at one
time it was no doubt taken very seriously.

Another interesting paper is that on the
controversy over the immortality of the soul in
mediaeval Chinese Buddhism. The anattā doctrine
in Indian thought was rather subtle, suggesting
that one candle-flame was handed on to light
another candle, at the same time transmitting
the load of karma which had been accumulated in
the previous existence. When the Buddhists
came into China, however, they found a very definite

doctrine of "souls" (the three hun and the seven
p'o) like beads strung on the thread of the body
itself. This doctrine was certainly important
in physiological alchemy (nei tan) and may have
had some connection with the profoundly rooted
idea of filial piety (hsiao) in Chinese thought.
In any case the +6th-century debates are of
abiding interest and Pachow gives us an interesting
introduction to them.

One of the most detailed studies is that
on the Chung Sheng Tien Chi (Dotted Record of
Many Sages), now lost, but dating from +486
or more probably +492, in translation from the
Pali. The idea was to add one dot for each year
since the death of the Buddha, so in this way,
by the knowledge we still have of it, it fixes
the death of Gautama Śākyamuni at -483.

One can also benefit by reading Pachow's
paper on "The Spirit of Zen Buddhism." I always
greatly enjoy the story in the novel Hsi Yu Chi
(Journey to the West) when all the sūtras that
Hsüan-tsang was bringing home got wet as his
party was fording a river. When they laid them
out to dry in the sun, they discovered that there
was nothing written on them at all, so they
decided that they had failed to tip the inferior
bodhisattvas enough, and they must therefore
return to Taxila or wherever it was and get the
proper sūtras. When they got there and told
their story, the bodhisattva on duty said, "Well,
as a matter of fact these are the real scriptures;
but if you want scrolls with texts written on
them you can of course have them." So they got
their load of sūtras and laboriously returned
with them to China. I always feel that this
story represents the spirit of Chan (Zen)
Buddhism, i.e., "as I should say," Buddhism
modified by Taoist mysticism. It always reminds
me of that French eighteenth-century story,
emanating from Voltaire, no doubt, of some man
who deposited in the form of a pli cacheté a
sealed book with the Perpetual Secretary of the
Academy, saying that it contained the entire

secret of Nature, but was not to be opened before a certain date. When eventually the Academicians got around to breaking the seal and opening it, they found that the pages were all completely blank. "Ah," said the Secretaire-Perpetual, "this is just what I expected."

I wish all success to Pachow's book, which I may say does not consist entirely of blank pages.

Joseph Needham

Director, East Asian History of Science Library, Cambridge University

The present collection of eleven articles
dealing with various aspects of Chinese Buddhism
were published in different journals. Their appearance covers a period of over thirty years,
and the geographical location of their publication
extends from China, India, and Ceylon to America.
Judging by the tremendous dimensions of Buddhism
in China, the area that has attracted our attention
is merely a drop in the ocean. However, since
the Himalaya mountains consist of specks of dust,
there would be no mountain at all if the insignificant dust particles were removed from the
total composition. It is our sincere wish that
this book may eventually lead to future worthwhile
contributions concerning this subject. "With
bricks one may trade for jade," as a Chinese
proverb suggests. It is hoped that such a dream
may materialize.

According to the nature of topics the articles
may be roughly divided into four classifications:

I.   Chinese Ch'an (Zen) Buddhism

II.   Chinese sources concerning the Buddha

III.   Development of Chinese Buddhism

IV.   International relations and Chinese
     Buddhism

Based on the above-noted considerations we have
the following arrangement:

Group I

1.   Zen Buddhism and Bodhidharma
2.   The Spirit of Zen Buddhism
3.   A Buddhist Discourse on Meditation

Group II

1. Lao Tzu and Gautama Buddha
2. A Study of the <u>Dotted</u> <u>Record</u>

Group III

1. Buddhism and Its Relation to
   Chinese Religions
2. The Development of <u>Tripiṭaka</u>-Translations
   in China
3. The Controversy Over the Immortality
   of the Soul in Chinese Buddhism
4. The Philosophical and Religious
   Elements in the <u>Red</u> <u>Chamber</u> <u>Dream</u>

Group IV

1. Ancient Cultural Relations Between
   Ceylon and China
2. The Voyage of Buddhist Missions to
   Southeast Asia and the Far East

The emphasis in two of the articles seems to be on the subject itself, such as the "Buddhist mission" and "Dream of the Red Chamber," but the essence of "interaction" is evident. Thus it provides us with interesting information concerning the cultural and social context of Chinese Buddhism.

Many of the articles are self-explanatory, that is to say, they are concerned either with "interaction" or "reinterpretation." We would like to point out the significance of two from the collection by way of illustration, viz., the "<u>Dotted Record</u>" and "The Controversy Over the Immortality of the Soul."

The former confirms the Pali tradition concerning the date of the Buddha and supports W. Geiger's research that the Buddha passed away in 483 B.C. This document also arouses our curiosity as to its original sources and the way in which it reached China. The latter demonstrates that certain Buddhist doctrines were misunderstood and misinterpreted. This suggests that the active forces of traditional beliefs overwhelmingly influenced the Chinese mind when it trod on unfamiliar philosophical grounds. It is in cases of this nature that we find evidence of interaction of Buddhism and Chinese culture. It indicates at the same time the intricate process of the development of Chinese Buddhism.

Originally the suggested title for this work was "Buddhology and Sino-Indian Buddhism." Owing to technical difficulties and other considerations, the articles on Indian Buddhism were withdrawn, hence our attention is focused on Chinese Buddhism. In a way this "purification" may be beneficial to everyone concerned, especially for those of us who are constantly threatened by the power of inflation and unmasked commercialism.

I take this opportunity to express my sincere thanks to Professor Joseph Needham of Cambridge University, for writing a foreword to the book, despite his extremely tight schedule of advanced research on Chinese civilization; to Professor James C. Spalding, former director of the School of Religion, to Professor John P. Boyle, present director, and to the faculty and staff for providing the necessary facilities; to Ms. Mary Lou Doyle for editing and producing the camera-ready copy; to Dale Wright, Arthur Emerson, and Scott Lowe for editorial assistance; to Dr. George Williams, editor-in-chief of New Horizons Press, for valuable suggestions; and to all my friends who rendered valuable advice when the articles were in the process of being completed at different locations and at different times.

Finally, I wish to express my unreserved gratitude and appreciation to Mavis for her constant encouragement and inspiration.

W. Pachow   Iowa City, January 1980

ZEN BUDDHISM AND BODHIDHARMA

In the Far East, there is no Buddhist influence so profound and penetrating as that of the
Ch'an (Dhyāna) school, popularly known as Zen
Buddhism. It has effected a change in the cultural life of the people as well as in their general
outlook regarding the method of attaining enlightenment. Not merely that; from the beginning of
the tenth century A.C., this school has gained
supremacy over all other schools in China, so
much so that the monks in the monasteries throughout the country claimed in one way or the other
to belong to the patriarchal lineage of celebrated
dhyāna masters. This phenomenon may be ascribed
to the fact that the Dhyāna school has been the
life and soul of Buddhism for over a thousand
years in China. As a result of its important
position, voluminous works have been produced by
various writers. Some of them are compositions
containing the sayings of dhyāna masters, mystical
and paradoxical in nature, and others are historical records concerning the patriarchal
genealogy, especially that of the various branches
of the disciples of Hui-nêng (1A), the sixth
Patriarch. However, all of them unanimously claim
that Bodhidharma, the sage from India, was the
twenty-eighth Patriarch of the Indian tradition
and the first Patriarch of the Chinese Dhyāna
school.

In the early Chinese Buddhist records there
is a great paucity of information concerning the
life of Bodhidharma. He was popularly known as
Ta-mo (2A) in China and Daruma in Japan. Tao-
hsüan, author of the Second Series of Buddhist
Biographies, states very briefly that Bodhidharma
belonged to a brahman family in south India,[1]
while Yang Hsüan-chih, author of Lo-yang chia-
lan chi (3A) (Record of the Buddhist Monasteries

in Lo-Yang; Taishō, No. 2092) says that he came
from Persia and was of an insignificant family.[2]
(This record was completed in 547 A.C.). However, the later Buddhist records of the eleventh
century A.C., such as,

   (1) Ch'i-sung: Ch'uan-fa chêng-tsung lun
       (A Treatise on the Right School of
       Transmitting the Law, Nanjio,
       No. 1528; Taishō, No. 2080);

   (2) Ch'i-sung: Ch'uan-fa chêng-tsung chi
       (Records of the Right School of Trans-
       mitting the Law, Nanjio, No. 1529;
       Taishō, No. 2078);

   (3) Tao-yüan: Ching-teh ch'uan-têng lu
       (Records of the Transmission of the
       Lamp up to the Ching-teh period--
       1004-7 A.C., Nanjio, No. 1524; Taishō,
       No. 2076),

unanimously claimed that he belonged to a kṣatriya
family and was the third son of the King of
Conjeevaram (Hsiang-chih) in south India. The
teacher of Bodhidharma, according to these records,
was Prajñātāra of eastern India, who commanded
him to proceed to China for the propagation of
Buddhism there. It took him three years to reach
Canton. He had an interview with Emperor Wu of
the Liang dynasty (4A), in 527 or 520 A.C.
Later, he met Hui-k'o and accepted him as his
chief disciple because the latter had cut off
his left hand and placed it before Bodhidharma
in order to show his sincere determination to
learn the sacred dharma. The official insignia
of the robe was handed over to Hui-k'o by him.
It is said that he was poisoned to death, and that
his ghost was seen by Sung-yün in the Pamirs.[3]
Also, there is a lengthy description of his life
in India, which narrates how he converted the
leaders of the six schools founded by pupils of
his classmate Buddhaśānta (Fu-ta-shêng-to) (5A).
The schools are:

(1) Yu-hsiang-tsung: The School of Form;

(2) Wu-hsiang-tsung: The School of No-form;

(3) Ting-hui-tsung: The School of Samādhi
    and Prajñā;

(4) Chiai-hsing-tsung: The School of Vinaya
    Practice;

(5) Wu-teh-tsung: The School of No-gain; and

(6) Chi-ching-tsung: The School of Silence
    (Taishō, No. 2076; Nanjio, No. 1524).

Further, he is said to have converted his
own nephew who showed hostility towards Buddhism,
but later repented of what he had done.[4]

However, the foregoing information on the
life of Bodhidharma should be regarded as pure
tradition, which was popularized in the eleventh
century A.C. by the followers of the Ch'an
school. These traditions may not stand the test
of critical inquiry.

Historically speaking, there is a simpler
picture of Bodhidharma, which may be framed in
the outline given below:

Bodhidharma was a Buddhist monk whose original home was in south India. He belonged to
a sect which observed early Buddhistic ascetic
practices. He advocated very strongly the practice of meditation and self-mortification, as is
well illustrated by some of his immediate disciples.
He appeared to have gone to China by sea. On
his way to Lo-yang (modern Honan province), the
capital of the northern Wei dynasty (386-532 A.C.),
he sojourned briefly in the territory of the Sung
dynasty (420-479 A.C.) whose capital was Nanking.
He taught Hui-k'o, his chief disciple, the
theory and practice of meditation and recommended
to him the Laṅkāvatāra Sūtra as a reference book.
He spent most of his time in two places, one the
Shao-lin ssǔ monastery in the Sung-shan mountain

3

(Honan) and the other Lo-yang, probably in the magnificent Yung-ning ssŭ monastery, because he had showered on it his profound admiration and declared that it was unsurpassed by any other in all the realms of the Buddhas. This monastery was built in 516 A.C., and destroyed by fire in 535 A.C.[5] This would indicate that about 520 A.C. Bodhidharma was still alive and at that time his age would be about sixty-five or seventy, if we accept the date of his arrival in China to be 480 A.C. He passed away in Lo-yang some time before 534 A.C. (T'ien-ping, 534-538 A.C.) (6A), because that was the time when his disciple Hui-k'o began to preach the new doctrine at Nanking.

This short sketch of Bodhidharma is naturally devoid of the colorful, fabulous tales linked with his life. We give below two of the tales as illustration:

1. When Emperor Wu of the Liang dynasty (502-549 A.C.) could not understand and appreciate the unusual answers given by him, Bodhidharma went across the Yangtse River riding on a reed. He then entered the Shao-lin monastery in Honan province and practiced deep meditation, facing the wall.[6]

2. He is said to have attained the hoary age of one hundred fifty years, and passed away after that. However, a Chinese envoy, while returning from India, saw Bodhidharma, with one shoe dangling from his monk's staff, on the Pamirs (Ts'ung-ling). When he reported this to the Emperor, his tomb was unearthed and to their surprise, they could not find anything in the coffin except a broken shoe.[7]

The stories mentioned above appear to indicate that he was credited with possessing supernatural powers, or, in the derogatory sense, that he was some sort of magician. This indeed is unfortunate. I shall endeavor to bring out the truth about this great sage. Special attention will be paid to the conditions of the Dhyāna school prior to his arrival in China and after his demise.

4

Was He the Founder of Chinese Zen Buddhism?

The answer to this question may be divided into two different categories. In one case, we may say "No," and in the other, "Yes," but partially.

It is a well-known fact that when Buddhism was introduced into China, it embraced all the three aspects of that religion, i.e., disciplinary observance, meditation and philosophy (śīla, samādhi and prajñā). As such, we find in the Chinese Tripiṭaka a large number of works on dhyāna or meditation. The earliest are probably those translated by An Shih-kao in 148-170 A.C. Take, for instance:

(1) The Sūtra spoken by the Buddha on keeping thought in the manner of great Anāpāna;[8]

(2) The Sūtra on perception in the law of practice of meditation;[9]

and the works on the same topic, translated by Chih Yao in 185 A.C. (Taishō, No. 608), by Buddhabhadra in 398-421 A.C. (Taishō, No. 618) and many other important texts, translated by Kumārajīva in 402-412 A.C. This would show clearly that the theory and practice of dhyāna had been known to the Chinese Buddhists quite early. Further, we find twenty-one dhyāna masters in Kao-sêng chuan (7A), or Biographies of Eminent Buddhist Teachers, completed in 519 A.C. by Hui-chiao, in which the name of Bodhidharma is not included,[10] while in Hsü kao-sêng chuan (8A), or the Second Series of the Biographies of Eminent Buddhist Teachers (Taishō, No. 2060, completed in 645 A.C. by Tao-hsüan), the names of 135 dhyāna experts are found, including a few of the immediate disciples of Bodhidharma.[11] These facts clearly show how popular and well known Dhyāna Buddhism was among the Buddhists at that time. They also show that to speak of Bodhidharma, who came to China about 480 A.C., as the founder of the dhyāna practices would not accord with the facts.

This, however, concerns only the early phase of the Dhyāna school in China, which had already a firm footing before the arrival of Bodhidharma and of which, therefore, he is not entitled to the honor of being the founder, as is usually supposed. We must make it clear, nevertheless, that the later-developed Ch'an school has much to do with him, though the honor seems to have been forced on him. When we say the later-developed Ch'an school we mean the particular form of Ch'an Buddhism which flourished during the T'ang and the Sung dynasties (619-905 and 962-1278 A.C. respectively), and was greatly popularized by Hui-nêng, the sixth patriarch of the Bodhidharma lineage. It was during the early part of this period that Japanese Buddhists came to China for higher studies and later took back with them the various Buddhist schools, including the Zen. (Zen is the Japanese term for "Ch'an" which, in turn, is derived from the Sanskrit word dhyāna). It is this form of Zen Buddhism that has become widely known in the West. It may be said of Bodhidharma that he was in some way associated with this school, though indirectly.

The Truth About Bodhidharma
Being the Twenty-eighth Patriarch

Several Chinese records of the biographies of the Patriarchs of the Zen school claim that Bodhidharma was the twenty-eighth Patriarch of the Indian tradition, starting from Mahākāśyapa. Ch'i-sung, author of two of these records, asserted that he was really the twenty-eighth Patriarch in India[12] and refuted the authority of Fu fa-tsang yin-yüan ching (9A) or Chuan or Sūtra on the Nidāna of transmitting the Dharmapitaka (Taishō, No. 2058), a Sanskrit text translated into Chinese in 472 A.C. by Chi-chia-yeh. This work gives us a list of the paramparā (lineage) tradition of twenty-three Indian Patriarchs, beginning with Mahākāśyapa and ending with Simha Bhiksu. In between, we have Aśvaghosa as the eleventh, Nāgārjuna the thirteenth, Vasubandhu the twentieth and so forth. In the biographical sketch of the

6

last Patriarch, Simha Bhikṣu, we are told that he
was killed by Mirakutsu (Mihirakula?), a king
belonging to the heretic faith, known for the
destruction he caused to Buddhist establishments
and the massacre of the Buddhist monks in Kaśmīr.
As a result, the line of paramparā was discontinued
after his death, because he could not, while he
was alive, find a suitable person to succeed him.[13]
On the evidence of this document, it is difficult
for us to accept the claim that Bodhidharma was
the twenty-eighth Patriarch of the Indian tradition. Moreover, as this claim was first made only
in the eleventh century A.C. by a staunch supporter of the Ch'an school in China, Ch'i-sung, it
can hardly convince us. We know that the motive
behind this claim was to enhance the prestige of
the school.

The Date of Bodhidharma's
Arrival in China

The popular tradition recorded in the literature of the Ch'an school tells us that Bodhidharma
reached Canton in 527 A.C. (or 520 A.C. in another
version) in the reign of Emperor Wu of the Liang
dynasty (502-549 A.C.). It is stated in the same
source that he met the Emperor. As this Emperor
chiefly devoted his attention to the building of
monasteries, giving alms to the monks and so
forth, he could not understand the mystical teachings of Bodhidharma, and, therefore, the latter
left him without being appreciated.[14] However,
other earlier and more reliable sources present us
with quite a different picture. The following
may be cited:

(1) Tao-hsüan (595-667 A.C.), author of
the Second Series of Buddhist Biographies, gives
us a life-sketch of Bodhidharma where he says:
"He first reached the territory of the Sung
Dynasty (420-479 A.C.) and then proceeded towards
the North. . . ."[15] This Sung dynasty came to
an end in 479 A.C. Moreover, he does not mention
anything about Bodhidharma's interview with the
Emperor of the Liang dynasty. If we accept this

7

version, we may safely place the date of his arrival somewhere between 420 and 479 A.C.

(2)   One of the chief disciples of Bodhidharma was Sêng-fu (10A), who met the Master when he was about seventeen years of age. Sêng-fu passed away in 524 A.C. at the age of sixty-one. This would put their meeting at about 480 A.C.[16]

(3)   Hui-shêng (11A), another pupil of Bodhi- dharma, learned all the meditation methods from him and observed ascetic practices strictly. He died sometime between 502-519 A.C. (T'ien-chien- nien-chung /12A7) at the age of seventy years.[17]

All the foregoing evidence leads us to the same conclusion, that is, that Bodhidharma reached China sometime around 480 A.C. If that is so, then the popular tradition about his arrival in 527 A.C. and about his meeting the Emperor of the Liang dynasty in the same year, falls to the ground.

His Teaching and Its Relation To the Later Zen Buddhism

According to general belief, the way of teaching adopted by Bodhidharma differed sub- stantially from that of all the Buddhist mis- sionaries who found their way into China. He seems to have been a bad linguist because he never translated any Sanskrit text into Chinese, nor did he compose any literary work. What was worse, judging by conventional standards, was that he preached an ultra-modern doctrine which seemed to harbor a profound hatred towards the traditional Buddhism as contained in the books. We give below an outline of the fundamental prin- ciples of Ch'an Buddhism:

A special tradition outside the Scriptures; Not to depend upon books or letters; To point direct to the heart of man; To see (one's own) nature and become Buddha.

These lines tell us of the Dhyāna school of the

developed form. The principles contained therein
seem to have been strictly observed by most of the
Zen followers in the Far East. However, to have
a glimpse of the simple teachings and practices
of early Zen, we have to go back to the sayings
and the mode of life of Bodhidharma and his immediate disciples.

In his short life-sketch (given by Tao-hsüan)
we find that he used to instruct Hui-k'o (13A), later
known as the second Patriarch, in the following
twofold doctrine: one is "reasoning" or the
basic principle, and the other "practice" (Êrh-ju-
ssŭ-hsing /14A/). As regards "reasoning" he says:

> I firmly believe that all living beings
> possess the same real nature (svabhāva).
> But in most cases it has been covered
> by the external dust of obstruction. I
> now ask them to give up falsehood and
> return to reality by gazing at the wall
> and meditating. They should not try to
> make any distinction between the self
> and others, between the saintly and the
> profane, but to stand firmly on these
> foundations and not to follow any
> other teachings. This, indeed, will
> be in accordance with the 'Tao' which
> is silent and devoid of activities.[18]

Among the "practices," there are four
in number:

(1) The attitude towards one's enemy:

> During the course of religious
> training, calamity may fall on the
> practitioner. Under such circumstances,
> he should think that in the previous
> kalpas he had been led astray and had
> many ties of attachment and hatred.
> In the present life he might have been
> freed from them, but the suffering
> should be regarded as the effect of
> deeds performed in one's former births.
> Therefore, one should willingly face

9

all the sorrows and should not harbor
any enmity toward the wrong-doer. . . .
When this occurs in one's mind, it is
in accordance with the 'Tao,' because
trying to understand what is the nature
of enmity is to enter the path of 'Tao.'[19]

(2)   To be content with one's lot:

    There is no ātman (soul) in living
beings.   Happiness and misery should be
received calmly as they come.   Even if
one is treated with honor, it is due to
his previous deeds: when their effect
is over, it would not come again.   Therefore, there is no occasion for rejoicing.
In the case of gain or loss, there should
not be any difference in the tranquillity
of the mind.   If the mind is calm and
gentle with regard to success or failure,
then, it is said to be in fitting accordance with the Dharma.[20]

(3)   The avoidance of hankering:

    The ordinary folk have for a long
time lost themselves in greed--that means
hankering.   A seeker after the Truth
should be different from them.   He ought
to rest his mind on inactivities and
let him face squarely whatever is his
lot.   Indeed, all the three worlds are
full of suffering and nobody is secure.
The sūtra says:

    "Whatever you hanker after,
    The sequel is suffering.
    There will be happiness,
    When one is devoid of greed."[21]

(4)   To be in accordance with the Dharma:

    By this is meant that the svabhāva
or real nature is inherently pure.

As Bodhidharma never wrote anything himself

10

this sums up the total output of his teachings.
In addition to this, we are told that he recommended to his disciples the study of the Laṅkāvatāra Sūtra.[22] This is the only Mahāyāna text
which had some connection with the Dhyāna school
in its early stages.

It may be mentioned here that in the early
years of this century, a large number of Chinese
manuscripts were discovered from the Thousand
Buddha Caves in Tun-huang in China. For a detailed account regarding this matter, one may
refer to my own work, Tung-huang yün-wên chi, or
An Anthology of Poetical Compositions from
Tun-huang (Taiwan, 1965). Later, these valuable
manuscripts were taken to Europe and kept in the
British Museum, London, and La Bibliothèque
Nationale, Paris. In these collections there are
several compositions ascribed to Bodhidharma.
However, after careful investigation, it was
found that they were forged and were actually
written by later Zen masters. The contents of
these texts are very contradictory, so much so
that one cannot believe they were written by the
same author. We may cite the following case as
an illustration. It is stated in one of the texts
that mind is the basic existence of all the phenomena. But at the same time another work by
the same author denies such a stand, and says
that there exists no mind. Shindai J. Sekiguchi
of Japan has listed in his Daruma daishi no kenkyū
(15A), or A Study of Bodhidharma, the following
texts from Tun-huang, and made a study of them:

(1)   Ta-mo ch'an-shih lun: The Discourses
      of Bodhidharma, the Dhyāna Master

(2)   Ta-mo ho-shang chüeh-kuan lun: The
      Venerable Bodhidharma's Discourses
      on Discarding Visualization

(3)   P'u-t'i-ta-mo wu-hsin lun: The
      Discourses of Bodhidharma on No-mind
      (Taishō, No. 2831)

11

(4)   Ta-mo ta-shih kuan-hsin lun: The
      Discourses of Bodhidharma, the Great
      Master, on Visualizing the Mind (Taishō,
      No. 2833)

(5). Chêng-hsin lun: A Discourse on the
      Realization of Mind

(6)   Ta-mo ch'an-shih kuan-mên: The Ways
      of Visualization of Bodhidharma, the
      Dhyāna Master (Taishō, No. 2832)

(7)   Ta-mo ta-shih ssǔ-hsing lun: A
      Discourse on the Four Practices by
      Bodhidharma, the Great Master.[23]

In addition, he also included three minor texts
from other sources, among which one was taken from
the Taoist Canon (Tao-tsang). It is interesting
to note the conclusion that was arrived at by
Sekiguchi. He is of the opinion that except for
Ta-mo-ch'an-shih-lun, the rest, as mentioned in
the list, are "not genuine," or were forged by
others.[24] I would, however, like to point out
that Bodhidharma cannot be the author of Ta-mo-
ch'an-shih-lun. This conviction is based on the
observation that this text has quoted more than
seven Mahāyāna and two Hīnayāna texts from the
Chinese translations, and one work from the Confucian classics. Given below are the original
titles:

(1)   Vimalakīrtinirdeśa Sūtra (Taishō,
      Nos. 474, 475)

(2)   Śrīmālā(devī)simhanāda Sūtra (Taishō,
      No. 353)

(3)   Vajracchedikāprajñāpāramitā Sūtra
      (Taishō, No. 235)

(4)   Mahāvaipulyatathāgatagarbha Sūtra
      (Taishō, No. 666)

(5)   Saddharmapuṇḍarīka Sūtra (Taishō,
      No. 262)

(6)   Mahāprajñāpāramitā Upadeśa (Taishō, No. 1509)

(7)   Mahāparinirvāṇa Sūtra (Taishō, Nos. 374, 375)

(8)   Laṅkāvatāra Sūtra (Taishō, Nos. 670, 671, 672)

(9)   Dharmapada (Taishō, Nos. 210, 211)

(10) Prātimokṣa Sūtra or Vinaya (Taishō, No. 1426)

(11) Lun-yü (Confucian Analects)

According to the biographical sketch written by Tao-hsüan, we understand that the Laṅkāvatāra Sūtra was the only text recommended by Bodhidharma, and that he did not show any interest in other books.[25] This was possibly due to the fact that his ability to read Chinese was very poor. That being the case, it is possible that he, all of a sudden, became a great writer and expert, not only on the Chinese Tripiṭaka, but also on Confucian classics? Further, the same manuscripts says "Chi-tz'ü-shên-hsin, ming-wei-ching-t'u(16A). This very body and mind are called the Pure Land."[26] The idea of "Pure Land is within oneself," was, for the first time, introduced by Hui-nêng the sixth Patriarch in the well-known work called Liu-tsu ta-shih fa-pao-t'an-ching, Sūtra spoken by the Sixth Patriarch on the High Seat of Dharma-ratna (Taishō, No. 2008, ch. 3).[27] It is likely that the text in question was influenced by the teaching of Hui-nêng. As Hui-nêng passed away in 713 A.C., the date for the composition of Ta-mo ch'an-shih lun cannot be placed earlier than the eighth century A.C. In other words, the authorship of this manuscript cannot be ascribed to Bodhidharma.

Judging by the rather curt outlines of his teaching and the ascetic way of life of his immediate disciples, it would appear that, theoretically, Bodhidharma had more or less based

his philosophy on the interpretation of Buddha-
nature in sentient beings as found in the Nirvana
Sutra. Therefore, he regarded the saintly and the
profane as being on the same level, because in-
trinsically there would not be any difference between them. However, there is not the slightest
hint of the theory of "Sudden Enlightenment" here,
though it is very prominent in the teachings of
the later patriarchs and their disciples. Moreover, the apparently eccentric ways of teaching,
such as giving a blow, a kick or tweak of the
nose, drawing a circle in the air, saying paradoxical things, answering questions with inco-
herence and all kinds of apparent absurdities
adopted by the Patriarchs after Hui-nêng the sixth
Patriarch (639-713 A.C.), cannot be said to have
originated with Bodhidharma, because he had nothing
to do with them. On the contrary, the emphasis
placed on austerity, self-contentment, self-
mortification, the curbing of desire, the belief
in the effect of karma, the insistence on concentration of mind by gazing at the blank wall, and
other ascetic trends appear more akin to the early
"Arhat" ideal than the Mahāyāna dhyāna practices
seen after the seventh century A.C. To substantiate our statement, we cite a few examples in order
to show what kind of austere life Bodhidharma's
disciples used to lead:

(1) Hui-k'o, his chief disciple and in
later generations known as the second Patriarch,
used to practice the teaching of Bodhidharma
very strictly. During the period of persecution
of Buddhism started by Emperor Wu-ti of the
northern Chou dynasty (Pei-chou-wu-ti, 561-578
A.C.) one of his arms was cut off by an assassin.
As he took it calmly, adhering to his master's
instructions, he did not feel any pain. To stop
the bleeding, he cauterized the wound with fire
and bandaged it with a piece of cloth. He went
on begging his alms as if nothing had happened.[28]

(2) Na Ch'an-shih (17A) or Na, the Dhyāna
master, was a disciple of Hui-k'o. Before his
renunciation he was a renowned Confucian scholar.
From the time he became a monk, he gave up

14

reading non-Buddhist literature and never touched
a pen. Regarding his personal possessions, he had
only a robe and a begging bowl. He ate only one
meal a day and observed the practice of dhūtaṅga
very strictly.[29]

(3) Hui-man (18A), a disciple of Na Ch'an-
shih and a great-grand-disciple of Bodhidharma,
devoted himself to the practice of non-attachment.
He had only a robe and ate once a day. There was
no property belonging to him except two needles.
He needed them for mending his rug in the winter,
but would discard them during the summer. Once
he was meditating on an open ground which was
covered by snow five feet deep. Someone saw him
and offered him free board and temporary lodging.
He refused that kind offer and said: "I would
accept your invitation only when no one else in
the whole world is alive!"[30]

Besides these, the lives led by his other
immediate disciples, like Sêng-fu (who died in
524 A.C.) and Hui-shêng (who died between 502-
519 A.C.), are more or less like the ones described
above. If we compare their spirit of self-mortification and quiet contemplation with the bois-
terous daring of burning a wooden image of the
Buddha (19A) (by Tan-hsia),[31] and the killing of
a cat (by Nan-ch'üan),[32] and other strange acts
performed by later dhyāna masters, supposedly
to contain the mystery of the dhyāna ideals, we
should come to the conclusion that there is hardly
any common ground between them. Thus, it would
appear to be an irony of fate that Bodhidharma
was placed as the first Patriarch of the Zen
school.

From the foregoing evidence, we are led to
believe firstly, that historically speaking,
Bodhidharma was very sober, simple-living and
comparatively less well known than most of his
contemporaries. (The story of his meeting with
the Emperor of the Liang dynasty and other fabulous tales associated with his life cannot stand
critical inquiry.) Secondly, Bodhidharma's
theories and practices concerning dhyāna differed

greatly from those of the later patriarchs and
their numerous disciples. If that is so, why was
he regarded as the first Patriarch of the Zen
school? Thirdly, the list of the six Patriarchs:

(1) Bodhidharma

(2) Hui-k'o

(3) Sêng-ts'an (20A)

(4) Tao-hsin (21A)

(5) Hung-jên (22A)

(6) Hui-nêng (or Shên-hsiu)[33]

popularly known from the beginning of the eighth
century A.C. and later on recorded in the Dhyāna
literature written by Ch'i-sung in the eleventh
century A.C. was not found in early Buddhist
historical records. Sêng-ts'an, the third
Patriarch on our list, was not known to any author
of the Buddhist Biographies. (The second series
was completed in 645 A.C. and the third series
in 988 A.C.). Tao-hsüan mentions very briefly
in his Biographies the names of Tao-hsin and Hung-
jên as teacher and pupil,[34] but he does not say
anything about their being the fourth and the
fifth Patriarchs in the Bodhidharma line.
Naturally, he could not, because he had already
recorded the life of Hui-man, the great-grand-
disciple of Bodhidharma.

NOTES

1. Tao-Hsüan, Hsü Kao-sêng Chuan (Second Series
of Biographies of Eminent Buddhist Teachers), in
Taishō Issaikyō, hereafter cited as Taisho (Taipei,
Taiwan: Chinese Buddhist Culture Institute, 1957),
vol. 50, ch. 16, p. 551.

2. Yang Hsüan-chih, Lo-yang Chia-lan chi (A
Record of Buddhist Monasteries in Lo-yang), in
Taishō, vol. 51, pp. 999ff.

16

3. Tao-yüan, Ching-teh chuan-têng lu (A Record of the Transmission of the Lamp of the Ching-teh Periods), in Taishō, ibid., pp. 217-18.

4. Ibid.

5. Yang Hsüan-chih, op.cit.

6. Tao-yüan, op.cit., p. 219.

7. Ibid., p. 220.

8. This translation can be found in Taishō, vol. 15, pp. 163-72.

9. This translation can be found in ibid., pp. 181ff.

10. Hui-chiao, Kao-sêng Chuan (Biographies of Eminent Buddhist Teachers), in Taishō, vol. 50, pp. 395-403.

11. Tao-hsüan, op.cit., p. 550.

12. Ch'i-sung, Chuan-fa chêng-tsung Chi (A Record of Transmission of the Dharma of the True School), in Taishō, vol. 51, pp. 715ff.; Ch'i-sung, Chuan-fa chêng-tsung Lun (A Treatise on the Transmission of the Dharma of the True School), in ibid., pp. 773ff.

13. Tao-yüan, op.cit., p. 219.

14. Tao-hsüan, op.cit., pp. 550-51.

15. Ibid.

16. Ibid.

17. Ibid.

18. Ibid.

19. Ibid.

20. Ibid.

21. Ibid.

22. Ibid., p. 552.

23. Shindai J. Sekiguchi, Daruma daishi no kenkyu (A Study of Bodhidharma) (Tokyo, 1957), pp. 9-11, 49-391.

24. Ibid.

25. Tao-hsüan, op.cit., p. 552.

26. Sekiguchi, op.cit.

27. Hui-nêng, Liu-tsu ta-shih fa-pao-t'an ching (Sūtra Spoken by the Sixth Patriarch on the High Seat of Dharma-ratna), Taishō, vol. 49, pp. 345-61.

28. Tao-hsüan, op.cit., p. 552.

29. Ibid.

30. Ibid.

31. T'ing Fu-po, ed., Fu-hsüeh ta-t'zǔ-tien (A Great Buddhist Encyclopedia (Shanghai: The Medical Book Co., n.d.), p. 699.

32. "Ku tsun-su yü-lu" ("The Sayings of the Ancient Venerable Sages") in Chi-tsang Chu, ed., Ta-tsang Ching (The Chinese Tripiṭaka) (Shanghai: Pin-chia Arama Publishing House, 1913), p. 70.

33. Shên-hsiu died in 706 A.C. The inscription on his tomb contains the above mentioned list. It is claimed that he was the Sixth Patriarch.

34. Tao-hsüan, op.cit., p. 606.

GLOSSARY

1A 慧能

2A 達摩

3A 洛陽伽藍記

4A 梁武帝

5A 佛大勝多

6A 天平

7A 惠皎：高僧傳

8A 道宣：續高僧傳

9A 付法藏因緣經

10A 僧副

11A 慧勝

12A 天鑒年中

13A 慧可

14A 二入四行

15A 關口真大：達摩大師之研究

16A 即此身心名為淨土

17A 那禪師

18A 慧滿

19A 丹霞焚佛，南泉斬貓

20A 僧璨

21A 道信

22A 弘忍

THE SPIRIT OF ZEN BUDDHISM[1]

The development of Buddhism in China is of great importance, though its progress is comparatively slow. It took almost 600 years and the indefatigable efforts of Chinese teachers at different times for the new religion to be thoroughly understood.

By the middle of the eighth century A.C. a large number of schools came into being. The more popular ones which may be mentioned here are: the Pure-Land, the Ch'an (or Zen), the T'ien-t'ai, the Dharmalakshna, the Three-Śāstras, and others. As they did not exist in India as separate schools, they may be termed Buddhist schools originating in China. But they have been directly or indirectly influenced by Indian Buddhist doctrines or practices.

To illustrate this point, we may examine the case of the following schools: The Pure-Land is based on the Sukhāvatī-vyūha Sūtra, the Dharmalakshna on the Yogācāra philosophy, the T'ien-t'ai and the Three Śāstras on the Mādhyamika philosophy, and the Ch'an or Zen on meditational practices. As new schools, they may have new interpretations or even new practices. This illustration may give the reader some idea as to the relationship between the original Buddhist doctrines or practices and the new schools in China.

However, among the schools, the development of Ch'an or Zen Buddhism is most outstanding. I shall endeavor to trace the various factors that brought about the achievement, and see what contributions the Zen school has made towards the cultural life in the Far East.

The Relation Between
Indian Dhyāna and Zen

There is very little connection between the Indian dhyāna and its counterpart in China after the sixth century A.C. Prior to that period we have evidence to show that right from the beginning of the second century A.C., many Sanskrit texts on Buddhist meditation were rendered into Chinese by scholars like An Shih-kao (148-170 A.C.), Chih Yao (185 A.C.), Buddha-bhadra (398-421 A.C.), Kumārajīva (402-412 A.C.), and others.[2]

Obviously this means that the practice of dhyāna has been known to the Chinese from very early times. Besides, we find that there are twenty-one dhyāna masters in the Buddhist Biographies[3] (completed in 519 A.C.) by Hui-chiao, and 135 dhyāna experts in the second series of the Buddhist Biographies[4] (completed in 645 A.C.) by Tao-hsüan.

All this would seem to indicate that the meditational practices in Indian Buddhism had been faithfully followed by the Chinese Buddhists. Probably there was hardly any difference between them. But it was altogether a different story when Bodhidharma and his followers, especially the disciples of Hui-nêng, the sixth Patriarch, appeared on the scene.

The Part Played by Bodhidharma

Bodhidharma has become a legend. We must, in the present context, mention briefly the part played by him and also the revolutionary spirit of the Chinese Buddhists in the fifth century A.C. Traditionally Bodhidharma was famed for being the first Patriarch of Zen Buddhism in China, and the twenty-eighth successor to the Indian Buddhist tradition. However, there is very little historical evidence to support this claim, except the fact that Zen followers at a later date forced on him this unsolicited honor.[5]

22

Nevertheless, Bodhidharma served as a bridge during the transitional period; that is to say, his dhyāna practices, in a way, had a faint resemblance to the early dhyāna tradition; and to a large extent, his theories inspired the imagination of future patriarchs. As Bodhidharma neither wrote anything, nor translated any Sanskrit text into Chinese, his sayings that have come down to posterity are rather scant. Fortunately Tao-hsüan preserved in the life-sketch of Bodhidharma a brief outline of his basic principles and practices. Below is a glimpse of his principles.

> I firmly believe that all living
> beings possess the same real nature
> (svabhāva). But in most cases it has
> been covered by the external dust of
> obstruction. I now ask them to give
> up falsehood and return to reality by
> gazing at the wall and meditating. They
> should not try to make any distinction
> between the self and others, between
> the saintly and the profane, but to
> stand firmly on these foundations and
> not to follow any other teachings.
> This, indeed, will be in concordance
> with the 'Tao' which is silent and
> devoid of activities.[6]

This outline of his theories lays great emphasis on the equality of the svabhāva of all sentient beings. It resembles, to a large extent, the doctrine of Buddha-nature in the Nirvāna-Sutra. His teaching of not-to-have-distinction between the self and others, and between the enlightened and the ignorant is probably a simplified version of the idea found in the Avataṁsaka Sūtra. There is a stanza in this sūtra which states that the Buddha, the sentient being, and the mind are identical.

Whatever may be the sources of his tenet, the influence of Bodhidharma was very great. A few instances will show its extensiveness.

Hsiang Chü-shih, an upāsaka and a friend of

23

Hui-k'o, the second Patriarch, used to declare that to get rid of kleśa in order to attain nirvāṇa is like finding a shadow without any substance; and to sever connections with living beings in order to attain Buddhahood is like searching for an echo without making any sound.[7] Hui-k'o approved this statement and said that there would not be any difference between wisdom and ignorance.

Hui-nêng, the sixth Patriarch of the Bodhidharma line, went a step further and said: "An ordinary man is a Buddha, and kleśa is bodhi. A foolish passing thought makes one an ordinary man, while an enlightened second thought makes one a Buddha. A passing thought that clings to sense objects is kleśa, while a second thought that frees one from attachment is Bodhi."[8]

This and many other utterances of Zen masters may be deemed to have continued the trend started by Bodhidharma, though the later patriarchs are more daring. Probably Bodhidharma would never have dreamt of the type of Zen Buddhism that took shape after his demise.

The Chinese Revolutionary Spirit and Zen

Western critics who know something of Chinese religions, but fail to grasp their inner significance and true spirit, often tend to make irrelevant remarks. The shower of stones rained by these critics is in no way justified. I am referring to an article entitled "The Problem of Chinese Buddhism."[9] Ch'an Buddhism is mentioned several times in that article. In one place, the author calls it a "Chinese religion under the cover of Indian Buddhism,"[10] and in another he says that the Ch'an Buddhists wanted to "discard most or all of Buddhist theory keeping only the practical rules, that is the commandments"[11] (emphasis mine).

A person who has studied thoroughly the

24

profundities of Zen Buddhism will testify, without
the least hesitation, that the last thing on
earth the Zen Buddhists would do is discard their
inner spiritual life and lead a life simply according to the letter of the Vinaya rules. And to
call it a "Chinese religion" in disguise, without
full explanation and literary evidence, is equally
misleading.

As regards the question of whether or not
Zen is a religion, we think that there is no
better answer than the one made many years ago
by D.T. Suzuki, a recognized authority on Zen
Buddhism. "For Zen has no God to worship, no
ceremonial rites to observe, no future abode to
which the dead are destined, and, last of all,
Zen has no soul whose welfare is to be looked
after by somebody else and whose immortality is
a matter of intense concern with some people.
Zen is free from all these dogmatic and 'religious' encumbrances."[12]

Having read this statement, if any one still
insists on calling Zen a religion or a "Chinese
religion" in disguise, we shall let him do it, if
he finds pleasure in this type of indulgence.

Further, we think it necessary to consider
the facts that contributed to the development
of Zen Buddhism in China.

In the early stages (from the first to the
fourth century A.C.) of introducing Buddhism
to China, the Chinese Buddhists, owing to their
respect for this new religion, reverentially
accepted all the Buddhist scriptures translated
from Sanskrit into Chinese, and never dared to
question the contradictory characteristics that
had existed in the Hīnayāna and Mahāyāna
doctrines.

However, as some of the texts were imperfectly rendered into Chinese, there was difficulty in arriving at the correct meaning. This
led to the dissatisfaction of the Buddhist
intelligentsia in the fourth century A.C. Some

of them wanted to get at the essentials in Buddhism and discard the comparatively unimportant trifles.

This could be well-illustrated in the case of Tao-shêng (who died in 434 A.C.). He was a disciple of Kumarajiva and Hui-yüan and possessed unusual insight in penetrating the inner meaning of Buddhist doctrines. After many years of study and research, he came to this conclusion: "The function of a symbol is to illustrate an idea, when one gets the idea, one may forget the symbol; and the purpose of a language is to explain the meaning, when one gets the meaning, the language may cease to function."[13]

He then complained that ever since the introduction of Buddhism into China, the translators had stuck to the letter, but failed to grasp the inner meaning. As for him, he would like "to forget altogether the fishing trap, once the fish was caught." That is to say, the Buddhist scriptures, rites and ceremonies and so forth should not occupy as important a place as the essentials and the true spirit of Buddhism. Surely the fish is more important than the fishing trap.

The other important pronouncements made by Tao-shêng (2A) which had a great influence over the Buddhists are: 1. Enlightenment may be attained suddenly; 2. An Icchantika possesses the potentiality of becoming a Buddha; 3. Good deeds may not get a reward; 4. The Buddha has no Sukhāvatī (or the western paradise).

However, at the beginning, the orthodox section disliked his daring utterances and found fault with him. They expelled him from the Saṅgha on the pretext that he had held heretical views. But they were fully convinced at a later date, when the complete version of the Nirvāna-Sūtra was translated into Chinese. This text clearly tells us that an Icchantika possesses Buddha-nature.[14]

The theory of "sudden enlightenment" had great appeal for the Zen Buddhists in the eighth century A.C. They accepted it as their own. Possibly their interpretation of this term is a little different from that of Tao-shêng. Nevertheless, the Zen school, undoubtedly, inherited from him this revolutionary spirit of getting-at-the-essentials. This is indicated by the sayings of the Zen masters. Moreover, we know that the sect of Hui-nêng was called the southern school of sudden enlightenment, and that of Shên-hsiu the northern school of gradual cultivation. Of course, the theory of svabhāva and Buddha-nature also influenced the Zen school to a large extent.

Other prominent teachers at that time, like Tao-an, Hui-yüan, and Sêng-chao, also made their contribution to the Buddhist revolutionary movement.[15] Some of them composed learned treatises on Buddhist philosophy; others founded new schools with the object of simplifying the complicated systems of dhyāna practices. The effort of these pioneers fired the imagination of the Zen Buddhists; and by following the footsteps of these early sages, the Zen school harvested glorious achievement.

The Spirit of Zen

Following is a brief outline which sums up the essential features of the Zen school:

A special tradition outside the scriptures;
Not to depend on books or letters;
To point direct to the heart of man;
To see /one's nature/ and become Buddha.

This has been traditionally attributed to the teachings of Bodhidharma. But if we examine carefully the type of Zen Buddhism that flourished after the eighth century A.C., we should say it better fits the Zen school in the well-developed form. Now let us analyze the special characteristics of Zen so that we may get a clear idea.

27

The usual way of spreading Buddhism in China was to spend a lot of time in rendering Buddhist Sanskrit works into Chinese: making commentaries on them, preaching them to the audience; establishing new theories and practices, and finally forming new schools on the basis of particular texts.

The Zen Buddhists would say that a tremendous amount of time and energy had been wasted in these activities. As some sūtras were imperfectly translated, they were rather difficult for people to understand; and not infrequently they had been misunderstood. If such were the case, they fell far short of fulfilling their function as originally intended.

Realizing the failure and limitations of the use of books, the Zen Buddhists decided not to depend on bookish knowledge as contained in the canonical literature. They also determined to do away with the dogma theories, logical reasoning, intellectual speculation, rituals, ceremonies, practices, and all the "isms" in Buddhism.

Having freed themselves from these fetters, they wanted to gain direct experience and realization of Bodhi, in the way the Buddha had attained his enlightenment. The technique or medium they adopted for this purpose is rather unusual. It may be a blow, a shout, a joke, a paradox, a gesture, or even a tweak of the nose.

To an outsider, this may be deemed sheer nonsense, but to them, if it comes in the right moment, it is full of meaning and probably as clear as a television picture. There and then, the seeker realizes the truth. He is enlightened! Compared to this, what purpose can the scriptures serve?

To put the direct method into effect, the Zen masters observed strictly the practice of not telling anything plainly to their disciples. The seeker must try to gain his realization by direct experience. The enlightenment may dawn upon him all of a sudden, when he least expects it.

The Zen Buddhists are generally iconoclastic to the traditional ways in Buddhism. They emphatically make it clear that everyone is endowed with Buddha-nature; everybody is a potential Buddha; both of these may be realized from within, and do not require any cultivation. Some of the more daring masters even deny the existence of the Buddha, dharma, nirvana, and bodhi.

According to them, the very idea of these high-sounding objects would be an obstruction which is like putting another head on your own head (t'ou-shang-an-t'ou /3A/--said by Lin-chi). To get rid of the conventional contradistinctions such as good and evil, or nirvāna and kleśa, Lin-chi (who died in 866 A.C.), one of the most outstanding Zen masters, advised the learner to kill the Buddha when he meets a Buddha, to kill the arhat, the patriarch, the parents and the relatives, when he meets all of them! Then the disciple will have no attachment to anything, and thereby he will gain real freedom.[16] Of course, here the word "killing" should be understood figuratively.

The other case of a Zen master (Tan-hsia)[17] making a bonfire of a wooden image of the Buddha may be viewed in the same light as stated above. According to the opinion of the Zen teachers, external and conventional practices will not contribute anything toward inner realization. Relying upon external aid is like trying to learn swimming merely from a book; he will probably find himself on the bottom of the river!

From the foregoing passages we have noticed the dominating feature in Zen Buddhism, namely, to break away from tradition; to get direct and immediate realization. Enlightenment should come from within and real experience is far superior to book-learning. All these may be said to belong to the "special tradition" which was initiated by the Buddha. Its transmission has been continued by the patriarchs through the ages.

This claim of a "special tradition" may sound weak from the historical standpoint, but history finds itself in a helpless position when it is face to face with Zen.

Many queer and strange ways, such as a blow, a shout, a push, a paradox, a counter-question, and drawing a circle in the air, have been employed by the Zen teachers as techniques for the guidance of their pupils. In most of the cases already recorded, it may not have any meaning at all, but at times it may have been of profound significance to certain individuals. We shall cite one or two instances in order to see whether we can understand the secret behind the strange acts of the Zen masters:

1. Once Lin-chi (4A) was invited to a military camp for lunch. Some of the officers of the camp gathered at the entrance to receive him. Pointing at a pillar nearby, he asked the officers whether it belonged to the class of the enlightened or the profane. The officers did not know what to reply. The Master struck the pillar with his staff and said: "Even if you could find an answer, it will not be anything else, but a wooden stump!"[18]

The meaning behind the words is obvious. It will be a lesson for the conventionalists.

2. Hsing-hua, a disciple of Lin-chi, once fell from horseback and injured his feet. He ordered a walking stick. Supporting himself with the stick, he walked along the corridor in the monastery and asked the monks whether they could recognize him. The monks acknowledged him and showed him respect. Then he said: "I am a lame dharma-master who can only talk, but cannot walk." On this point, he expected a reply from them. The monks were silent and did not know what to say. Therefore he threw away the stick and passed away then and there.[19]

If that question is put to us, we may say that it probably has something to do with the

30

"special tradition" which does not place any faith
in the human talking-machine, because it is not
the truth itself. If our guess were right, possibly that Master would not have died so soon!

There are hundreds of instances of such
nature. To us, they may appear very strange, but
to the initiated, I am sure, quite normal and
simple. In fact, Zen is very simple, though some
of the early Zen scholars tried to dress it with
mystic garb. They used to say that Zen is intuitional and beyond the comprehension of the in-
tellect. This may be partially true, if it implies
the technical aspect of Zen. The essence of Zen
may be something else which could not be described by any known medium, except direct experience. Zen is ubiquitous. Lin-chi gave us the
hint by saying: "Gentlemen, there is no place
for exertion in Buddha-dharma. And Buddha-dharma
is nothing but the daily ordinary affairs of no
importance such as to answer the call of nature,
to dress, to eat and lie down when one feels
tired. The ignorant may laugh at me, the wise
alone will understand. 'Any one who devotes
himself to external activities,' as the proverb
runs, 'is definitely a fool.'"[20]

Ma-tsu (5A), another great teacher of Zen,
in the same trend, showed us a clearer picture.
He said: "Whatever you do: you smile, wink,
sneeze or snore--all are in accordance with
Buddha-nature; and things like anger, hatred
and kleśa--also belong to the Buddha-nature. . . .
you let yourself be perfectly at ease and free.
That is called freedom. In that freedom, nothing
will be able to bind you, and you know there is
no Buddha-hood."[21]

On another occasion when the question of
"enlightenment" was put to him, he even denied
its existence by saying: "We speak of enlightenment, because there is ignorance. Originally
there is no ignorance, therefore, enlightenment
cannot be established."[22]

Just see, how simple and free! Is it not

the true spirit of Zen Buddhism?

The foregoing evidence leads us to the conclusion that Zen Buddhism is the most simple and
straightforward form of Buddhism. It can be
practiced and realized by any individual if he
cares to experience the inner awakening. It is
revolutionary, progressive and free from conventional theories and practices. Moreover, it has
been a living force in the cultural life of the
Far East for centuries, though originally it
began in the confines of the meditation halls.

NOTES

1. "Zen" is a Japanese word for the Chinese
"Ch'an," which in turn is a transliteration of
the Sanskrit "Dhyāna." I use the word "Zen"
here, because of its popularity among Western
scholars.

2. See Taishō, nos. 602, 608, and 613.

3. Hui-chiao, Kao-sêng Chuan (Biographies of
Eminent Buddhist Teachers), in Taishō, vol. 50,
pp. 323a-324c.

4. Tao-hsüan, Hsü Kao-sêng Chuan (Second Series
of Biographies of Eminent Buddhist Teachers),
in Taishō, vol. 50, p. 551.

5. See W. Pachow, "Zen Buddhism and Bodhidharma,"
Indian Historical Quarterly, vol. XXXII, nos. 2-3,
p. 333.

6. Tao-hsüan, op.cit.

7. Ibid., p. 552.

8. Wing-tsit, Chan, trans. and ed., The Platform
Scriptures (New York: St. John's University
Press, 1963), p. 73.

9. See Walter Liebenthal, "The Problem of Chinese Buddhism," Visva-Bharati Quarterly, vol. 18, no. 3 (1953), pp. 233-46.

10. Ibid., p. 241.

11. Ibid., p. 243.

12. D.T. Suzuki, An Introduction to Zen Buddhism (London: Rider and Co., 1948), p. 14.

13. Hui-chiao, op.cit., p. 366.

14. Ibid.

15. Tao-an and Hui-yüan were two of the most out- standing teachers in the history of Chinese Buddhism. The former was a great thinker, and the latter was the founder of the Pure Land School. In the early stage of this school, it was closely connected with the Dhyana practices.

16. "Ku tsun-su yü-lu" (6A) ("The Sayings of the Ancient Venerable Sages") in Chi-tsang Chu, ed., Ta-tsang Ching (The Chinese Tripiṭaka) (Shanghai: Pin-chia Arama Publishing House, 1913), pp. 86a, 87b.

17. T'ing Fu-po, ed., Fu-hsüeh ta-t'zǔ-tien (A Great Buddhist Encyclopaedia) (Shanghai: The Medical Book Co., n.d.), p. 699.

18. "Ku tsun-su yü-lu," op.cit., p. 866.

19. Ibid., p. 92A.

20. Ibid., p. 87n.

21. Ibid., p. 66b.

22. Ibid., pp. 66a, b.

II

GLOSSARY

1A 菩提達摩

2A 道生

3A 頭上安頭

4A 臨濟

5A 馬祖

6A 古尊宿語錄

A BUDDHIST DISCOURSE ON

MEDITATION FROM TUN-HUANG

The discovery of the Thousand Buddha Caves at Tun-huang in northwestern China by L. de Loczy and Count Szechenyi of Hungary in 1879, and the subsequent collection of a large number of Chinese Buddhist manuscripts by Sir Aurel Stein in 1907, were two great events in the history of modern Chinese studies.[1] According to Stein's report the size of the pile of manuscripts and other objects of art was about 500 cubic feet. Undoubtedly Stein was fortunate enough to secure the best selection of manuscripts from Tun-huang. He collected over 6,000 scrolls and sent them to the British Museum in London, as his expedition to the Tun-huang region was financed by the British and Indian governments. In Stein's wake Professor Paul Pelliot, a noted French Sinologist, went to Tun-huang in 1908 and carried away another 2,000 scrolls of manuscripts, paintings and other objects of art to France. These are housed in the Bibliothèque Nationale, Paris. Realizing the importance of these literary documents, the Chinese government hastened to collect whatever was left behind. A final collection of over 8,000 scrolls was made and sent to the National Peiping Library in Peking. However, it is obvious that the best collections of Tun-huang manuscripts and other art objects are to be found in England and France and not in China. China had failed to take prompt action to prevent these priceless treasures from falling into the hands of private parties.

Each of the collections of Chinese manuscripts kept in London, Paris, and Peking consists of two main divisions, Buddhist and non-Buddhist. In the Buddhist section, the majority are texts from the Chinese Tripiṭaka, i.e., Sūtras, Vinaya

and Śāstras, in addition to the philosophical,
doctrinal, historical and literary compositions
made by Chinese scholars. Among the writings a
special literary creation called pien-wên, or
dramatized versions of Buddhist topics, such as
the life of the Buddha, the subdual of Māra by
Mañjuśrī Bodhisattva, the story of Maudgalyāyana's
rescuing his mother from hell, the Jātaka stories,
and the popularized version of the Saddharma-
puṇḍarīka-Sūtra, the Sukhāvatī-vyūha-Sūtra, the
Vimalakīrti nirdeśa-Sūtra, and so forth, has made
a great contribution to Chinese folk literature.
It is generally written in prose and poetry, and
has a great beauty of its own. Because of its
popular appeal, the Chinese Buddhists from the
eighth century onward used to recite this type of
composition to large audiences for the purpose of
propagating Buddhism. Consequently other writers
adopted this form to write literary pieces on
non-Buddhist topics which are also known as
pien-wên.[2] There is a good collection of such
works in the three centers mentioned above.

In the non-Buddhist section are found
literary writings on diverse topics, ranging from
texts of Taoism, Confucianism and Manicheism to
history, topography, poems, songs, ballads,
biographies, divination, measurements, club
rules and a host of miscellaneous subjects. For
further information on this matter, L. Giles'
exhaustive list of topics may be consulted.[3]

The present translation is taken from one of
the Tun-huang Chinese manuscripts kept in the
British Museum. There are three slightly different versions of the same text in the Stein
Collection bearing Nos. S.2669, S.3558 and S.4046.
I have used No. S.4046 as the base and consulted
the other two whenever necessary. The author
of this essay, Hung-jên (1A), was a well-known
figure in Zen history. He was the teacher of
Hui-nêng (2A), the sixth Patriarch of the Zen
school. Historically speaking Bodhidharma was
not the first Patriarch of Zen Buddhism in
China, as his teachings and practices are quite
different from those of the later Zen masters.[4]

That being the case, this discourse of Hung-jên becomes all the more important. Probably he was the first Chinese teacher to write a treatise on meditation, and it must have influenced greatly some of the later Zen masters, including Hui-nêng. This work will help students of Buddhist history in tracing the early teachings of Zen Buddhism. Regarding the date of composition, we are not in a position to say anything definite at this stage. As Hui-nêng, his pupil, passed away in 713 A.D.,[5] it must have been completed by that time.

With regard to the principal arguments found in the discourse, the author was of the opinion (1) that the mind is inherently pure and is in a state of neither existence nor non-existence; (2) that the common folk and the Buddha are placed on an equal footing, as both possess a similar kind of mind. The reason for their being in a different state is due to the fact that the Buddha has realized the nature of the dharma, whereas other living beings are ignorant of it, and thereby they wander on the path of birth and death. The way which will lead the common folk to attain enlightenment is to undergo a course of meditational practice retaining mindfulness. "Mindfulness" has occupied a very important place in this essay. It is, according to the author, the foundation of, and stepping-stone to, Buddhahood and nirvāna.

Generally speaking, the teaching of Hung-jên is fairly close to the early Buddhist tradition of dhyāna, though it has been influenced, to a certain extent, by the theory of Buddha-nature which is inherent in every individual. We are, however, unable to agree with the statement that the self and nirvāna are ultimately void, whereas the dharmatā is not so, or it exists permanently. Normally dharmatā and nirvāna are considered to be similar in character and both are asamskrta-dharmas. The author's attempt to make a distinction between them appears unnecessary.

Finally we hope that the discourse of Hung-jên will enable us to understand the theory and

practice of Zen as known in the seventh century
in China. It is very clear that the particular
type of Zen practiced by most of the Zen masters
after the eighth century has very little to do
with Hung-jên, and has nothing to do with Bodhidharma, the so-called founder of Chinese Zen
Buddhism.

The Text

An Important Discourse on the
Cultivation of the Mind Which
Leads the Profane to Holiness
and to the Realization of Mukti

by

Upādhyāya Hung-jên of Ch'ichow

Regarding the cultivation of the essence of
Tao, one should know that the self is originally
pure. It is neither born, nor destroyed, nor has
it any differentiations. To see one's own Teacher
with the inherent, perfect and pure mind is much
better than keeping remembrance of the Buddhas
of the ten quarters.

(1) Question: How do you know that one's
own mind was originally pure?

Answer: The Daśabhūmi-Śāstra says:
"In the body of the living beings there exists
the vajra-like Buddha-nature which resembles the
bright, full, perfect, immense and endless Sun.
On account of its being obstructed by dense
clouds of the five skandhas, the Sun cannot
shine, just as the flame of a lamp inside a jar."

To dwell further on the simile of the Sun,
we may cite the example that, when clouds and
mist rise from the eight quarters, the whole
universe becomes dull and cloudy. Why is there
no sunshine? Is it because the Sun is defective?
In reply to this, we say that the sunshine is
not defective, but that it is being obscured by

38

the dense clouds of attachment, false thoughts
and diverse views. If one is able to maintain mindfulness distinctly, the false ideas
will not emerge and the nirvāṇa-dharma-sun will
automatically appear.   We know, therefore,
that one's own mind was originally pure.

(2) Question: How do you know that
one's own mind was originally neither
existent nor non-existent?

Answer: It is stated in the Vimalakīrti-Sūtra: "Suchness (Tathatā) has no
existence nor non-existence. This suchness
is the Bhūtatathatā Buddha-nature, and the
source of self-existent pure mind. Bhūtatathatā
is self-existent and not produced by the conditioning causation." Further, it is said:
"All living beings are in a state of suchness, the sages and saints are also in a
state of suchness."

We are the living beings while the
sages and saints are the Buddhas. They may
be called differently; however, in them, the
dharmatā of suchness which is neither existent,
nor non-existent is the same. Therefore, I
say, all are in a state of suchness. Hence
we know that one's own mind was originally
neither existent nor non-existent.

(3) Question: What do you mean by
calling the mind to be one's teacher?

Answer: The true mind is self-
existent, not coming from outside, nor does
it accept any restrictions.[6] In the three
periods of existence there is no one who sur-
passes the most intimate relationship of the
mind. If any one recognizes the bhūtatathatā
and retains it, he will reach the Furthershore:
the confused one who misses it will fall into

the three inferior states of suffering.
Therefore, we know that the Buddhas of the
three periods take the self-existent true mind
to be their teacher.

It is stated in a śāstra: "Living
beings exist on the basis of the waves of
false ideas." Having realized this false-
hood, one clearly retains mindfulness.[7] When
false ideas do not arise, one reaches a state
of no more birth. Therefore, we know that
the mind is one's teacher.

(4) Question: What do you mean by
saying that the mind of the ordinary people
is better than that of the Buddhas?

Answer: One will not get rid of
birth and death if one constantly thinks of
other Buddhas. However, if one retains one's
mindfulness, he is sure to reach the Furthershore. It is, therefore, said in the
Vajracchedika-prajñāpāramitā-Sūtra: "If any
one wishes to see me in form, or to seek
me in sound, this person is treading an evil
path and he cannot see the Tathāgata."
Therefore, to retain true mindfulness is
better than the remembrance of other Buddhas.
Further, the word "better" is merely intended
to give encouragement to people who devote
themselves to practice. In fact, the
characteristic of the ultimate fruition
is the same, and is on an equal footing.

(5) Question: Since the true characteristic of living beings and the Buddhas is
the same, how is it that the Buddhas are in
a state of neither existence, nor non-existence,
free from obstruction and enjoy immense
bliss, whilst we, ordinary beings, sink into
the depth of birth and death suffering various
kinds of miseries and sorrows?

40

Answer: Having realized the nature of the dharma, the Buddhas of the ten quarters comprehend the source of the mind. Thus false ideas will not arise, righteous thought will be retained and the conception of what-belongs-to-me will disappear. Thereby they will not be subject to birth and death. As there is no birth and death, it will be the ultimate nirvāṇa. Being in a state of nirvāṇa, the ten thousand forms of bliss will flock to it of their own accord.

Being ignorant of what is truly holy, all the living beings do not know the diverse false causations of the mind, and do not cultivate righteous thought. As there is no righteous mindfulness, there emerges hatred and affection; because of hatred and affection, the mind-vessel is cracked and leaking; because of the damage to, and leakage of the mind, one undergoes birth and death. Since there is birth and death, all the sufferings are present. The Hṛdaya-rāja-Sūtra says: "Suchness of the Buddha-nature is buried in knowledge and views. In the ocean of the six senses, one is sunk to the depth of birth and death, and shall never be freed from it." Be earnest! When one retains true mindfulness, false thoughts will not arise, and the conception of what-belongs-to-me will disappear. Thus one will naturally attain the same state as the Buddhas.

(6) Question: Since suchness of the dharma-nature /of the Buddhas and the living beings/ is the same, bewilderment and enlightenment should be applicable equally to both. Why do only the Buddhas attain enlightenment, whereas the living beings are in a state of illusion and confusion?

Answer: /Some of/ the foregoing passages may be classified into the wondrous region which cannot be reached or comprehended by people who are still in a state of profanity. Knowing the mind, one is enlightened, losing one's nature, one is confused, and there will be union when the conditioning factors are put together. These are the things which cannot be

41

said definitely. However, the transcendental truth, indeed, is in one's retaining true mindfulness. The <u>Vimalakīrti-Sutra</u> says: "It is not the self-existent nature, nor anything from outside. The dharma does not come into being, so now it has no cessation." This means the realization of the two extremes of attachment and detachment and the attainment of the wisdom of non-discrimination. If one understands this meaning, and always concentratedly retains the original pure mind while walking, standing, sitting and lying down, false ideas will not arise, the conception of what-belongs-to-me will disappear, and one will naturally attain mukti or liberation. If one wishes to raise further questions and get answers thereby, the terms and their meaning will multiply manifold. However, if one is desirous of knowing the essence of the dharma, the retaining of the mind should come first. This mindfulness is the foundation of nirvāna, the main gate to the Path, the principle of the twelve divisions of Sūtras, and the ancestor of the Buddhas in the three periods.

(7) Question: How do we know that mindfulness is the foundation of nirvāna?

Answer: The term "nirvāna" means the characteristic which is a state of peace, cessation, non-activity and bliss. Since the mind of one's self is true, false ideas will come to an end; when false ideas are no more, righteous mindfulness will take its position; when there is righteous mindfulness, wisdom of silent comprehension will emerge; when that wisdom is born, one understands thoroughly the dharma-nature, and because of that understanding, one attains nirvāna. Therefore, one should know that mindfulness is the foundation of nirvāna.

(8) Question: How do we know that mindfulness is the main gate to the Path?

Answer: /Among the various means/, either one draws the image of the Buddha with one's fingernail, or performs meritorious deeds

42

as numerous as the sands of the Ganges, it is
merely the convenience of the Buddha for teaching
the ignorant people to prepare for future excellent ground, /to receive/ the reward of karma,
as well as to prepare them to meet the Buddha.
If these persons wish to attain Buddhahood early,
they should understand this true mindfulness which
is not subject to cause. There are innumerable
and endless Buddhas in the three periods; there
is not even a single instance to show that any one
who had attained Buddhahood could do away with
true mindfulness. It is, therefore, said in the
Sūtra: "Everything will be done, if the mind is
concentrated." Thus we know that true mindfulness is the main gate to the Path.

(9) Question: How do we know that true
mindfulness is the principal of the twelve
divisions of Sūtras?

Answer: In all the Sūtras, the Tathāgata speaks extensively on sins and merits,
causations and fruitions, or cites unlimited
similes of mountains, rivers, plants and the
universe and so forth, or manifests innumerable
supernatural powers. These diverse transformations
are meant for one purpose only, to teach the ignorant beings who have many cravings and desires,
and wish to perform innumerable meritorious deeds.
It is on account of this that the Blessed One
leads them to permanent bliss in accordance with
their mental conditions. Having realized that
the Buddha-nature in living beings is originally
pure, and similar to the sun being covered by
clouds, one should consciously retain true mindfulness, so that the sun of wisdom will appear
when the clouds of false thoughts are swept away.
It is unnecessary that one should try to acquire
more knowledge for knowing the doctrines and
affairs of the three periods, because all these
belong to the suffering of birth and death. It
is like the polishing of a mirror,[8] when the dust
is wiped off, naturally one sees the self-nature
/svabhāva/. It will be absolutely useless,
even if one has learned something with the
ignorant mind now. If, however, one could

43

consciously retain right mindfulness, and learn
it with the mind which is not subject to cause,
then this is true learning. When we say "true
learning" it means that ultimately there is
nothing to be learned. Why? Because the self and
nirvāna are both void. There is neither one nor
both. Therefore there is nothing to learn. But
dharmatā is not void, one should consciously
retain true mindfulness, so that false thoughts
will not arise, and the conception of what-
belongs-to-me will disappear. Thus, it is stated
in the Nirvāna-Sūtra: "The one who knows that
the Buddha does not preach is called a man of
accomplished learning." Therefore, we know that
true mindfulness is the principle of the twelve
divisions of Sūtras.

(10) Question: How do we know that mindfulness is the forefather of the Buddhas of the
three periods?

Answer: The Buddhas of the three
periods are born from consciousness, but false
thought is not born from consciousness. When
the idea of what-belongs-to-me is discarded, one
recognizes the mind in consciousness. First of
all, one retains true mindfulness, and later
one will become a Buddha. Therefore, we know
that mindfulness is the forefather of the Buddhas
of the three periods.

If we wish to explain extensively the four
foregoing questions and answers, indeed, there
will be no end to it. I simply wish that you
should recognize your original mind, and
therefore, be diligent about it. Even if you have
read hundreds and thousands of sūtras and śāstras,
there is nothing better than true mindfulness.
This, however, needs effort. I cite a quotation
from the Saddharma-puṇḍarīka-Sūtra as follows:
"I have shown you vehicles, treasures, bright
jewels, wondrous medicines and so forth, but you
do not take and use them. You pretend to be
poor and suffering, how could anybody help you?"
When this is realized, false thought will not
arise, and the conception of what-belongs-to-me

will disappear; then, all merits will naturally
become perfect and will not depend on any external
seeking; /if it does/, it will return to the
suffering of birth and death.

Under all circumstances and at every moment,
the mind should be well-controlled. One should
not experience the pleasure of the present, which
may sow the seed of suffering in the future. Thus
one may swindle oneself, as well as others, but
it will not lead any one to the liberation from
birth and death. One should strive hard. It
may not be of much benefit now, but it prepares
the ground for the future. One should not spend
/the lives/ of the three periods uselessly, and
allow one's effort to go to waste. The Sūtra
says: "Living constantly in hell, he behaves
as if he is strolling leisurely in the parks and
palaces, and remaining in the other inferior
states of suffering, he likes them as if they are
his home." It is rather strange that we ordinary
beings, having seen it clearly, are not aware of
the terrifying state of affairs. We do not have
the faintest idea of running away from it.

If one is a beginner in the practice of
meditation, he should follow the instruction given
in the Sukhāvatīvyūha-Sūtra: "Let him sit up-
rightly closing the eyes and mouth. At a certain
distance from the front, as well as at the same
level of his chest, he visualizes a sun. That
image must be retained and he should not allow
himself to rest even for a moment." This will
enable the practitioner to harmonize the breathing and silence any sound. He should not allow
the breathing to become heavy or fine all of a
sudden, as this will cause illness to him.

If one practices meditation in the night,
one may see good or bad mental reflections, or
enter the samādhis of blue, yellow, red and
white color and so forth, or see illuminations
issuing from, and entering one's own body, or
see the image of the Tathāgata, or there are manifestations of transformations; one should know
what is proper, control the mind and not have any

45

attachment to them. All these are void, and they
appear through false thoughts. Thus, it is said
in the Sūtra: "Countries in the ten quarters
are like the empty sky." Further it says: "The
three worlds are unreal and illusive; they are
merely creations of the mind."

If one is unable to gain samādhi, and does
not see the objective mental projections, he should
not be surprised, but should always consciously
retain true mindfulness while walking, standing,
sitting and lying down. When one realizes this,
false ideas will not arise, and the conception
of what-belongs-to-me will disappear. The dharmas
amounting to 10,000 are nothing beyond one's
own mind. The reason for the Buddhas to explain
it in many similes, is that among the living beings, each is different from the other. Therefore, the ways for teaching them are not the same.
In fact, the 84,000 ways of the doctrine, the
positions and substance of the three yānas and
the principal practices of the seventy-two sages
are nothing beyond one's own mind. If one is
able to comprehend his own mind, and train it at
all times, he is, in each conscious moment, making
constant offerings to the Buddhas of the ten
quarters who are as numerous as the sands of the
Ganges, and the twelve divisions of the Sūtras.
He makes the wheel of the Dharma turn at every
moment.

If one understands the source of the mind,
then the meaning concerning the mind will be
inexhaustible; he will be endowed with everything
and become perfect in practices. He has done all
that ought to be done, and he will experience
no further birth. When this is realized, false
ideas will not arise, the conception of what-
belongs-to-me will disappear, this physical
frame will be given up and one is sure to attain
the state of birthlessness which is beyond our
comprehension. One should strive hard.

There is no speech greater and more important
than this, which is rare to be heard. Among
those who have heard it, there is only one, in a

crowd like the sands of the Ganges, who will put
it into practice; having practiced it and reached
the final goal, there is hardly any one in one
hundred million years. /Therefore/, one should
be perfectly tranquil, control the sense organs
well, look sharp at the fountain of the mind,
make it constantly function and pure, and not
allow it to remain unrecorded /Wu-chi; 6A/
or neutral.

(11) Question: What do you mean by the
unrecorded /Wu-chi/ or neutral mind?

Answer: Owing to external conditions
the gross mind of those practicing concentration
is temporarily coming to rest, but internally
the true mind is fettered. When the mind is not
in a tranquil state, the practitioner always
consciously keeps a watch over it; that means he
has not yet obtained perfect purity and independently comprehended the fountain of the mind.
This is called unrecorded /Wu-chi/ or neutral.
It is also the mind with a discharge /asrava/
which will not be able to escape from the great
disease of birth and death. /This is bad enough/,
not to speak of those who know nothing at all
concerning mindfulness. These people will sink
into the suffering ocean of birth and death. No
one knows when they will be able to emerge from
it. It is a pity. One should strive hard. The
Sutra says: "If the living beings are not sincere, and have not made aspiration from within,
even if they come across the Buddhas like the
sands of the Ganges in the three periods /of
existence/, there is nothing that could be done
for them."

And another Sutra says: "The living beings
who know the mind will gain salvation by themselves; the Buddhas cannot give salvation to
them."

In the past, there were as many Buddhas as
the sands of the Ganges; in spite of that, why
have we not yet attained Buddhahood? It is
simply because there is no sincere aspiration

from within, and thereby we are submerged in the
sea of suffering. One should strive hard.

It is rather late to repent the past errors
of which we are aware. Now in the present life
we happen to listen to speeches of a distinctive
character. We should understand them quickly and
comprehend that mindfulness is the only way.
Those who are unwilling to seek Buddhahood with
sincere heart, from which immense and unfettered
bliss would be enjoyed, begin seriously to search
for fame and riches by following worldly practices.
They will, in future, fall into hells to undergo
various pains and sufferings. What can we do
for them? One should strive hard.

It would be of great service to the world,
if one is able to wear tattered rags, take coarse
food, be consciously mindful and pretend to be
insane; these are the best ways to conserve one's
energy and strength. The unenlightened folk
who do not know, seeking the reason from the
ignorant mind, have undergone great hardship by
performing extensively visible meritorious deeds,
with the hope of gaining mukti. But they return
to the sorrows of birth and death.

"Clearly not to lose sight of righteous
thought, and let the living beings gain salvation," is the Bodhisattva of Great Might speaking
to you in clear language which means that mindfulness is the best. I wish to hear from you
that you are unwilling to bear the pains of the
present life, but desirous of undergoing sufferings of ten thousand kalpas. What have you
to say?

With regard to "Not to be blown off by the
eight kinds of wind," it is indeed a rare[9]
mountain of treasure (7A). If one is desirous
of knowing the characteristic of fruition /it
may be tested in this manner that/ while in
various conditions one is able to multiply the
functions as numerous as the sands of the Ganges,
while one exhibits great eloquence, and while
one gives medicines to the sick according to the

48

disease, no false thought will arise in him and the conception of what-belongs-to-me will disappear. If one can do that, he is really a person who has gone beyond the world, and the Tathāgata will freely and endlessly bless him. I say this, because I am sincerely glad that you have no false thought, and have discarded the conception of what-belongs-to-me.

(12) Question: What do you mean by the conception of what-belongs-to-me?

Answer: It is the conception that when one is a little better than the other, one thinks: I am able to be in such a position. The Parinirvāna-Sūtra says: "It is like the space which can accommodate everything. However, the space itself will not say 'I am able to do this.'" This means that the conception of what-belongs-to-me is gone and it will lead to the vajra-samādhi. These two conditions will function at the same time.

(13) Question: The sincere practitioners seek the true and permanent cessation /nirvāna/. But the world is impermanent and not delighted in the transcendental truth; its goodness is gross, as the permanent and subtle one has not yet manifested. Whenever one is about to aspire and take to reasoning, there arises the thinking consciousness, that is the mind of discharge /āsrava/ or imperfection; whenever one tries to guide the mind towards dwelling on nothing, there prevails the ignorance and darkness which are devoid of reason. However, if one does not guide the mind to the right path and to reasoning, there emerges the false view of void. In that case, one may possess a human body, but behave like an animal. At this stage, if one has not got samādhi and wisdom, he will not be able to see clearly the Buddha-nature, and it will be the drowning spot for him only. How could one proceed to the anupadhiśesa-nirvāna? I request you to show the true destination.

49

Answer: When faith is complete and the sincere vow is accomplished, you slowly quiet your mind, then I shall instruct you further: Pacify your mind and body well, so that they will not have any attachment; let yourself sit in an upright position and allow your breathing to become fine and well-controlled; the mind is neither within, nor without, and it is not in between; see it nicely and steadily, then you see the mobility of consciousness. It is like the flowing of water and the mirage which do not stay even for a moment. Having noticed that consciousness is neither internal nor external, you look at it leisurely, steadily and firmly. Then it will melt away, settle down and become motionless. That being so, the mobile consciousness will suddenly disappear. The disappearance of this consciousness means the destruction of obstacles for the bodhisattvas in the ten stages (daśabhūmi), or, when the characteristic of the consciousness and so forth has gone, one's mind will become perfectly tranquil, detached, bright and serene. I cannot describe its conditions any further. If you are desirous of knowing it, I refer you to the chapter on vajrakāya of the Mahāparinirvāṇa-Sūtra, and the chapter on paying a visit to Akṣobhya Buddha of the Vimalakīrti-Sūtra. Think carefully that these words are true.

If any one retains mindfulness either while walking, standing, sitting and lying down, or when he is face to face with the five desires, or the eight winds, this person has achieved the brahmacārya and completed what he ought to perform. He will ultimately receive no further physical frame which is subject to birth and death. The five desires are form, sound, smell, taste, and sensation, and the eight winds are gain, loss; defamation, eulogy; praise, ridicule; sorrow and joy. This is the training and testing-ground of the Buddha-nature for the practitioners. One should not be surprised that the present life is not free. The Sūtra says: "If there is no Buddha staying in the world, the bodhisattvas of the ten stages will not be able to obtain the benefit of what they are."

Regarding the getting rid of this rewarded body due to karma, the living beings in the past had sharp and dull intellectual qualities which could not be equalized. With those belonging to the higher grade, it is a matter of seconds, and with those of the lower grade, it may take innumerable kalpas. If one has the ability one should, according to the nature of the beings, arouse their good qualities of bodhi /intelligence/. This will bring benefit to one's self as well as to others.

To adore the Path of the Buddha, one should understand the four necessaries, so that one may know fully the characteristics of reality. If one sticks to the letter, he will miss the true spirit.

With regard to the bhiksus who renounced the home and took to religious practices, this home-renouncing means leaving the home of birth and death. This is called leaving the home.

Those who are endowed with right mindfulness, and have accomplished the religious practices, will retain that mindfulness at the time of the final passing away, even if the joints and limbs of their bodies are cut into pieces. These are the disciples of the Buddha.

"The foregoing discourse merely speaks about the mind; it derives its meaning from the letter." If any one speaks in this manner it shows that he does not really and clearly understand and realize it. In case one misunderstands the holy teaching, he should make a confession and discard it. If, however, one understands properly the Holy Path, he should divert that merit to living beings, with the hope that they will understand their own minds and at once attain Buddhahood.

Any one who has heard this should strive hard for the Goal. If one attain Buddhahood in the future, he should lead in securing deliverance for my disciples.

(14)   Question: From the beginning to the
end, this treatise dwells on the theme that one's
mind is the Path. In what ways does it include
the practice and fruition?

Answer: This treatise chiefly shows
the characteristic of Ekayāna. However, full
attention of this discourse is directed toward
guiding the unenlightened to liberation. First
of all one should get rid of birth and death, then,
he will be able to provide deliverance to others.
Finally it speaks of self benefit, and not the
benefit of others. This may, roughly, be included
in the division of practice. If any one practices
it according to this text, he will become a
Buddha right away. If I am telling you a lie,
I shall swear by Heaven and Earth that I may
fall into the eighteen hells. If any one does
not believe my words, he will be eaten by the
tigers and wolves in every birth!

NOTES

1.   Chou Shao-liang, Tun-huang Pien-wên Hui-lu
(A Collection of Pien-wên from Tun-huang)
(Shanghai: Shanghai Publication Co., 1954),
pp. 1-2; Aurel Stein, On Central Asian Tracks
(London: Macmillan and Co., 1933), p. 193.

2.   Wang Ch'ung-min, ed., Tun-huang Pien-wên Chi
(A Collection of Pien-wên from Tun-huang)
(Peking: People's Publishing House, 1957).

3.   This list can be found in Lionel Giles,
Descriptive Catalogue of the Chinese Manuscripts
from Tun-huang of the British Museum (London:
Trustees of the British Museum, 1957).

4.   A more complete discussion of this may be
found in W. Pachow, "Zen Buddhism and Bodhidharma,"
The Indian Historical Quarterly, vol. XXXII,
nos. 2-3, pp. 329-37.

5.   Wing-tsit Chan, trans. and ed., The Platform Scriptures (New York: St. John's University Press, 1963), p. 7.

6.   "Pu-so-shu-shiu" (3A) (see Appendix) has the meaning of "not to ask for any salary due to a teacher." This does not make any sense here. Possibly it is a mistake for "pu-shou-shu-hsi" (4A) (see Appendix) which means "not to accept any binding." If we accept the second possibility, the sense is more clear.

7.   "Shou-hsin" (5A) (see Appendix) means "to keep," "to retain," or "to watch over the mind"; hence we render it as "mindfulness."

8.   This refers to the mirrors made of metal in ancient China.

9.   "Shu-shih" (7A) (see Appendix) means "distinguished or different times." I think "rare" is a suitable rendering here.

III

GLOSSARY

1A 弘忍

2A 慧能

3A 不索束脩

4A 不受束縛

5A 守心

6A 無記

7A 殊時

54

IV

LAO TZU AND GAUTAMA BUDDHA

An Inquiry into the Authenticity
of Lao Tzu's Mission to India

After the introduction of Buddhism to China
in the first century A.C. the cultural impact
of Buddhism was deeply felt by the local religious sects in that country, especially Taoism.
The founder of this religion, according to tradition, was Lao Tzu. It is Lao Tzu's mission to
India to convert the Buddha with which we are
chiefly concerned. The spurious character of
the composition entitled, Lao Tzu hua-hu ching (1A)
or The Sutra on Lao Tzu's Converting the Barbarian
or the Buddha has been a subject of heated discussion and controversy throughout the centuries
and many times the debates were officially pre-
sided over by Chinese emperors and kings. The
outcome of these disputations was generally defeat and humiliation for the Taoists. The motive
for the fabrication of this story naturally
arouses curiosity. I shall endeavor to trace the
likely causes that led to the composition of the
text in question and discuss the spuriousness
or authenticity of the alleged mission.

It is quite obvious that in the first two
or three centuries after the introduction of
Buddhism, people in China did not understand the
true characteristics of this religion and took it
to be something similar to Taoism or its sub-
divisions, which were closely associated with
superstitious practices such as witchcraft,
divination, necromancy, animism and the performance of various rituals. In the Chinese
historical and Buddhist writings there is ample
evidence to show that Buddhism and Taoism were
practiced side by side, not merely by the masses,
but even by members of the royal family. For

instance, Prince Ying of Ch'u, who flourished
in the middle of the first century A.C., was
famed for his keen interest in the doctrines of
Huang-ti (the Yellow Emperor) and Lao Tzu, and
also for his observing the Buddhist practices
of fast and purification. This is officially
recorded in the Annals of the Later Han Dynasty.[1]
And in 166 A.C. Hsiang K'ai (2A) in his official
memorandum to Emperor Huan-ti (146-167 A.C.)
mentioned that he had heard of the establishment
of shrines for the Yellow Emperor, Lao Tzu, and
the Buddha in the latter's place.[2] From Buddhist
sources we notice that the early Buddhist missionaries from India and Central Asian countries,
such as An shih-kao (who reached China about
148 A.C.), and Lokaksin (who reached China in
176 A.C.), were famed for their secular learning
and magical powers, such as interpreting the
planets, medical healing, understanding the sounds
of birds and animals, and prophecy, in addition
to their exposition of Hīnayāna and Mahāyāna
doctrines.[3] Strictly speaking, the performance
of miracles in any form, and the dabbling in
secular arts, are prohibited by the Buddha. The
biographies of these missionaries stressed these
features, which probably indicate what the popular
taste in religious matters at that time was, hence
the assumption that there was something common
to Buddhism and Taoism. Later this idea was
crystallized in the story that Lao Tzu had been
to India and had converted the Buddha to Taoism.
Obviously such a story was intended to demonstrate
teacher-pupil relationship between the two sages.
This relationship may be pure imagination--it
cannot stand any critical investigation. However, it has been a controversial issue between
the Taoists and Buddhists in China for centuries,
and at times it provides very interesting reading.

To examine the claim for Lao Tzu's mission
to India, we should first of all ascertain whether
Lao Tzu was an historical figure , and if so,
when did he flourish and who were his contemporaries?
The earliest record ever found was a short biography written by the famous historian Ssŭ-ma
Ch'ien. We are told that Lao Tzu was originally
of K'u district in Ch'u Kingdom, but later became a librarian or keeper of archives in the

Imperial Court of the Chou dynasty.[4] He was an
elder contemporary of Confucius. This inference
is based on the fact that in the biographies
of both Lao Tzu and Confucius, the latter was
said to have paid visits to the former in order
to make inquiries regarding rites and proprieties.
From the fatherly advice given by Lao Tzu and
the praise showered on him in which Confucius
compared him to the cloud-riding dragon, it appears that Lao Tzu was much older than Confucius.[5] The time of their interview is not quite
certain. However, indications suggest that it
must have taken place some time after Confucius'
retirement from government service, perhaps sometime in his fifties. This is hinted at in Lao
Tzu's advice: "When a superman," says he, "gets
the proper opportunity, he will ride on a chariot;
and if he does not get it, he will walk with his
hands supporting a straw hat."[6]

This seems to be a sort of consolatory advice. In another place Lao Tzu is reported
to have said: "Indeed, it is rather difficult
to propagate the Tao."[7] These instances make
us believe that Lao Tzu was definitely very much
senior to Confucius. There is no doubt that Lao
Tzu and Confucius were historical figures,
though at a later stage legendary attributes crept
in and their lives were shrouded in fantasy and
myth.

Confucius passed away in 479 B.C. He
enjoyed a fruitful life of seventy-three years
(551 or 552 B.C. would be the date of his birth).[8]
Unfortunately the precise dates of Lao Tzu's
birth and death were not recorded anywhere. As
he was an older contemporary of Confucius he must
have lived before 479 B.C. If we assume he lived
about eighty years, and if he were thirty years
older than Confucius, his probable dates would
be 582-502 B.C.

Regarding the later phase of activities of
Lao Tzu, Ssŭ-ma Ch'ien mentions briefly that,
noticing the fortunes of the Chou dynasty to be
declining, he left for the Kuan (the Pass)

in northwest China, and at the request of Yin Hsi,
the commanding officer at the Pass, Lao Tzu made
his immortal composition dealing with Tao-teh
or The Path and Virtue, consisting of over 5,000
words.[9] "Then he left the place and nobody
knows how he met his end," as Ssŭ-ma Ch'ien puts
it.[10] The last sentence here is very significant, i.e., that in 104 B.C. when Ssŭ-ma Ch'ien
completed his Shih-chi (3A), he was not aware
of the whereabouts of Lao Tzu in the later phase
of his life. Of course, it is out of the question to speak at all of Lao Tzu's mission to
India at that time.

When Did the Mission Story Begin?

The story of Lao Tzu's conversion of the
barbarian to Buddhahood presupposes the existence of Buddhism in China. If that is the
case, it would mean that this story cannot be
dated earlier than the date of the introduction
of Buddhism itself to that country, traditionally
held to be 64 A.C., during the reign of Emperor
Ming-ti (57-75 A.C.), though its authenticity
has been questioned by scholars. According to
the Record of Western Barbarians in the Wei-lioh
(4A) by Yŭ Ch'üan, it is stated that in 2 B.C.
in the reign of Ai-ti (7-1 B.C.), Ching-lu,
a learned scholar, received Buddhist sūtras
orally from I-tsun, a Yüeh-ch'i envoy to the
Chinese Court.[11] This indicates, at least, that
in 2 B.C. Buddhism was known in China, though
perhaps not widely known. If this is accepted,
it would definitely exclude the faintest possibility of Lao Tzu's going to India to convert
the Buddha for the simple reason that in the
sixth century B.C. the name of Gautama Buddha
was not known to the Chinese in general, and in
particular, Lao Tzu had not yet been recognized
as the founder of Taoism. At that time, he was
simply a keen observer of worldly affairs and
a philosopher of negativism. There was not
the slightest hint in his writings that he had
any religious inclination or missionary zeal to

convert others. As a matter of fact, he had no
school or following at all during his lifetime.

Further, when Chang Ch'ien (5A) visited
Fergana and Bactria in 129 B.C., the name of India,
in the form of Shên-tu (6A), or Sindu, was introduced to the Chinese for the first time.[12]
Before that, it is known for certain that there
was hardly any cultural or religious intercourse
between India and China; Lao Tzu would not have
gone to India to carry out any missionary propa-
ganda. There is, however, a coincidence between
Lao Tzu and Gautama Buddha, i.e., both of them
lived contemporaneously in the sixth century B.C.,
although they didn't know each other.

The Earliest Traditions
Concerning This Story

From the foregoing paragraphs, it is evident that there was not the slightest likeli-
hood of Lao Tzu's travelling to India. Obviously
this tradition must have originated much later.
It is very likely that Hsiang K'ai's statement
in his memorandum to Emperor Huan-ti in 166 A.C.,
"Someone said that Lao Tzu had entered the regions of the Barbarians to become a Buddha,"[13]
might be regarded as the first definite statement
of Lao Tzu's mission, though he did not make it
clear who had said it. Whomever that may be,
it is quite likely that it was influenced to a
certain extent by Liu Hsiang's work entitled
The Biography of Immortals (7A). According to
this text, Lao Tzu and Yin Hsi went on a tour
to the west of the Flowing Sand and nobody knew
what happened to them afterwards.[14] Liu Hsiang
was an official of Emperor Yüan-ti (48-33 B.C.)
and flourished in the middle of the first century
B.C. He was famed for his literary talent and
his interest in astronomy. Obviously he did not
suggest that Lao Tzu had gone to India as a
missionary. He clearly indicated that he had
no knowledge whatsoever regarding the end of
Lao Tzu. I am of the opinion that someone at
a much later date misinterpreted "the west of the

Flowing Sand" to be "the land of India." The
term "Flowing Sand" may mean any one of the
"deserts" found in great abundance in northwestern China. Not very far from Sian (ancient
Ch'ang-an), along the border of the Shensi and
Kansu provinces and Inner Mongolia, there is a
vast expanse known as the Gobi Desert. Further,
between Tun-huang and Lobnor, there is the
"River of Sand," as Fa-hsien calls it, which took
him seventeen days to cross.[15] According to his
rough estimate, this stretch of sand might be
about 5,000 li or nearly 1,600 miles. And if
one enters Sinkiang or Chinese Turkestan, there
is the famous Taklamakan Desert.[16]

In all the cases, whether it is the Gobi
Desert or the desert near Tun-huang or even
that of Taklamakan that Lao Tzu had travelled, it
does not suggest that he had gone to India. At
most one may say he had been to Sinkiang or Central
Asia. To take it to be India is to stretch the
imagination a bit too far. This misconception,
however, has been persistent and was elaborated
in later centuries, as is seen in the following
quotation from Yü Ch'üan's Wei-lioh, or the
Outline of the History of the Wei Kingdom: "The
contents of Buddhist /texts7 are similar to that
of the Classics of Lao Tzu in China. Why? It
is because Lao Tzu went beyond the west of the
Pass, traversed the Western Regions /Central
Asia7, reached India and taught the barbarian to
attain Buddhahood and to become his disciple--
whose epithets amounted to 29."[17]

The Wei kingdom flourished from A.C. 220
to 265. The Outline of History concerning this
dynasty must have been composed some time after
265 A.C., though the actual date of composition
is not known. Naturally, by that time Buddhism
was fairly popular in China, and the Chinese had
improved their geographical knowledge of India
as well as of the doctrines of Buddhism. It
is no wonder, therefore, that the author of this
work made a detailed itinerary of Lao Tzu's
mission. If it was not based on pure imagination, then the mission story must have been very

popular at that time, so much so that he could not
help but record whatever he had heard without
using his critical judgment. To go deeper into
the problem, we think that an examination of the
sūtra of Lao Tzu's converting the barbarians is
very essential.

Lao Tzu-hua-hu-ching or The
Sūtra on Lao Tzu's Converting
the Barbarian

This work is attributed to Wang Fou, a Taoist of the western Tsin dynasty (265-316 A.C.).[18]
Regarding the causes which prompted him to write
it, it appears that Wang Fou and Pai-tsu (or
Po Fa-tsu?), Buddhist scholars of Kucī origin,
had many disputations on Buddhism and Taoism,
but unfortunately the former was frequently de-
feated by the latter. To take revenge for this
defeat, Wang Fou resorted to the fabrication of
the story of "converting the barbarians" and
adopted in his work some of the geographical
names appearing in the "Record of the Western
Regions" of the Han-shu. The motive for doing so
was his hatred for the Buddhists. This was
pointed out by Ching-t'ai in the presence of
Emperor Kao-tsung in 660 A.C.[19] In the short
period of the western Tsin dynasty no person
coming from Kucī was known as Pai-tsu (8A). However, a Buddhist missionary by the name "Po Fa-
tsu" during this time was well known. He translated the Buddha-Parinirvāṇa Sūtra   into
Chinese in 290-306 A.C.[20] If Po Fa-tsu is identical with Pai-tsu, then Wang Fou, the author of
Hua-hu ching, must have lived toward the end of
the third century and the beginning of the fourth
century A.C. His composition was chiefly based
on legend, mythology and imagination, and partly
copied the Buddhist traditions, especially the
birth of the Buddha. The following points will
substantiate this statement:

In the first place the text tries to show
that Lao Tzu was a great immortal who had lived
for several centuries. He is said to have been

born during the reign of King T'ang-chia of the
Yin dynasty (2205-1154 B.C.). However, none of
the kings of that dynasty had such a name. A
further statement found in the same text says
that about one hundred years after the birth of
Lao Tzu, the Yin dynasty was overthrown by King
Wu-wang (1122-1116 B.C.) of the Chou dynasty.
This would mean that he was born sometime in 1222
B.C. Later, during the reign of subsequent kings,
he was reported to have frequented India and China
as if he were paying visits to his next-door
neighbor. The notable events, according to this
text, are: (1) During the reign of King K'ang-
wang (1078-1053 B.C.) of the Chou dynasty, he
was serving as an official in that court. (2)
During the time of King Chao-wang (1052-1002 B.C.)
he travelled west and reached the city called
Ve-ma in Khotan. It was there that, with his
supernatural powers, he summoned the kings of
over eighty kingdoms in India and its neighboring
countries, including Persia, to come to Khotan.
In that assembly, he taught them to refrain from
taking life and to cut off their beards and
hair. Later he crossed over the Pamirs, reached
Udyāna and visited the five divisions of India.
(3) During the reign of King Mu-wang (1001-947
B.C.) he returned to China, and later during the
reign of King Huan-wang (719-697 B.C.) he did
some extraordinary things: "I asked Yin Hsi,"
says he, "to ride on the back of the Moon-Spirit
and to descend to the mouth of Queen /of/
Suddhodana /i.e., Mahāmāyā/, so that a prince
will be born to her who will be called Siddhārtha.
After some time he will renounce the high position of a prince and retire to the mountains for
religious practices. When he attains enlightenment, he will be called the Buddha."21

It is understood that he was in India again
until he returned to China in 659-651 B.C. in
order to teach Confucius the doctrine of bene-
volence and justice.

In this manner, the author of this work
goes on to elaborate the missionary activities
of Lao Tzu for a period of over five hundred

years (from 1222 to 651 B.C.). How far can we accept the statement that a human being could manage to live for more than five centuries? If we refuse to believe it, then we may say that the Hua-hu ching is sheer imagination, and devoid of any historical truth.

In addition to this, the author presents a colorful picture of the birth of Lao Tzu which is almost an identical version of the birth scene of the Buddha.[22] It reads as follows: "On the full-moon day of the Second month when Lao Tzu was born in Po, nine dragons poured water over him in order to wash his body. Later these dragons transformed themselves into nine wells. Soon after his birth he walked on the ground, and a lotus sprang up at each step, until it amounted to nine. With his left hand pointing at the sky, and his right hand at the earth, he declared: 'Both above and below the heaven, I am the most supreme. I shall preach the highest Tao and give salvation to all living and inanimate beings . . .'"[23]

As the Buddha had ten titles, the same number of high-sounding designations has also been conferred on Lao Tzu by the author, though there are slight differences from those of the Buddha. In the case of Lao Tzu, he is called the Teacher of emperors and kings, a great Immortal, Father of gods and men, and so forth.

All these indicate that Taoist writers have borrowed substantially from Buddhist sūtras concerning the birth of the Buddha, and the custom of addressing the Master. Such practices and conceptions were not found in Chinese literature before the introduction of Buddhism in the first century A.C. This clearly shows that the Taoist imitated the Buddhist institutions, and makes it obvious that there is no truth regarding Lao Tzu's mission to India to convert the Buddha or the barbarians.

Further, the Buddha was not born during the reign of King Huan-wang, i.e., between

719-697 B.C., as students of Buddhism know it today. The dates which modern scholars give to the birth and the death of the Buddha are closer to 543 and 483 B.C. This does not mean, however, that Lao Tzu was not an historical person. We have to distinguish between the "historical" Lao Tzu and the "deified" Lao Tzu. The historical Lao Tzu was a contemporary of Confucius (552-479 B.C.) and had left behind him a large portion of his sayings as found in the Tao-teh Ching; the deified Lao Tzu of the later Taoists was created from the phantom of the historical one whose glory and supernatural manifestations were substantially borrowed from Buddhism. To say that he converted the Buddha is really a great irony of fate which undoubtedly reflects the credulity of the author of this story. No historically-minded person would accept it as containing a grain of truth.

The Imperial Inquiries on the Authenticity of Lao Tzu's Mission

Since the mission story in itself provides sufficient ground for suspicion, there is nothing unusual, therefore, if the intelligent rulers in China probed this question from time to time. The earliest official debate on Lao Tzu's mission took place during the reign of Emperor Hsiao-ming-ti (516-627 A.C.) of the northern Wei dynasty. It was at the request of Liu Shêng-hsüan, a high official of the Emperor, that a debate was arranged between T'an-mo (9A), the Buddhist scholar, and Chiang Pin, the Taoist. In reply to the Emperor's query whether or not the Buddha and Lao Tzu were contemporaries, the Taoist answered in the affirmative that when Lao Tzu went to the West to convert the barbarians, the Buddha was his attendant.[24] Regarding the date of birth of Lao Tzu, the Taoist said that he was born in the third year of King Ting-wang (604 B.C.) and went to the West in the first year of King Ching-wang (519 B.C.). To contradict this claim, T'an-mo said that the Buddha was born in the twenty-fourth year of

King Chao-wang (1029 B.C.) and passed away in
the fifty-second year of King Mu-wang (948 B.C.).
In other words, the birth of the Buddha was over
four hundred years earlier than that of Lao Tzu.
Therefore, it was not possible for the latter to
convert the former. The sources quoted by both
parties are dubious. Probably they could not
verify the date of the Buddha as we are able to
do it today. When the authority of the Taoist
was doubted, and when the ministers informed
the Emperor that Lao Tzu had composed the Tao-teh
ching only and there was nothing concerning
his mission, Chiang Pin, the Taoist, was on the
verge of being doomed to capital punishment, when
Bodhiruci intervened. The accusation against
him was that he had cheated the public by making
a false statement. Obviously the Emperor and
his ministers did not believe the story of
Lao Tzu's mission.[25]

The question of Lao Tzu's converting the
barbarians was taken up again in 660 A.C. by
King Kao-tsung (659-683 A.C.) of the T'ang dynasty.
The disputants who participated in this debate
were Ching-t'ai from the Buddhist side and Li Yung
representing the Taoists. The arguments forwarded
by Ching-t'ai were comparatively more forceful
and convincing than that of his opponent. The
former quoted many references from well-known
works such as Tsin-tai tsa-lu, Chuang-tzŭ,
Hsi-ching tsa-chi (10A) and so forth, to prove
that the story of Lao Tzu's mission was invented
by Wang Fou; that Ch'in Shih paid a condolence
call when Lao Tzu had passed away and that Lao Tzu
was buried at a place called Huai-li.[26] Accordingly, if these records were to be believed, it
would mean that it was not possible for Lao Tzu
to go to India as a missionary. The outcome of
the debate was that the Taoist lost the favor
of the Emperor and was removed from the capital,
because his statement concerning the issue was
patently ambiguous. Comparatively, he was better
off than his predecessor Chiang Pin as he was
not threatened with capital punishment.

These are the two instances which have been

directly concerned with this topic. They generally lack the solid foundation of accuracy regarding the dates of Lao Tzu and the Buddha. For the sake of defending the honor of their religions, the disputants tried very hard to make a good show out of a hopeless case. If their religious fervor had been less ardent, and if they had cared to take an objective view, probably they would have realized where the truth lay.

NOTES

1. T'ang Yung-tung, Han-wei Liang-tsin Nan-pei-ch'ao Fu-chiao Shih (History of Buddhism in the Han, Wei, Eastern and Western Tsin, and Northern and Southern Dynasties) (Peking: Chung Hwa Book Co., 1972), p. 53.

2. Ibid., p. 56.

3. Hui-chiao, Kao-sêng Chuan (Biographies of Eminent Buddhist Teachers), in Taishō, vol. 50, pp. 323-24.

4. Ssǔ-ma Ch'ien, Shih-chi (A Historical Record), (Peking: Chung Hwa Book Co., 1972), pp. 2139-43.

5. Ibid., p. 1909.

6. Ibid., p. 2140.

7. Ibid.

8. Ibid.

9. It is very likely that this may be the earliest version of the extant Tao-teh ching.

10. Ssǔ-ma Ch'ien, op.cit., p. 2143.

11. T'ang Yung-tung, op.cit., p. 60.

12.   P.C. Bagchi, India and China (New York: Philosophical Library, 1951), pp. 5-6; T'ang Yung-tung, op.cit., p. 9.

13.   T'ang Yung-tung, op.cit., p. 56.

14.   Ibid., pp. 14-15.

15.   Fa-hsien, The Travels of Fa-hsien, in Taishō, vol. 51, pp. 857-65.

16.   Bagchi, op.cit., pp. 8-16; see also the maps attached to Wang Chun-heng, A Simple Geography of China (Peking: Foreign Languages Press, 1958).

17.   T'ang Yung-tung, op.cit., p. 60.

18.   Ibid.

19.   Tao-hsüan, Chi ku-chin fo-tao lun-hêng (A Collection of Controversial Discussions from Ancient to Modern Times Between the Buddhists and the Taoists), in Taishō, vol. 52, p. 391c.

20.   This translation can be found in Taishō, vol. 1, pp. 160ff.

21.   Wang Fou, Lao-tzu hua-hu ching (The Sūtra on Lao Tzu's Converting the Barbarians), in Taishō, vol. 54, pp. 1266-67.

22.   Cf. E.J. Thomas, The Life of the Buddha as Legend and History (London: Routledge & Kegan Paul, 1952), p. 31; P'u-yao-ching (Lalitavistara Sūtra), in Taishō, vol. 3, pp. 483ff.; Tao-hsüan, Shih-chia p'u (The Genealogy of the Śākyas), in Taishō, vol. 50, pp. 1ff.

23.   Wang Fou, op.cit., p. 1266b.

24.   Tao-hsüan, Chi-ku-chin-fo-tao-lun-hêng, p. 369b.

25.   Ibid.

26.   Ibid., pp. 391-92.

IV

GLOSSARY

1A 老子化胡經

2A 襄楷

3A 司馬遷：史記

4A 魚豢：魏畧西戎傳

5A 張騫

6A 身毒

7A 刘向：神仙傳

8A 白祖（白法祖）

9A 曇謨，姜斌

10A 晉代雜錄…西京雜記

V

A STUDY OF THE DOTTED RECORD

It is nearly seventy years since J. Takakusu
mentioned the Dotted Record in the Journal of the
Royal Asiatic Society in 1896. His main purpose
at that time was to show that some of the Buddhist texts translated into Chinese were of
Pali origin. To prove his theory, he cited the
case of Samantapāsādikā. This text is a commentary on the Vinaya by Buddhaghosa, the well-
known Pali commentator closely associated with
Ceylon.[1] The Chinese translation is entitled
Shan-chien-lü p'i-p'o-sha (1A) (Taishō, no. 1462).
While describing the circumstances under which it
was translated, he briefly mentioned the title
Chung-shên tien-chi (2A) or A Dotted Record of
Many Sages. From that time on many Western
scholars came to know of the existence of such a
document. On account of its relative importance
concerning the date of the Buddha, orientalists
such as Wilhelm Geiger,[2] V.A. Smith,[3] J.F. Fleet,[4]
Gopala Aiyer,[5] and others have in one way or
another cited the Dotted Record. Probably their
interest in this connection was comparative in
nature. This is because most of the above-
mentioned scholars who suggested dates of the
Buddha came to the conclusion that the Buddha
passed away about 480 B.C. The date shown in
the Dotted Record, as it stands today, is 486 B.C.

However, the information given in J. Takakusu's article was inaccurate to a certain extent. As a matter of fact, there was a dis-
crepancy in calculation due to an oversight of
another important document which concerns the
same Record. It is my intention to make a com-
prehensive survey of all the relevant facts
regarding this matter, so that an impartial
conclusion may be drawn. In addition to this,
observations will be made as to the authenticity
of the Record itself.

69

According to J. Takakusu, in the year 489 A.C. there were 975 dots on the Record and "The Buddha's death therefore falls, according to this Record, in the year 486 B.C."[6] But it was a serious mistake when he agreed with the statement made by Fei Ch'ang-fang that no more dots were added to the Record after 489 A.C. Apparently neither J. Takakusu nor Fei Ch'ang-fang (3A) (from whose book the former drew all his information) were aware of the fact that in 493 A.C. (4A) a bhikṣuṇī by the name of Ching-shiu (5A) added a dot to that Record. This is stated in Sêng-yu's (6A) Ch'u san-tsang chi chi (7A), and below is a translation of the relevant passage:

On the 10th of the 3rd Moon, in the 10th year of Yung-ming /8A/ of the Ch'i dynasty /492 A.C./, Bhikṣuṇī Ching-hsiu of Ch'an-lin /ssŭ?/ /9A/ learnt that the Venerable Saṅghabhadra, assisted by the Venerable Sêng-wei /10A/ translated the Sanskrit/7/ text Samantapāsādikā /11A/ into Chinese, consisting of 18 fascicles. As it was not available in the capital, she was very eager to see it. In that year, in the 5th Moon, Saṅghabhadra returned to the South /12A/. On the basis of that translation, she made a copy of it /at Canton/, and returned to the capital with the Vinaya /viz., Samantapāsādika/ on the 10th of the 4th Moon, in the 11th year of Yung-ming /493 A.C./. Making due obeisance, she held and read it, and deferentially copied it for distribution. On the 15th day of the 7th Moon /of that year/, after the ceremony on the conclusion of the Summer's Retreat /13a/, in the presence of an assembly, showing her humble estimation in regard to the years after the Parinirvaṇa of the Buddha, she respectfully set down another dot, as had been the annual practice previously. She was so overwhelmed by her sentiment of adoration that unknowingly she burst into tears.[8]

From this passage it is obvious that the addition
of a dot to the Record in question was carried out
as late as 493 A.C. This will certainly contradict the statement made in Fei Ch'ang-fang's
Li-tai san-pao chi, and a similar view expressed
by J. Takakusu, that the practice of adding a
dot to the Record was discontinued after 489 A.C. [9]

On account of the newly discovered evidence,
we think, the number of dots in the Record in
489 A.C. has to be studied afresh and recon-
structed in a critical manner. Accordingly we
would like to pose the following questions and
thereby arrive at a suitable solution:

1) Was it true that there were 975 dots
    in 489 A.C.?

2) When Fei Ch'ang-fang made the state-
    ment in 597 A.C. (14A), did he include
    the dot that was added by Bhiksuni
    Ching-hsiu?

3) Were any dots added to the Record
    during the period 490-492 A.C.?

Before answering these questions, we
should have a better understanding of how this
episode came into being. To achieve this, we
can do no better than refer to the original
statement made by Fei Ch'ang-fang in 597 A.C.,
in the eleventh chapter of his Li-tai san-pao chi
(15A). A translation of the relevant passage
is given below:

        During the reign of Emperor Wu-ti
    /ōf the Ch'i dynasty, 482-493 A.C./,
    there was a foreign Śramana bearing the
    name Sêng-ga-pa-t'o-lo /16A/ /Sanghabhadra/.
    It means 'Sêng-hsien' /17A/ in Chinese.
    According to him, there was a tradition
    which had been handed down from teacher
    to teacher for generations, viz., after
    the passing away of the Buddha, Upāli
    collected the Vinaya and observed the
    Pavaraṇa on the 15th of the 7th Moon

of the same year. Having offered flowers
and incense to the Vinaya on that occasion,
he marked a dot /on a Record/ and placed
it close to the Vinaya text. Thereafter
this was repeated every year. When Upāli
was about to depart from this world, he
handed it over to his disciple Dāsaka,
and in similar circumstances Dāsaka to
Sonaka, Sonaka to Siggava, Siggava to
Moggalīputta Tissa, and Moggaliputta
Tissa to Candavajjī. In this manner the
teachers in turn handed it down to the
present Master of Tripitaka. This Master
brought the Vinaya-piṭaka to Canton.
When he was about to disembark /10/
he decided to return to his /native land/,
and handed over the Vinaya-piṭaka to his
disciple Saṅghabhadra. With the assistance
of Sêng-wei /11/ Saṅghabhadra began
translating the Samantapasādikā Vinaya
at the Bamboo Grove Monastery /18A/in
Canton, in the 6th year of Yung-ming
/488 A.C./, and on account of that they
stayed together for the Rain-season
Retreat /19A/. Having observed the Pavāraṇā
and offered flowers and incense to the
Vinaya-piṭaka at midnight /on the 15th/,
of the 7th Moon, in the 7th year of
Yung-ming[12] /489 A.C./, he added a dot
/to the Record/ as a traditional practice.
The total amounted to 975 dots in that
year. A dot is counted as a year.

In the first year of Ta-t'ung /20A/
/535 A.C./ of the Liang dynasty, Chao
Pê-hsiu /21A/ met Hung-tu /22A/, the
Vinaya master, famed for his ascetic
practice, at Mt. Lu-shan /23A/, and
from whom he obtained the number of
years as shown in the Dotted Record
of Many Sages. This was initiated after
the passing away of the Buddha, and continued up to the 7th year of Yung-ming
/489 A.C./. "How was it that after the
7th year of Yung-ming /489 A.C./ no
dots were added to it?" Pê-hsiu asked

72

Hung-tu. "Before that year, the dots were added personally by the enlightened sages. As I am an ordinary mortal, I may pay my respects and keep it safely, but I dare not add any dot on my own," replied Hung-tu. On the basis of the age-old dots /975 dots in 489 A.C./ Pê-hsiu made a calculation, and it amounted to 1028 years/13/ in the 9th year of Ta-t'ung /543 A.C./ . . . ./14/

Being familiar with the background, we may now proceed to answer the questions.

To answer question one, "Was it true that there were 975 dots in 489 A.C.?": Most probably the counting of dots did not take place in 489 A.C., but between 494 and 535 A.C. This is inferred from the fact that Hung-tu was not aware that in 493 A.C. a dot was added to the Record by Bhiksunī Ching-hsiu. Therefore, there were either 974 or 972 dots in the Record in 489 A.C., but not 975 dots. (Regarding the figure of 972 dots, a lengthy explanation will be given in the answer to the third question in this article.)

The answer to the second question, namely, "When Fei Ch'ang-fang made the statement in 597 A.C., did he include the dot that was added by Bhiksunī Ching-hsiu?", is as follows:

It appears that he relied heavily on the statement made by Hung-tu, and was not aware of the fact that a dot was added to the Record in 493 A.C. If our judgment is correct, obviously he was responsible for making the statement that "The total amounted to 975 dots in that year /489 A.C./." He said this as if he were absolutely sure of it. This being so, naturally he must have included the dot that added in 493 A.C. Had he been aware of this particular addition, he would have said that there were 974 dots in 489 A.C.

Unfortunately, Sêng-yu, author of Ch'u

san-tsang chi chi, did not mention the number of
dots when he recorded the event of Bhiksunī
Ching-hsiu's addition in 493 A.C.[15] As he
flourished in 444-518 A.C. and was the Resident
Abbot of the Chien-t'su-ssŭ (24A) Monastery in
the capital (Nanking), in addition to his being
a renowned Master of Vinaya, he must have had
a firsthand and personal knowledge of the episode.[16]
To our mind, the Record in question is a genuine
one, though the number of dots was not indicated
in the earlier and more trustworthy document of
Sêng-yu.

Regarding the third question, "Were any
dots added to the Record during the period
490-492 A.C.," it appears that no literary
documents mentioned anything of this nature.
However, it may be argued that, as Sanghabhadra
returned to the South (his native land) in the
5th Moon in 492 A.C., there was a possibility
that he might have followed his own example
shown in 489 A.C. in adding two dots for 490
and 491 A.C.[17] As the Pavāraṇā ceremony is
usually held in the 7th Moon, it was not possible
for him to make the addition in 492 A.C. Further,
we notice that Bhiksunī Ching-hsiu met Sanghabhadra at Canton between the 3rd and the 5th Moon
in 492 A.C., and the Dotted Record was obviously
handed over to the former by the latter. Consequently she followed the example of Sanghabhadra
and added a dot to it in 493 A.C. at Nanking.
The task of copying the newly translated Chinese
version of the Samantapāsādikā took her nearly
a year to accomplish. This is seen from the
fact that she went to Canton in the 3rd Moon
of 492 and returned to Nanking in the 4th Moon
of 493 A.C. It is unlikely that she added any
dot to the Record in 492, since she was very
busy in copying the text in eighteen fascicles,
and probably she would not have done it in
private, as she added a dot to the Record in 493
in the presence of an assembly with great ceremony. In any case, the literary sources did not
say anything definite about this point.

Thus we see that probably two more dots

74

have been added to the Record in 490 and 491 A.C.
This fact has not been taken into account in calculating the date of the Buddha by scholars of the
preceding generation. If this view is accepted,
it would mean that three dots were added to the
Record after 489 A.C., or that is to say, there
were 972 dots in the Record in 489 A.C. By sub-
tracting 489 from 972 we get 483 years, which
means that the death of the Buddha falls in
483 B.C. This agrees with the calculation made
by W. Geiger as stated in his introduction to the
Mahavamsa,[18] and at the same time, this corrects
the error made by J. Takakusu that "The Buddha's
death therefore falls, according to this Record,
in the year 486 B.C."[19]

However, if there is any solid evidence to
prove that no dots were added to the Record in
490 and 491, we would say that there were 974
dots in 489 A.C. If we accept this view, then
the death of the Buddha took place in 485 B.C.
Even in this case, it still corrects J. Takakusu's
theory that 486 B.C. is the year in which the
Buddha passed away. But, until such evidence is
presented we would maintain that 483 B.C. is
a reasonable calculation of the Parinirvana date
of the Buddha. There is reason to believe that
the substance of the Dotted Record is closely
associated with the tradition of the Pali chronicles
of Ceylon.

The Origin of the Tradition
Concerning the Date of the Buddha

As the Dotted Record is directly connected
with the translation of the Samantapasadika, it
calls for reference to its author Buddhaghosa
and the tradition prevalent in Ceylon during the
time when he made his commentaries on the
Canonical texts. This is a necessary step by
which we can assess the degree to which the Dotted
Record tradition is acceptable.

Regarding the teachers who were responsible
for transmitting the Vinaya in succession in

India, the Dīpavamsa[20] gives us a list of names
including the founder of Buddhism. It is said
that Upāli received it from the Buddha. After
that, Upāli handed it over to Dāsaka, Dāsaka to
Sonaka, Sonaka to Siggava and Candavajjī,
Candavajjī to Tissa Moggalīputta and Tissa Moggalīputta to Mahinda. According to the Pali tradition, we know that Mahinda was the son of King
Aśoka, and the person through whom Buddhism was
introduced to Ceylon. This list is comparable
with the names given by Fei Ch'ang-fang,[21] except
that Fei was confused regarding the relation between Tissa Moggalīputta and Candavajjī. According to the Dīpavamsa, Candavajjī was the
teacher of Tissa Moggālīputta, but Fei Ch'ang-fang
made him a pupil of Tissa Moggalīputta; and the
name of Mahinda was not mentioned at all. This
error should be corrected, and naturally, the
Pali tradition should be preferred.

The Mahāvamsa list is in close agreement
with that of the Dīpavamsa, i.e., 1) Upāli,
2) Dāsaka, 3) Sonaka, 4) Siggava and Candavajjī,
5) Tissa Moggalīputta, and 6) Mahinda,[22] with
the exception that Candavajjī was mainly an
expert in the Sutta and Abhidhamma Pitakas. It
was to learn these sections of Buddhist literature
that Siggava sent Tissa Moggalīputta to him.
In other words, it means that Siggava was officially the fourth teacher who transmitted the
Vinaya. It is on this point that the Mahāvamsa
differs from the Dīpavamsa.

When Buddhaghosa composed the introduction
to the Samantapāsādika, he made a list of seven
teacher which is almost identical with that of
the Mahāvamsa, i.e., 1) Upāli, 2) Dāsaka, 3)
Sonaka, 4) Siggava, 5) Tissa Moggalīputta, 6)
Mahinda, and 7) Arittha.[23] However, he elimi-
nated altogether the name of Candavajjī, a
fellow disciple of Siggava. Later, Fei Ch'ang-
fang adopted the first five names given in this
list. But it is significant that he named the
sixth teacher as Candavajjī. As pointed out
earlier, this was a mistake. However, we are
inclined to ask the question: Whence did he get

that name? It may be an oral tradition given
by Saṅghabhadra, but certainly it was not from
the Samantapasādika.

Among the Pali works mentioned above the
Dīpavamsa appears to be the oldest, according
to its date of composition. It must have been
completed some time about the beginning or middle
of the fourth century A.C., as by the middle of
the fifth century A.C., during the reign of King
Dhātusena (495-497), it was recited in public
at the annual Mahinda festival, and it was quoted
several times by Buddhaghoṣa.[24] Concerning the
relative interval of composition between the
Dīpavamsa, Mahāvamsa, and the works of Buddhaghoṣa, G.P. Malalasekera, author of The Pali
Literature of Ceylon, is of the opinion that it
was about 100-150 years between the first two,
and the works of Buddhaghoṣa came in between
them.[25] This would indicate the order of antiquity in the following manner: 1) Dīpavamsa,
2) Samantapasādika, and 3) Mahāvamsa. It is,
however, interesting to note that while the
Dīpavamsa and Mahāvamsa were in full agreement
with regard to the names of teachers, Samantapasādika dropped the name of Candavajjī altogether, but mentioned Arittha, the seventh
teacher, of Ceylonese origin.[26] There is something in common among these works, that is, they
point to a tradition concerning the transmission
of the Vinaya by these teachers. Later, when
Saṅghabhadra went to China in 486 A.C., he was
regarded as a teacher who had succeeded to the
line of teachers transmitting the Vinaya. This
claim made by the translator of Samantapasādika
seems reasonable and acceptable. If such is the
case, the Dotted Record, which was closely associated with this translator, may have a genuine
origin, or perhaps have belonged to an ancient
Buddhist tradition. But the way in which it
was preserved, handed down from generation to
generation, and carried about from one country
to another appears to be rather mysterious and
suspicious. I cannot but express doubts concerning its authenticity. I state my reasons
as follows:

1) The Pali chronicles and Samantapāsādikā
speak of the transmission of the Vinaya by the
teachers initiated by Upāli, but in them we do
not encounter any reference to the practice of
adding dots to a record every year after the
rain season retreat. Such being the case, how
can one believe that the Dotted Record was started
by Upāli and handed down in succession by the
Vinaya teachers?

2) If there was really such a Record initiated by Upāli, then Mahinda, the sixth teacher
of the Vinaya succession, on coming to Ceylon,
should have brought it with him, and continued
to add dots each year throughout his life. If
so, such a Record would have been safely preserved in Ceylon as a sacred object like the
Bo-tree, or the Tooth Relic. But this was not
known to the writers of either the Pali or the
Sinhalese works, nor was it noted in the Travels
of Fa-hsien, when Fa-hsien visited Ceylon in the
beginning of the fifth century. Did Mahinda
really bring such a thing to Ceylon?

3) If we say that there was no Record of
such nature in ancient Ceylon, how can we account for its journey to China, especially in
connection with the translation of the Samantapāsādikā? The Chinese Buddhist works are not
very helpful in determining the nationality or
native land to which Saṅghabhadra belonged. From
the Li-tai san-pao chi of Fei Ch'ang-fang, and
Ch'u san-tsang chi chi of Sêng-yu, we are given
to understand that he was a "foreign Śramaṇa"
(25A) who went to China by sea, in the company
of his teacher. He stayed at Canton from 488
to 492, and in 493 he returned to Nan (26A)
(South).[27] Of two other works of later date, one
mentions that he was an Indian Śramaṇa,[28] and
the other states that he was a Śramaṇa of the
Hsi Yu (27A) or Western Regions.[29] As they were
dated in 1341 and 802 respectively, we cannot
attach much importance to them. I am, however,
inclined to think that there is some omission in
the sentence of "Saṅghabhadra returned to the
South. . ." (28A). I would venture to suggest

78

that "Nan" (29A) might be a part of the proper
noun Fu-nan (30A), which is the ancient name for
Cambodia. The meaning in "Saṅghabhadra returned
to the South" is rather ambiguous, but if we say
"Saṅghabhadra returned to Fu-nan /Cambodia/,"
it would suit the circumstances under which the
event took place.

In support of this hypothesis, we observe that
Fu-nan had Buddhism and diplomatic relations with
China from the end of the third century A.C. In
the Fu-tsu t'ung-chi (31A) it is stated that
"During the reign of Wu-ti of the Tsin dynasty
/280-290 A.C.7 Fu-nan sent her envoy to China with
presents of a gold statue of the Buddha, and an
ivory stupa."[30] Later in the fifth and sixth
centuries there were Buddhist missionaries who
went to China from Fu-nan. For instance, 1)
Saṅghapāla reached the capital (Nanking) some
time during the period of 435-468.[31] Among the
works translated by him, Vimukti-mārga Śāstra
was one, and among the official buildings where
he undertook his translations was the Hall of
Fu-nan (32A).[32]

2) At the beginning of the Liang dynasty
(ca. 502), Mandra or Mandrasena brought a number
of Sanskrit texts to China, and translated three
works in cooperation with Saṅghapāla.[33]

3) During 535-545 A.C. Emperor Wu-ti of
Liang appointed Chang Fan (33A) as an escort to
accompany the Fu-nan envoy back to his country.
To express her gratitude, Fu-nan requested Paramārtha of India to take many sūtras and śāstras
to China. The date of Paramārtha's arrival in
China was about 545 A.C. (34A).[34]

The evidence mentioned above indicates the
great possibility that Saṅghabhadra might have
come from Fu-nan, especially when we consider
that Fu-nan possessed a large collection of both
Mahāyāna and Hīnayāna texts at that time. This
appears to be more convincing than the suggestion
made by J. Takakusu that Saṅghabhadra was a
Sinhalese or Burmese.[35] Thus, the Dotted Record

might have been taken to Cambodia from India, if it did not go there via Ceylon. However, it is impossible to make a definite statement in regard to its mysterious journey to China.

4) It may be said that a period of 975 years is a very long time in history. Is it possible that during this lengthy space of time no mistake or omission was ever made in respect to the dots marked on the Record? This may be a difficult question to answer. However, as a result of the investigations indicated elsewhere in this article, it appears that there may be many omissions and errors regarding the addition of dots by different persons at different times. Also, the Record itself was carried about from country to country over a period of nearly 1,000 years. Therefore, the accuracy of the Record in calculating the years after the Buddha's Parinirvāna may not be accepted without further careful investigation.

In conclusion, we would like to make it clear that, in spite of all the defects, the Dotted Record says something noteworthy. It indicates that the date of the passing of the Buddha is about 483 B.C., which coincides and agrees with the calculation made by W. Geiger on the basis of the Pali chronicles. It seems to have a genuine origin closely associated with either the Indian Buddhist tradition or with that of the Pali chronicles, although we are not quite certain as to how it went from India to China. With regard to its mysterious journey, there may be two possibilities. 1) It may have gone to Fu-nan or Cambodia from Ceylon along with the Samantapāsādikā, as this Vinaya commentary is definitely of Ceylonese origin. However, the Pali chronicles and Sinhalese works are silent about it. 2) It may have gone to Cambodia directly from India. The Chinese Buddhist literary documents which described the names of Vinaya teachers, especially the name of Candavajjī, lend support to this view. This shows that Fei Ch'ang-fang did not obtain this information concerning the Vinaya teachers from the

Samantapāsādikā, but from elsewhere: it may have been from Fu-nan.

Another point which should be clarified here is that the Dotted Record must have existed independently, at least for some 500 years, until the composition of the Samantapāsādikā in the fifth century. Therefore, we may suggest that the association between the Dotted Record and the Samantapāsādikā which took place in China was by mere accident.

It is very unlikely that Saṅghabhadra was a Burmese and brought the Record to China from Burma, as we know that his journey to China, as well as the return voyage from China, was by sea.[36] Normally a Burmese would not travel all the way from Burma to Canton by sea for the purpose of reaching China. Such a journey would be similar to a person's going to San Francisco from New York via the Panama Canal.

In passing, it may be mentioned that the conclusion made by P.H.L. Eggermont regarding the date of the death of the Buddha on the basis of The Dotted Record of Canton, and his suggestion that "The Buddha-era of the Dotted Record of Canton was used in Ceylon before it was replaced by the one based on the epoch 483 B.C.,"[37] appears to be very unsatisfactory. He would probably have arrived at a quite different conclusion had he devoted more time to a study of the episode of Bhiksunī Ching-hsiu's addition of a dot to the Record.

NOTES

1. G.P. Malalasekera, The Pali Literature of Ceylon (London: Royal Asiatic Society of Great Britain and Ireland, 1928), p. 94.

2. Wilhelm Geiger, trans., The Mahāvamsa (Colombo: Ceylon Government Information Department, 1950), p. xxvi.

3. V.A. Smith, Early History of India (Oxford: The Clarendon Press, 1914), p. 49.

4. J.F. Fleet, "The Day on Which Buddha Died," Journal of the Royal Asiatic Society (1909), p. 9.

5. Gopala Aiyer, "The Date of the Buddha," Indian Antiquary (1908), pp. 341ff.

6. J. Takakusu, "Pali Elements in Chinese Buddhism," Journal of the Royal Asiatic Society (1896), pp. 415-39.

7. Actually this was written in Pali.

8. Sêng-yu, Ch'u San-tsang chi chi (A Collection of Records Concerning the Translating of the Tripitaka) in Taishō, vol. 55, p. 82a, b.

9. Takakusu, op.cit., p. 437.

10. The Chinese words are "to embark" (38A), but it must be an error for "to disembark" (39A).

11. "Sêng-yi" (35A) here, but it was "Sêng-wei" (36A) in Sêng-yu, op.cit., p. 82a, b, and in Chih-shêng, K'ai-yüan Shih-chiao Lu (37A;45A) Catalogue of Buddhist Texts of K'ai-yüan Period), in Taishō, vol. 55, p. 535a.

12. The text reads as (40A). In fact, the years should be (41A). See Chih-chang, ed., Fu-tsu Li-tai T'ung-tsai (42A , (A General Survey of All Dynasties of Buddhism), in Taishō, vol. 49, p. 341a; and Chih-shêng, op.cit., p. 535c.

13. Actually this should be 1029 years.

14. Fei Ch'ang-fang, Li-tai san-pao Chi (A Record of the Triple Gem of All the Dynasties), in Taishō, vol. 49, p. 95b, c.

15. Sêng-yu, op.cit., p. 82a, b.

16. Hui-chiao, Kao-sêng Chuan (43A) (Biographies of Eminent Buddhist Teachers), in Taishō, vol. 50, p. 402c.

17. Sêng-yu, op.cit., p. 82a, b.

18. Geiger, op.cit., p. xxvi.

19. Takakusu, op.cit., p. 437.

20. Hermann Oldenburg, ed. and trans., The Dīpavaṃsa (London: Williams and Norgate, 1879), pp. 144-45.

21. Fei Ch'ang-fang, op.cit., p. 95b, c.

22. Geiger, op.cit., pp. 34-37, 39.

23. Buddhaghoṣa, Shan-chien-lü P'i-p'o-sha (The Samantapāsādika Vinaya) in Taishō, vol. 24, p. 684b, c.

24. Malalasekera, op.cit., p. 138.

25. Smith, op.cit., p. 49.

26. Malalasekera, op.cit., p. 44; see also Geiger, op.cit., pp. 34-37, 39, 133.

27. Fei Ch'ang-fang, op.cit., p. 95b, c; Sêng-yu, op.cit., pp. 82, 83.

28. Chih-chang, op.cit., pp. 543-44a. The text states, "In foreign countries there is a so-called Saṅghabhadra who is a Śramaṇa of India" (44A).

29. Chih-shêng, op.cit., pp. 535-36a; Fung Ch'eng-chün, Les Moines Chinois et Étrangers qui ont Contribué à la Formation du Tripiṭaka Chinois (Shanghai: The Commercial Press, 1931), p. 42.

30. Chih-p'an, Fu-tsu T'ung-chi (46A) (Records of the Lineage of the Buddha and the Patriarchs), in Taishō, vol. 49, ch. 52, p. 456c.

31. This was the period during which Saṅghapāla
flourished. As Saṅghapāla was a disciple of
Guṇabhadra, the former's arrival in China cannot
be later than 468 A.C.

32. Tao-hsüan, Hsü Kao-sêng Chuan (47A), (Second
Series of Eminent Buddhist Teachers), in Taishō,
vol. 50, ch. 1, p. 426.

33. Ibid.

34. Ibid., p. 429. The text states, "the twelfth
year of Ta-t'ung" (48A). As there were only
eleven years in the Ta-t'ung period, ending in
545 A.D., this statement is a mistake.

35. Takakusu, op.cit., p. 435.

36. Ibid.

37. P.H.L. Eggermont, The Chronology of the
Reign of Aśoka Moriya (Leiden: E.J. Brill, 1956),
pp. 141-43.

GLOSSARY

1A 善見律毘婆沙	14A 開皇十七年
2A 眾聖點記	15A 歷代三寶記
3A 費長房	16A 僧伽跋陀羅
4A 齊永明十一年	17A 僧賢
5A 淨秀	18A 竹林寺
6A 僧祐	19A 安居
7A 出三藏記集	20A 大同
8A 齊永明十年	21A 趙伯休
9A 禪林比丘尼淨秀	22A 弘度
10A 僧璟	23A 廬山
11A 善見毘婆沙律	24A 建初寺
12A 南	25A 外國沙門
13A 受歲	26A 南

27A 西域

28A 僧伽跋陀羅其年五月
　　　　還南

29A 南

30A 扶南

31A 佛祖統記

32A 扶南館

33A 張氾

34A 大同十一年

35A 僧猗

36A 僧禕

37A 開元錄

38A 上舶

39A 下舶

40A 永明七年庚午

41A 己巳

42A 佛祖歷代通載

43A 高僧傳

44A 外國有祈謂天竺沙門
　　　　僧伽跋陀羅者

45A 開元釋教錄

46A 佛祖統記

47A 續高僧傳

48A 大同十二年

BUDDHISM AND ITS RELATION

TO CHINESE RELIGIONS

The Religious Trends in Early China

Buddhism was the earliest foreign religion, having been introduced to China in the first century A.C., when its philosophical tenets, religious organization and practice became known to the Chinese. In the initial stage, it attracted the attention of men of high position like Prince Ying of Ch'u and Moutzu, although neither of them understood the Buddhist doctrine very correctly.[1] This was due to the fact that the Prince was deeply interested in magical arts and the worship of spirits. He believed that Buddhism was a branch of the Taoist cult. Possibly he was influenced by the popular story that the Buddha appeared in a dream to Emperor Ming-ti of the Han dynasty in the form of a golden man.[2] From this one may gauge his knowledge concerning Buddhism. In the case of Moutzu (1A), he regarded the doctrine of karma, or cause and effect, to be the same as the continuity of the soul.[3] It was a misinterpretation of the doctrine of anattā or non-soul. If the understanding of these two well-known supporters of Buddhism could be superficial to such an extent, naturally one cannot expect anything better from the masses at that time. On account of this ignorance, when great Buddhist missionaries like An Shih-kao, Fu Tu-têng (2A), Kumarajīva, Buddhabhadra and others reached China at different intervals, they were thought to be magicians for their unusual ability to interpret the language of the birds, to cause the growth of a blue lotus from a begging bowl, to predict the arrival of foreign boats from India, to make damp ashes float on the surface of water,

and many other surprising magical feats.[4] There
were only a few learned scholars who showed great
respect for their learning and pure conduct in
the observance of the Vinaya or discipline. Besides, their secular knowledge of astronomy,
geography, the cosmic principles of yin and yang
and the five elements, the preparing of the
calendar, the interpreting of prophecies, and the
art of healing was considered to be their normal
training and qualifications, although secular
learning was not encouraged by the Buddha.[5] The
fact that Kao-sêng chuan, or the Biographies of
Eminent Buddhist Teachers, repeatedly publicized
the unique achievement of performing magical
feats leads us to suspect that there must be a
certain motive behind it. Looking deeper into
the matter, we notice that supernatural powers
ascribed to these teachers coincided with the
traditional Chinese belief in immortality. This
is illustrated in the cases of the Han magicians
such as Li Shao-chün, Shao Ong, Luan Ta and
Hsü Fu, who were supposed to be able to command
the spirits and ghosts,[6] to reach the Fairy Islands
and gather the life-giving herbs for preparing
a concoction so that one could become an immortal.[7]
On the basis of this observation, and since
Buddhism was regarded as a branch of Taoism, it
was able to gain a footing on Chinese soil.
Hence, it received friendly treatment from the
Chinese public in its initial stage.

Doctrinally, there is a great similarity
between the two religions. The Buddhist concept
of leading a life of purity, having no desires
for worldly pleasure and being freed from moral
blemish is not much different from that of Lao
Tzu's taking no notice of a sage and his wisdom,
and remaining in inactivity and self-contentment.[8]
We are also aware of the fact that the story of
Lao Tzu's mission to India to convert the Buddha
had a profound influence on the Chinese masses
who believed that Gautama Buddha was the disciple
of Lao Tzu.[9] That being so, Buddhism was identified with Taoism. But on the other hand, it was
due to the striking similarity between Taoism
and Buddhism that the latter was enabled to spread

far and wide in China in its early years. This
is the other side of the coin, we need not feel
shy or uneasy about it.

Its Relation to the State

        During its existence in China for a period
of nearly two thousand years, occasionally
Buddhism was harshly treated and persecuted by
several emperors bearing the title "Wu." It began with Emperor T'ai Wu-ti (424-450) of the
northern Wei dynasty (3A); then he was followed
by Emperor Wu-ti (561-578) of the northern Chou
dynasty (4A), Emperor Wu-tsung (840-846) of the
T'ang dynasty (5A), and Emperor Shih-tsung (954-
959) of the Later Chou dynasty (6A).[10] During
the periods of persecution Buddhism suffered
immense damage and great humiliation. However,
this does not mean that the Buddhists kept quiet
without showing any sign of protest. Actually
many of them did register their protest, even
at the risk of their lives. Take, for instance,
Hu-yüan (7A), an eminent Buddhist teacher who
wrote a learned treatise against paying homage
to the king when Huan Hsüan (8A), prime minister
of the eastern Tsin dynasty (317-420) was carrying
out a purge of the Buddhist Sangha.[11] This is a
complicated topic involving many causes and factors
which may be summed up as follows:

        (1) The Chinese think that they are the
descendants of the Yellow Emperor; that they
have had a glorious civilization for thousands
of years, and that they have also long ago left
the primitive ways of the caveman and entered
into a civilized world, where man wears silk
dresses, eats tasty meat dishes and stays in
palatial buildings. Further, holding the view
that China was situated in the center of the earth,
they regard its neighbors as barbarous, uncivilized, and unable to contribute anything worthwhile to Chinese learning. As Buddhism came
from India, which was a country of the barbarians,
and as Gautama Buddha, the founder of Buddhism
was an Indian, he was of course a deity of the
barbarians. How could it be possible for the

civilized to adopt a religion of the uncivilized?
Under these circumstances, if China was to be
restored to the pristine purity of the virtuous
ancient sages and sage-kings such as Yao, Shun,
Yü, and T'ang (ca. 2536-1766 B.C.), the first
step in this direction would be to reject any
institution of a foreign origin. When this was
put into effect, Buddhism was the first victim.
This trend of national superiority is clearly seen
in the official statement made by K'ou Ch'ien-
chih (9A) who was a Taoist teacher of Emperor
T'ai Wu-ti (424-470) of the northern Wei dynasty.[12]
Unfortunately this sparked off the first persecution of Buddhism in China. On account of their
national pride, the Chinese were unable to tolerate
the culture of a foreign nation, therefore, all
foreign elements were subjected to unkind treatment and rejection. Consequently Buddhism was
the chief target of attack.

(2) Considering the sayings of Lao Tzu
such as "The Tao constantly does nothing, but
everything is done,"[13] and "Man models himself
after Earth, Earth models itself after Heaven,
Heaven models itself after Tao and Tao models
itself after Nature,"[14] as found in the Tao-teh
ching, there is a certain amount of philosophical
and metaphysical elements. They deserve our
deep respect and admiration. But Taoists of the
Han, Wei, and Tsin dynasties (from the second
century B.C. to the fifth century), like Chang
Tao-lin, Wei Po-yang, Kao Hung and Tao Hung-ching,
were of a different type.[15] Chang Tao-lin claimed
that Lao Tzu was the founder of Taoism and hence
he established the Taoist cult of Five-Bushels-
of-Rice;[16] the rest contributed generously to
the final formation of the Taoist sects of
Alchemy and Amulets. The theory and practice of
these sects are very superficial and not of much
value to society. At the most one may say that
their function is similar to that of a shaman or
an old-fashioned physician. Consequently the
ancient emperors and kings either attended
a religious ceremony for the purpose of receiving
a sacred text on magic, and then called themselves
the True-King-of-the-Peace,[17] or held to the

belief that Lao Tzu was their ancestor and, therefore, a posthumous title called "The Mysterious Primordial Emperor" was conferred on that great philosopher.[18] It seems this was not enough. In order to demonstrate their filial piety for the great ancestor young princesses of the royal house of the T'ang dynasty (seventh to ninth century) were ordered to join the Taoist church and became female Taoists. By this means they blissfully believed that they could attain immortality. We are not sure as to the final attainment of their goal. But one thing is clear, that is to say, Taoism gained the status of a national religion of China in the Northern Wei and T'ang dynasties, whereas Buddhism and Confucianism were in a subordinate position.

On other occasions emperors of various dynasties used to convene conferences in order to discuss the superiority of the three existing religions in China (Buddhism, Taoism, and Confucianism) and accordingly seats of precedence would be allocated to them at official functions.[19] This measure was apparently a whitewash, because they regarded Buddhism as a foreign religion, which meant that it could not possibly amount to anything worthwhile. To them it was obvious that Taoism or Confucianism should occupy the first position. In other words, from the standpoint of national pride and the preservation of national culture, Buddhism should be looked down upon and it deserved the third and the last position because it was a foreign religion.

(3) Contrasting most sharply with the traditional Chinese culture is the relationship between Buddhism and conservative Confucianism. They look like ice and burning coal, and therefore, there is hardly any possibility of a compromise. These Confucianists talk about the observance of social relations, that there should be love between the parents and children, justice between the sovereign and subjects, and distinctive duties between the husband and wife.[20] They also lay great emphasis on the teaching "Of the

91

three infilial sins, the one being without a son is the worst." And "Everyone within the empire, including those who live in the remotest corner, is a subordinate to the king,"[21] and many other Confucian ethical standards. They regard the family as the basic unit of society. It is the duty of every man to observe filial piety while at home and to fulfill one's obligations in respect to one's country.[22] If a person renounces the world and becomes a Buddhist mendicant, it means that he is disloyal to his parents and the state by neglecting his obligations and duties. Further, according to the Confucian definition of the word "subject," it appears that anybody who lives within the boundary of a country is a subject, and is obliged to pay allegiance to the king.[23] Accordingly a mendicant is also a subject, and therefore he should pay homage to him, too. Owing to this interpretation the question rose of whether or not a Buddhist monk should salute the emperor. Had it been in India, the question would be whether the parents should or should not worship the children who had entered the Buddhist monastic order. As customs differ from country to country, entanglements and mis-understandings occur which are beyond the compre-hension of outside parties. It may be imagined that when Buddhism was first introduced to China, it had experienced great difficulty on account of the differences in national tradi-tions and customs.

However, after a time, Buddhism was able to overcome these tremendous obstacles. It was not only highly honored by the kings, ministers, the intelligentsia and the masses, but throughout the ages eminent and outstanding Buddhist teachers were produced by the Saṅgha, and the teaching of the Buddha spread extensively in all directions. The various series of Kao-sêng chuan or the Biographies of Eminent Buddhist Monks can be cited as evidence in this respect.[24] The popu-larity of Buddhism may be due to its profound philosophy, boundless compassion or universal love, religious ceremonies, including Buddhist art and sculpture and the organization of the

Saṅgha.   It was also due to the translation of
two popular Buddhist texts, i.e., The Sutra on the
Original Vows of Ksitigarbha Bodhisattva and
The Ullampana Sūtrā.   The former describes the
Bodhisattva's visit to the Land of Darkness to
rescue his mother who was undergoing painful
sufferings, and the latter concerned itself with
the salvation of the departed and helpless souls.[25]
When these Buddhist stories became popular they
made a deep impression on the people, so much
so that they were inclined to think that Buddhism
also showed interest in filial piety.   Thus it
was in no way against the Confucian ethics, but
it would, on the other hand, help improve the
morality of the people.

        (4)   The main causes which led to the enforce-
ment of control over the Saṅgha by the state
were, 1) the controversy about paying allegiance
to the king, and 2) the economic drain on society.
Han Yü, a Confucian scholar of the T'ang dynasty,
was a formidable opponent of Buddhism under the
second classification.   Besides, the Saṅgha was
partially to be blamed for the decadent trends
as shown by some of its members.   In the fifth
century there was a bhikkhunī by the name of
Miao-yin (10A).   At that time the members of the
royal household, including some of the kings of
the Tsin dynasty (317-420), showered on her
honors and respect.   Taking advantage of this, she
frequented the palace, making alliances with the
influential nobles.   People who desired favors
from these high officials often approached her
and made her their intermediary.   She too, was
deeply involved in the game for earthly considerations.   It is said that the number of people
who went to pay her visits amounted to many
hundreds per day.   Their horse-drawn vehicles
were parked just outside her monastery, and this
made the place look like a market square.[26]
If this is correct, then where was the Buddhist
principle of observing a life of purity, non-
activity, non-attachement and the freedom from
worldly possessions?   The unbecoming behavior
of this bhikkhunī and her associates seems
responsible for bringing disgrace on the Buddhist

Saṅgha. As a consequence there was an official
purge to eliminate the undesirable elements.
Perhaps the Buddhists have learned a lesson.

The Contribution of Buddhism
To Chinese Culture

Buddhism's unique contribution to Chinese
culture is, perhaps, in the form of an organized
religion and the doctrine of karma, which means
good or evil action. Through action one may
either be rewarded with a happy birth in heaven
or degraded to undergo sufferings in hell.
Further, by the practice of reciting the names of
Amitābha Buddha, the devotees will be born in his
Paradise of Bliss called "Sukhāvati." Since this
is very easy and simple to practice, the heavenly
paradise is within the reach of everybody. In
addition to this, by constructing stūpas and
monasteries, by making statues and translating
Buddhist sacred texts, it helped introduce to
China Indian literature, philosophy, fine arts
and architecture, and sometimes these objects
served as a memorial dedicated to one's departed
ancestors or men of distinguished service to
the nation. In any case, the awe-inspiring
monuments enhance the scenic beauty of a particular locality, and it was stated by one of
the emperors of the Ch'ing dynasty (1616-1911)
that most of the famous mountains in China were
occupied by the Buddhist Saṅgha. It means that
wherever there is a beautiful spot, one is sure
to find an ancient Buddhist monastery in excellent traditional architecture. It is obvious
that the daily life of the Chinese people has been
directly or indirectly influenced by an atmosphere
which is thoroughly immersed in Buddhist culture.
According to poet Po Chü-i (11A) of the T'ang
dynasty even a three-year-old child knows of the
Buddhist saying from the Dharmapada, "To perform all the good deeds and avoid doing the
evil ones."[27] This is definitely an indication
of the profound penetration of Buddhism to the
Chinese masses. This Buddhist atmosphere has
become a part and parcel of Chinese culture, so

94

much so that one could hardly make out any difference in respect to its Indian origin.

Among the Buddhist schools which were developed in China, the Pure Land, T'ien-t'ai, and Ch'an or Zen are essentially Chinese products, although some of their tenets could be traced to Indian origin. As these schools suit the Chinese temperament and climate so well, they are identified with Chinese beginnings. Take the case of Ch'an (Zen). It has done away with bookish learning; it points to the mind of man in order to see his inner nature and thereby to achieve sudden enlightenment.[28] How simple, bold and straightforward! This Zen of the Chinese patriarchs, which allows one's mind ample freedom, is definitely superior to the Indian traditional dhyāna or meditation. People call this school the "Chinese Ch'an." As it is tinged with strong Chinese characteristics, it adds splendid glory to Chinese culture.

Among the other contributions made by Buddhism to Chinese culture which may be mentioned here are: the translation of Sanskrit texts, phonology, linguistics, imaginative literature, architecture, sculpture, painting, astrology, calendar-computing, mathematics and medicine.[29] Moreover, in terms of its influence on religions of Chinese origin, it caused Taoism and Confucianism to formulate their new concepts and philosophy and bring about a religious systematization.

Thus we see that Chinese Buddhism, in its initial stage, was a lonely and helpless visitor to the Land of Confucius and Lao Tzu. For quite a long while it attached itself to the wagon of Taoism, perhaps with a purpose. But finally it firmly established itself in China and made outstanding contributions to Chinese culture.

NOTES

1. T'ang Yung-tung, Han-wei liang-tsin nan-pei-ch'ao fu-chiao shih (History of Buddhism in the Han, Wei, Eastern and Western Tsin, and Northern and Southern Dynasties) (Peking: Chung Hwa Book Co., 1972), p. 153.

2. Ibid., p. 17.

3. Ibid., pp. 73-79, 88.

4. Hui-chiao, Kao-sêng chuan (Biographies of Eminent Buddhist Teachers), in Taishō, vol. 50, pp. 322ff.

5. "The Brahmajāla-Sūtra," trans. T.W. Rhys Davids, in Max Müller, ed., The Sacred Books of the Buddhists, vol. II (London: Routledge & Kegan Paul, 1973), pp. 16-26.

6. T'ang Yung-tung, op.cit., pp. 51-53; Wang Chih-hsin, Chung-kuo tsung-chiao ssǔ-hsiang-shih ta-kang (A Brief History of Chinese Religious Thought) (Taipei, Taiwan: Chung Hwa Book Co., 1960), pp. 68-69, 74-75.

7. D. Howard Smith, Chinese Religions (New York: Holt, Rinehart, and Winston, 1968), p. 99.

8. Wing-tsit Chan, trans., The Way of Lao Tzu (New York: Bobbs-Merrill, 1963), pp. 132, 232.

9. T'ang Yung-tung, op.cit., pp. 59-60; W. Pachow, "Laotzu and Gautama Buddha, an Enquiry into the Authenticity of Laotzu's Mission to India," in N.A. Jayawickrama, ed., Paranavitana Felicitation Volume (Colombo: M.D. Gunasena & Co., 1965), pp. 293-303.

10. Chiang Wei-ch'iao, Chung-kuo fu-chiao shih (History of Buddhism in China) (Shanghai: Commercial Press, n.d.), pp. 36-39; T'ang Yung-tung, op.cit., pp. 493-538.

11. Hui-chiao, op.cit., pp. 322ff.

12. T'ang Yung-tung, op.cit., pp. 493-94.

13. Chan, op.cit., p. 166; Fung Yu-lan, Chung-kuo che-hsüeh shih (History of Chinese Philosophy), vol. I (Shanghai: Commercial Press, 1944), p. 224.

14. Chan, op.cit., p. 144.

15. Wang Chih-hsin, op.cit., pp. 75-77.

16. Chiang Wei-ch'iao, op.cit., p. 33; Sung Pei-wei, Tung-han tsung-chiao shih (Religious History of the Eastern Han Dynasty) (Shanghai: Commercial Press, n.d.), pp. 66-77.

17. T'ang Yung-tung, op.cit., p. 494.

18. Chiang Wei-ch'iao, op.cit., p. 9.

19. T'ang Yung-tung, op.cit., p. 541.

20. The Confucian Analects, in James Legge, trans. and ed., Hwa-yin Ssŭ-shu (The Four Books in Chinese and English) (Shanghai: Commercial Press, n.d.), p. 121; cf. The Works of Mencius, in Legge, op.cit., pp. 122-32, 189.

21. The Works of Mencius, in Legge, op.cit., pp. 170-71. In quoting the Book of Poetry, it says: "Under the whole heaven,/To the borders of the land,/Every spot is the sovereign's ground;/Every individual is the sovereign's minister (subject)."

22. The Confucian Analects, in Legge, op.cit., p. 120.

23. The Works of Mencius, in Legge, op.cit. pp. 170-71.

24. See Taishō, nos. 2059, 2060, 2061, and 2062.

25. See Śikshānanda, trans., The Sūtra on the Original Vows of Kṣitigarbha Bodhisattva, and The Ullampana Sūtra, in Taishō, vol. 13, pp. 777ff.

26. T'ang Yung-tung, op.cit., pp. 348-50.

27. Chiao-an, Shih-shih chi-ku lüeh (Outline of Investigation of Buddhist Antiquities), in Taishō, vol. 49, pp. 832-33 (from the biography of the "Bird's Nest Ch'an Master"); cf. Irving Babbitt, trans., The Dhammapada (New York: New Directions, 1965), p. 30.

28. W. Pachow, "Zen Buddhism and Bodhidharma," The Indian Historical Quarterly, vol. 32, nos. 2, 3 (1956), p. 29.

29. Kenneth Ch'en, Buddhism in China (Princeton, NJ: Princeton University Press, 1972), pp. 471ff.

GLOSSARY

1A 牟子

2A 安世高, 佛圖橙

3A 北魏太武帝

4A 北周武帝

5A 唐武宗

6A 後周世宗

7A 慧遠

8A 桓玄

9A 寇謙之

10A 妙音

11A 白居易

VII

DEVELOPMENT OF TRIPIṬAKA-
TRANSLATIONS IN CHINA

The institution of translating Buddhist
Tripiṭakas into Chinese from both Sanskrit and Pāli
sources has a long history, reaching back to the
formal introduction of Buddhism into China in
67 A.C., when Emperor Ming-ti of the Han dynasty
accorded his imperial welcome to the first two
Indian sages, Kāśyapa Mātaṅga and Dharmānanda,
at Lo-yang, capital of the Han dynasty.[1]   It is
recorded in several historical and non-canonical
works that the first Buddhist text translated into Chinese by them was the Sūtra of the Forty-Two
Chapters, along with Buddhacarita-Sūtra, Daśa-
Bhūmi-Kleśa-cchedikā-Sūtra, Dharma-Samudrakosha-
Sūtra, Jātaka, and other texts of the Vinaya.
However, except for the first one, the remaining
texts, so far as our knowledge goes, were either
lost or disappeared without any trace. Under
the auspicious inauguration of Mātaṅga, the noble
sages of both the countries laboring constantly
for a long period of 1500 years did perform a
great wonder in bringing about the monumental work
of the Chinese Tripiṭaka. It may not be an
exaggeration to say that it is a rare, priceless
relic of Indian culture being carefully preserved
and protected in the soil of China. Not only by
its highly developed philosophy and literature
did it influence the thought and mode of life of
the Chinese people to a large extent, but also
it furthered the intimate and everlasting cultural
relationship between the two great sister nations,
India and China. To the scholars who toil   in
the field of ancient Indian history and culture,
it will prove to be an inexhaustible mine, because it is directly connected to all subjects
and branches of Indology. Owing to the misconception that the Chinese language is the most

difficult one in the world, the foreign scholars, therefore, are barred from reading these translations directly, and as a matter of fact, they have been blissfully ignored by the outside world.

To have a clear idea of the development of these canonical works, the following points may be made here.

The Three Stages of Development

1. The First Stage

The inception of such meritorious enterprise, as we have mentioned above, is dated back as early as the first century A.C. At that time Buddhist missionaries began to pour into China from different kingdoms of the western region-- central Asia, i.e., An Shih-Kao (1A) from Parthia (148-170 A.C.), Lokaraksa from Yüeh-chí (164-186 A.C.), Káng Chu from Káng-ch'ü or Ulterior Tibet (187 A.C.), Kumārajīva (2A) from Kharajar (401 A.C.), Buddha-yaśas from Kabul (403 A.C.) and so forth.[2] This short period from 67 A.C. to the arrival of Kumārajīva in 401 A.C. was little more than 330 years, yet there were about sixty foreign Buddhist masters whose translations were counted to be over 400 separate works. In these books we find every branch of Buddhist doctrine which belongs to both Hīnayāna and Mahāyāna schools, though the former has been delineated comparatively in a more dominant form. Of course, it is impossible to expect perfect translations (either in accuracy or in style) at this experimental stage. We are given to understand that they were confronted with great difficulties which could not be easily overcome.

First, they had no manuscripts with them. It was probably not their custom to translate a work from a written or printed copy, as it is done today, but they did it simply by depending upon their wonderful memories. But however strong such memory might be, sometimes it would betray them, and the text thus translated may not be in accordance with the original one. Writing down the sacred texts on paper or other materials was a very late practice. The whole collection of the Pāli Canon was committed to writing only in 25 B.C., during the reign of Vattagāmini Abhaya in Ceylon.[3] And there was no written Vinaya text in northern India till late in 400 A.C. That is what Fa-hsien informed us in his Travel[4] and we believe it to be true, comparing it with the following record which states how the Abhidharma-vibhāsha-śāstra[5] was first translated into Chinese: "The text was recited from memory by Saṅghabhūti /381-385 A.C.7, put down in Sanskrit by Dharmānanda, orally translated into Chinese by Dharmarakṣa and finally made into a Chinese version by Śramana Ming-chih of the eastern Chin dynasty /317-420 A.C.7."[6]

Under such circumstances, it would not be surprising if slight errors were found in the translations.

Second, when the foreign missionaries came to China their first difficulty was the language. They, of course, could not hope to speak Chinese correctly in a short time, nor could the scholars of the country easily master Sanskrit, especially its most complicated system of grammar. As their desire to preach and spread the Buddhist doctrine was very great, so they had somehow or other to get the work done through the cooperation of the Chinese scholars. The results of such translation were partly comprehensible and partly ambiguous, because, at that time, the Buddhist doctrine and its terminology were absolutely foreign to the minds of the Chinese people.

Third, at the beginning the translations were not carried out on a grand scale or in any critical or systematic manner. It continued to be a private enterprise of the missionaries for a long time. During that period they had no proper residence, nor any support or protection from the government. They had, therefore, to complete their undertakings in a hurried way,

103

even at the cost of extracting the essential parts
from the bigger works and calling them by their
original titles. In some cases the translators
forgot to put down their names on the works which
they had done. Why it was so, is still a puzzle.

Fourth, we suspect that some of the translations were not directly done from Sanskrit, but
indirectly from the language of central Asia.
For instance, the Chinese term for Upādhyāya is
Ho-shang (3A), which may be a transliteration of
Hua-She in the language of Haskal and a direct
import from Khotan, because in Khotan Upādhyāya
is called Ho-Shang.[7] It would not be impossible,
if some works in the Chinese Tripitaka were translated from languages other than Saṅskrit or Pāli.

The above facts show how hard it was for the
forerunners to proceed with such an important
task with the imperfect knowledge they had at
that stage. It is universally recognized that
An Shih-Kao and Dharma-rakṣa were the two great
representatives of this period.

2. The Second Stage

This stage probably began with the arrival
of Kumārajīva in China in 401 A.C. and lasted up
to the days when Haüan-tsang (4A) returned to
China and began to translate the works which he
had brought with him in 645 A.C. The rich experiences of the forerunners who toiled in the
first period of Tripitaka, translating for over
300 years, had certainly helped Kumārajīva and
his co-workers in their own works, so far as
Buddhist terminology, idioms and phrases are
concerned. As a sign of general improvement,
the foreign teachers by then could understand a
good deal of Chinese, and the scholars of the
country also learned sufficient Sanskrit. When
setting to work, they could proceed very smoothly,
without feeling any difficulty about the language.
However, there were occasions for heated discussions over a certain philosophical topic such
as "Is an Icchantika also possessing the nature

104

of the Buddha?" and the like.

Another feature of this period was that the general public, especially the intelligentsia, took a keen interest in Buddhism and Buddhist activities. To undertake any service in connection with translating Buddhist scriptures was considered a meritorious deed, and also it used to be a spell of protection for those who were bored and tired of the political chaos at the time. From a political point of view, the history of China from 302-589 A.C. was not a very happy one. During this period there were fourteen dynasties which were established in different parts of the country by different rulers, and most of them were "alien" or "Hu"--the barbarians, as the historians used to call them. It is interesting to note how Kumārajīva came to China. Fu Chien (5A), the ruler of the former Ch'in dynasty (350-394 A.C.) ordered his commander-in-chief Lu Kwang (6A) to bring Kumārajīva to Ch'ang-an. The latter went to Kharajar, conquered the kingdom, killed the king and brought Kumārajīva with him as a captive. But fortunately or unfortunately, the aforesaid ruler was dethroned by another powerful king just before their arrival. In such a state of affairs, Kumārajīva had however to put up with his surroundings and could not set to work. It was in 401 A.C., after the capital and headquarters of Lu Kwang had been destroyed by the second ruler of the later Ch'in dynasty (384-417 A.C.) that he arrived at Ch'ang-an.[8] This shows the political tumult at that time and the unrest of the country.

In spite of all these, the rendering of Buddhist Canon progressed well. Under the king's patronage in the later Ch'in dynasty, Kumārajīva translated over fifty works in the famous Hsiao-yao garden with the help of only one penman who put down the translated sentences in the Chinese language. The most important works of Buddhism, such as Mahāprajñāpāramitā-Sūtra (Nanjio, No. 3), Saddharmapundarīka-Sūtra (No. 134), Vimalakīrti-nirdeśa (No. 146), Śata-Śāstra (No. 1188), Dvādaśanikāya-Śāstra (No. 1186), Prāṇyamūla

Śāstra-tīkā (No. 1179) and Mahāprajñāpāramitā-
Śāstra (No. 1169) and others were translated during
this period by Kumārajīva.[9] It was his mastery
over both the languages of Sanskrit and Chinese,
his excellent style and subtle rendering of the
texts that had given a new impetus and inspiration
to the world of translation.

The representatives of great translators in
the second stage were Kumārajīva (401 A.C.),
Buddhabhadra (398-421 A.C.) and Paramārtha (548-
557 A.C.). Moreover, this period is considered
to be a period of cooperation between the foreign
Buddhist teachers and Chinese scholars.

3. The Third Stage

From what has been shown in the previous
two stages, it is very clear that the foreign
missionaries took the initiative. Undoubtedly
they had their own merit, so far as their enthusiasm for spreading Buddhist doctrine and their
religious aspiration in undertaking such noble
services are concerned, yet there were defects
in the translations which they had done. Even
great experts such as Kumārajīva would not escape
criticism if some of his works were compared with
the original texts, as would others who were not
as critical and efficient as he was. Taking a
distrustful attitude toward the translations
Fa-hsien (7A) was the first person among the
Chinese Buddhists to go to India in search of
Vinaya texts and sūtras in 401 A.C.[10] and in
518 A.C. another Chinese traveller, Sung-Yün
by name, was sent by the empress of northern
Wei dynasty (386-534 A.C.) to India to look for
scriptures of Buddhism.[11] Following in their
steps, a large number of Chinese Buddhists did
go to India for the same purpose at different
times. The most celebrated among them was
Hsüan-tsang, who went to India in 631 A.C. and
stayed in the holy land for fifteen years. The
Indian sages honored him with the title of
Mahāyānadeva. He was a great Sanskritist and
used it to defeat learned Indian pundits. While

returning, he brought with him 520 bundles of 657 separate books and translated seventy-three of them, consisting of 1,330 fasciculi. The most voluminous work among them is Mahaprajñaparamita-Sutra. It consists of 600 fasciculi and 200,000 stanzas in verse.[12] Because of his perfect knowledge of both the Sanskrit and Chinese languages and his deep penetration into the vast ocean of Buddhist philosophy and literature he laid once and for all the reliable and authentic foundation for interpreting the Sanskrit scriptures into Chinese. It is he who created a revolution in the field of Tripitaka-renderings and snatched away, not by force, but by merit, the sovereignty of the translation-kingdom from the hands of the foreign missionaries. By this time, the rendering of Tripitakas had reached its zenith of perfection in truthfulness, in reliability, in expression, in excellency of style and in so many other ways.

This was called the golden age in the field of translation and Hsüan-tsang was the great representative of the third period. Of course there were at that time many other good scholars fluent in both Sanskrit and Chinese, such as I-tsing and Amoghavajra, who also contributed much of their talents to the glory of the Chinese Tripitaka.

At the end of the T'ang dynasty (618-907 A.C.), there was a tendency to decadence in this noble service, though in other aspects, such as copying the sutras and printing the canonical works, there was good progress. It is only during the Sung dynasty (960-1127 A.C.) that there appeared a flash of light in the revival of such undertakings. That is to say, there were a few learned Indian teachers, namely Fa-t'ien (8A) (Dharmadeva) or Fa-t'ien of Nālandā (973-1001 A.C.), T'ien-hsi-tsai (9A) of Jalandhara (982 A.C.), Dānapāla of Udyāna (980 A.C.) and Fa-hu (Dharmaraksa) of Magadha (1004 A.C.), who came to China in quick succession and together translated 269 separate works.[13] Along with their contributions, the history of Tripitaka-translations came to a close. The glow of a lamp, at the moment of its extinction, is

107

usually brighter than ever. But, alas! it shines
no more.

The table given below will give a concrete
view of the scriptures translated by different
persons at different periods.

Date	Translators	Works	Fasciculi
A.C. 67-730	176	986	4507
A.C. 730-789	8	127	242
A.C. 789-1037	6	220	532
A.C. 1037-1285	4	20	115
Total	194	1353	5396*

How Were the Texts Translated?

To have more than four persons laboring over
a text in the earlier stages of scripture-rendering
was not a luxury but sheer necessity. Later on,
it developed. The number of office-bearers
steadily increased from three to four and finally
it went up to nine. This very complicated and
systematized organization has a characteristic
of its own, and it claims our attention for the
purpose of rendering modern literature into
different languages.

In the first period, beginning from the
first century A.C. to the fourth century A.C.,
a translation was generally completed through the
efforts of four persons. That is, 1) one recites
the Sanskrit text from memory, 2) one records
the recitation in Sanskrit, 3) one orally inter-
prets it into Chinese, and 4) one makes a Chinese
version. And three persons would suffice if a

---

*These statistics are based on the Comparative
Catalogue of the Buddhist Sacred Books in the Chih-
yüan Period, 1264-94 A.C. See Nanjiō, No. 1612.

manuscript were available. In that case, (1) and (2) would be replaced by a person who could read out the text and explain its meaning, and the rest would remain as they were.[14]

When it entered into the second stage, with Kumārajīva taking a leading role on the scene of action, the translations became critical and re-fined, and more members were admitted to such translation committees, especially for works which were completed after Kumārajīva's time. During this period, the new member being added was called Chêng-i (10A), whose office was to examine the meaning of the translated manuscript and see whether it agreed with the original text. Between 590 and 907 A.C. there are the following addi-tions: one specialist was appointed to verify the correct significance of the translated text, another to examine it from the linguistic point of view. And also there used to be a proofreader, a revisor, and general directors.

Some time later, in 982 A.C., by the order of Emperor T'ai-tsung (976-998 A.C.) of the Sung dynasty, a Translation Hall was established. In that hall, we are told that there were nine members who sat side by side, rendering a Buddhist work into Chinese. Below is listed the function of each member therein:

1. I-chu or the translator-in-chief, who took his seat in the center, facing outside, and loudly recited the Sanskrit text.

2. Chêng-i or the examiner of meaning, who sat on the left of I-chu and discussed the sense of the text with him.

3. Chêng-wên or the examiner of text, who sat on the right of I-chu and listened carefully to his recitation of the Sanskrit text, in order to find mistakes, if there were any.

4. Shu-tzŭ or the transcriber, who listened attentively to the recitation of the Sanskrit

text and wrote down its pronunciation in Chinese characters, i.e., "Ha-ri-da-ya" for "Hrdaya."

5. Pi-shou or the penman, who translated the transcribed letters into the Chinese language, i.e., "Hsin"--mind or heart--for "Hrdaya."

6. Cho-wên or the text-composer, who arranged the translated words in syntactical order and made suitable Chinese sentences.

7. Ts'an-i or the text-comparer, who compared both the original and the translated texts and saw that there was nothing wrong in the translations.

8. K'an-ting or the text-censor, who cut off all the superfluous expressions and finally decided the doubtful meanings of the sentences.

9. Jün-wên or the revisor of the composition, whose function was to improve the language and make the translations more excellent and refined in style.[15]

When all these had been properly executed, the text then was sent to be printed and later on to be distributed.

Having read the descriptions above, we cannot but admire the scientific spirit and religious zeal of these workers in involving themselves in the vast field of Buddhist literature. It is said that before their setting to work they had to perform various sorts of rituals, which included homa, mandala, arghya, and offerings of different kinds, taking a bath daily, wearing three garments, behaving as properly as possible, and so forth.[16] No doubt they were supported by the state, but they would not take what was more than necessary for their simple life and maintenance. They were self-denying sages for the noble cause of Buddhism.

Principles of Translation

Before Hsüan-tsang's taking part in the field of translation, there was constantly the problem of stiff translation and paraphrase. As a matter of course, during the earlier stages, the translations could not help but be stiff. In the first place, there was the difficulty of gaining mastery over both the languages. Secondly, they dared not make the style literary because of religious piety. So they had to let the translations remain in the simple, faithful, straightforward but unpolished state.

Tao-an (about 330-386 A.C.), a very learned and authoritative Chinese Buddhist scholar, was of the opinion that except for the following five points, the translation should be strictly faithful to the original text.

The points are: 1) the syntactical order, 2) the habit of employing literary words, 3) the abridgement of praise repetitions, 4) the omission of explanatory sentences which could belong to the text proper, and 5) the exclusion of paragraphical repetitions.

In addition he also made remarks on the difficulties of translating a text. First, he said that a translation should not merely be true to the original one, but should also be easily accessible to the common people. Second, the profound wisdom of the Buddha is rather hard to understand in its esoteric meanings. And third, the Buddha who preached the doctrines had passed away long ago, and therefore the controversial views of Buddhism had very little chance to be corrected.[17]

The method of translation being employed by Kumārajīva was somewhat different from Tao-an. His works are mostly paraphrases. When translating the Saddharmapuṇḍarīka-Sūtra, we are told that he was purposely following the phraseology of the Chinese language, though he made it a point not to allow the ideas of the original

111

work to suffer any misinterpretation. Since he was such a great pundit, it is not to be expected that he be satisfied with the simple form of stiff translation.

Hsüan-tsang, the great Chinese Sanskritist, was very particular about the transliteration of Sanskrit words. One will find, especially in his Si-yu ki, or the Buddhist Records of the Western Kingdoms, the corrections of proper names, and he would point out that such transliterations were absolutely defective. While translating, he would simply instruct the penman to write down the sentences in Chinese as though he were reading typed sheets of such dictations. It is in no way exaggerating to say that his translations are perfect in every aspect, and naturally, the question of stiff rendering and paraphrase would not in any case be applied to them. However, there are rules laid down by him regarding certain Sanskrit words which may not be interpreted but only transliterated. He would not translate a word if 1) it had a connection with esoteric doctrine, such as "Dhāraṇī"; 2) if it had many meanings, like "Bhagavan"; 3) if an article was not to be found in China, such as "Jambu Tree"; 4) following the terms of the old, if it was widely known and adopted, and lastly, for the sake of producing good faith, i.e., the word "pañña"-- prajñā is much better than its translated words "Chih-hui"--wisdom, for, as he explained, they would awaken the people's faith in Buddhism.[18]

Leaving aside what has been stated above, there were scholars who upheld the view that the best way of penetrating to the heart of Buddhism was to abandon the institution of translation, and learn directly the Sanskrit language. We too approve and agree with such a proposal, but alas, the dream never came true. And the Chinese Tripiṭaka in the present day is regarded as one of the invaluable legacies of Sino-Indian culture which will undoubtedly make a proper contribution to the enrichment of the civilization of the world.

Thus far, we have been able to gather materials as to how the Chinese Tripitaka-translation had its growth and development. It is our sincere hope that the Indian scholars should shoulder the burden in restoring them to Sanskrit or Pali, and translate some of them, if not the whole collection, into the different vernaculars of modern India. One day, when this noble object shall fully be attained, we are quite sure that China would feel happier, because in preserving this priceless treasure of Indian culture, her effort was not in vain.

NOTES

1. T'ang Yung-tung, Han-wei Liang-tsin Nan-pei-ch'ao Fu-chiao Shih (History of Buddhism in the Han, Wei, Eastern and Western Tsin, and the Northern and Southern Dynasties) (Peking: Chung Hwa Book Co., 1972), p. 21; Hui-chiao, Kao-sêng Chuan (Biographies of Eminent Buddhist Teachers), in Taisho, vol. 50, pp. 322-23.

2. Hui-chiao, op.cit., pp. 323-24, 333-34.

3. G.P. Malalasekera, The Pali Literature of Ceylon (London: The Royal Asiatic Society of Great Britain and Ireland, 1928), pp. 43-47.

4. Fa-hsien, The Travels of Fa-hsien, in Taishō, vol. 51, p. 864n.

5. This śāstra can be found in Taishō, vol. 28, pp. 416ff.

6. Hui-chiao, op.cit., p. 328b.

7. Tsan-ning, Sung Kao-sêng Chuan (Biographies of Eminent Buddhist Teachers of the Sung Dynasty), in Taishō, vol. 50, p. 723c.

8. Hui-chiao, op.cit., pp. 230-33.

9.   Ibid., p. 232b.

10.   Fa-hsien, op.cit., p. 864b.

11.   Fung Ch'eng-chün, Les Moines Chinois et Étrangers qui ont Contribué à la Formation du Tripitaka Chinois (Shanghai: Commercial Press, 1931), p. 40.

12.   Tao-hsüan, Hsü Kao-sêng Chuan (Second Series of Biographies of Eminent Buddhist Teachers), in vol. 50, pp. 446-58.

13.   J. Takakusu, et al., eds., Hobogirin: Fascicule Annexe, Tables du Taishō Issaikyo (Tokyo: Maison Fransco-Japonese, 1931), p. 138.

14.   Tsan-ning, op.cit., p. 724b, c.

15.   Chih-p'an, Fu-tsu T'ung-chi (11A) (Records of the Lineage of the Buddha and the Patriarchs), in Taishō, vol. 49, p. 398a.

16.   Ibid., p. 398b; Chiang Wei-chiao, History of Chinese Buddhism (Shanghai: Commercial Press, 1935), pp. 13-14.

17.   Tao-hsüan, op.cit., p. 438a, b.

18.   Tsan-ning, op.cit., p. 723b.

GLOSSARY

1A 安世高

2A 鳩摩羅什

3A 和尚

4A 玄奘

5A 苻堅

6A 呂光

7A 法顯

8A 法天

9A 天息災

10A 證義

11A 佛祖統記

VIII

THE CONTROVERSY OVER THE

IMMORTALITY OF THE SOUL IN

CHINESE BUDDHISM

From time immemorial the restless human mind
has been searching for the unknown, mystical and
metaphysical. The earnest quest for an answer
to the question of existence after death in
philosophy and religion must have originated from
the same urge. It seems natural that humans
should love existence and make attempts to achieve
immortality. However, as death is inevitable,
some ancient thinkers refused to admit defeat and
propounded theories on immortality of the soul.
To them, the physical frame may perish, but the
soul or the spiritual being will exist eternally.
The Upaniṣadic philosophers created the doctrine
of ātman and Brahman, viz., the individual soul
will reunite with the cosmic soul. Thus, a host
of allied ideas such as transmigration, rebirth,
and causes for being born in a particular state
of existence began to emerge. This concept does
not confine itself to advanced civilizations in
the East and West, but is equally applicable to
primitive cultures and less developed regions in
the world.

Regarding the controversial topic concerning
the existence of the soul after death in Chinese
Buddhism in the fifth and sixth centuries, it
should be noted that the supporters of this view
were Buddhist intellectuals. These scholars might
have been influenced by the Mahāyāna theory of
Dharmakāya or the transcendental body of the
Buddha on the one hand, and the Taoist notion of
immortality as found in the writings of Chuangtzǔ
on the other. They consolidated their efforts
in refuting the thesis of destructibility of the
soul set forth by Fan Chên. If a comparison is

117

made regarding the position taken by the Buddhist in India and his counterpart in China, it appears that the Indian Buddhist, a follower of Gautama Buddha, was a front runner in opposing the theory of ātman or the soul, whereas his co-religionist in China was a strong supporter of such a doctrine. This naturally generates curiosity in the mind of Buddhist historians. One wonders what was wrong with the Chinese Buddhists in upholding a theory that is in direct opposition to the teachings of the Buddha. Undoubtedly there exists great complexity in the matter. This may involve the doctrines of Hīnayāna and Mahāyāna that were introduced to China at different levels, and their interpretations concerning karma, the causes for, and the process of, rebirth. In addition, the syncretistic approach to local religious traditions and beliefs was also a contributing factor. Moreover, the proponent of the destructibility of the soul was dissatisfied with the unusual attention shown to Buddhism and the Buddhist way of life as well as certain religious practices. All this seemed to have hurt his national pride, viz., China has an advanced civilization. The bitterness of resentment in him brought about the anti-Buddhist expressions.

For the convenience of presentation, we shall first clarify the meaning of the word "soul" from the Upaniṣadic literature and the Pali canon. It is well known that Theravāda Buddhism takes great pains to deny the existence of a soul. Next we shall take up the main discussions concerning the controversy in China over the indestructibility of the soul. On a comparative basis we may be able to see for ourselves what went wrong, and the possible reasons the Chinese Buddhist has in taking such a position. Having examined the various facts related to the historical development of Sino-Indian Buddhism, one may arrive at a suitable conclusion.

The Theory of Ātman in
Indian Literature

In the Vedic literature it is unmistakably
evident that the word "ātman" was not shrouded
in mystery in the initial stage. It is a philosophical concept of the subject "self" in relation
to the objective external reality. The etymology
of this term has not yet been determined. According
to the Ṛg veda x.16,3, ātman means breath or the
vital essence, and in course of time it acquired
the meaning of soul or self.[1] Still later it is
interpreted as "a sort of subtle manikin inside
the body but separate from it, and continuing,
after it leaves the body, as a separate entity."[2]

We may first examine the philosophical interpretation of the term, and next look into its
animistically associated connotations. In the
philosophical sense the general characteristics
of the true self are assumed to be permanence,
continuity, unity and eternal activity. The true
self is free from sin, old age, death, grief,
hunger and thirst. It is a world which is complete
in itself.[3] This may be the ideal self that is
seen in its highest perfection. In general, however, the self is identified with the following
four categories: (1) The bodily self that is
seen when one looks into another's eye, or a pail
of water, or a mirror.[4] It is subject to suffering, misfortune and imperfections, and it is
simply a material phenomenon with which we are
familiar. (2) The empirical self--the self that
moves happily and freely in dreams.[5] It enjoys
unusual freedom and is not restricted by time,
space and living conditions. However, dream
states do not seem to be self-existent, although
they are independent of body. (3) The transcendental self--this is the state when a man being
asleep, reposing and at perfect rest, sees no
dreams.[6] In such a state both the waking and
dreaming experiences are suspended. Thus the
self transcends and there is no object to con-
template. However, the danger in such a situation is what the critics call a state of utter

annihilation and "there is no self at all."[7] And
(4) The absolute self--this is the universal self
which is immanent and transcendent. There is
nothing in the universe which is not involved in
this infinite self in us. It "can be looked upon
as the permanent subject persisting in waking and
dreaming, death and sleep, bondage and liberation.
It is present throughout, surveying all the world.
It is the universal subject and yet the universal
object. It sees and yet it sees not."[8] The self
in this category is also called the intuitive
self or pure consciousness, which is freed from
all bodily and mental limitations. This self or
ātman which is the inner essence of man is later
on identified by the Upaniṣadic thinkers with
Brahmā, the ultimate reality and the inner essence
of the universe.[9] This identification, bringing
about the unity between the individual soul (ātman)
and the cosmic soul (brahman), and between the
physical principle of the universe and the spiritual
essence of man is one of the highest achievements
of Indian philosophical speculation. The various
theories concerning the soul, either for or against
it, at later times, must have in some way been
associated with this original concept.

The Belief in Soul and
Folk Religion

At the popular level, the belief in a soul
in relation to death is deeply rooted in primitive
religions. This belief is universal in character.
It appears that the fanciful descriptions about
the soul in early Indian literature may have originated from Indian folk religion.[10] This is
evidenced by the fact that the belief in spirits
is found in almost every primitive culture all
over the world; on the contrary, some of these
cultures may not possess a philosophy at all.
It may be justifiable if we say that the identification of the cosmic soul with the individual
soul is a philosophized sophistication based on
popular religious beliefs. By way of illustration,
we shall sample a few of the descriptions of the

120

soul from the Upaniṣads and other sources:

The Katha Upaniṣad informs us that the "person" not larger than a thumb, the inner Self, is always settled in the heart of man.[11] It is "smaller than small, greater than great." However, the movement of the soul is mysterious and its activities are not confined to the inner regions of the heart, because "though sitting still, he walks far; though lying down, he goes everywhere."[12] Rhys Davids made a careful study of the subject, and as a consequence, more information is available about the physiology and nature of the soul. We are told that the size of the soul is like a grain of rice or barley; its shape is like that of a man; its appearance is "like smoke-coloured wool, like cochineal, like flame, like white lotus, like a flash of lightning, like a light without smoke. . . ,"[13] its substance is "a subtle, material homunculus, or manikin," but it "wanders from body to body."[14] It performs unusual activities in dreams, including meeting with dead relatives and friends while away from the body. On account of this information it is believed that "death and trance and disease could be ascribed to the absence of the soul."[15] When an individual passes away, his soul "flies away from the body through an aperture in the top of the head, it was apparently regarded as a subtle and very impalpable, but still material, double of the body of the deceased."[16] This indicates that man may die, but the soul is immortal, or it will take up residence elsewhere, or will be reborn into different planes of life in accordance with the individual's karma performed in past lives.[17]

Regarding the future destiny of a soul after death, the Upaniṣads and other traditions suggest three possibilities: (1) One may be born into the plane of Brahmā through the path of light (devayāna). It will enjoy the fruits of its good deeds done in its lifetime on earth. From this there is no return.[18] (2) One may be born in the region of the moon (candraloka), through the path of the fathers (pitryāna). Having enjoyed the fruits of its good deeds there, it will come back to the earth and resume the various forms of existence, ranging from man to inferior beings, in accordance with the quality of their work and degree of knowledge. (3) The third path which differs from the previous two, will lead to the joyless regions enveloped in darkness.[19]

It is discernible that the first two are heavenly planes where one may lead a divine existence of ease and comfort, and may even enjoy forever such heavenly blessings in Brahmā's paradise. In the third category it may be identified with hell, although the horror of purgatory, as found in Buddhist literature, was not exemplified. The moral value of good or evil deeds is the principal cause which determines the future destiny for the soul. In general, it is the soul of the evildoer or the hypocrite that goes to the land of darkness and assumes the form of worms, insects and creeping things.[20] As the soul is the essence of living beings transmigrating from one existence to another, it played a very important part in the moral and philosophical spheres of Indian thought. The concept of saṁsāra, liberation, karma and rebirth are directly associated with it. In regard to its origin, Radhakrishnan is of the opinion that before the arrival of the Aryans, the aborigines in India already had the belief of existence of the soul after death. They believed "after death their souls lived in animal bodies."[21] This may be considered the primitive and initial stage of this concept. The vital force of this notion, however, has been persistently powerful throughout the centuries, in spite of the convincing denial put forward by the founder of Buddhism.

The Soul Theory in
Buddhist Literature

Gautama Buddha, founder of Buddhism, appeared on the scene in the fifth century B.C. During this period the speculation about the soul became more sophisticated and popular. The central focus was on whether or not the soul exists eternally after death, its origin and the ideal conditions for the soul in the present life. Among these, the theories of eternality and annihilation of the soul is of special interest to us. The Eternalists who supported the permanent existence of the soul put forward their theory in sixteen ways, stating:

The soul after death, not subject to decay, and conscious,

    (1) has form,
    (2) is formless,
    (3) has, and has not form,
    (4) neither has, nor has not form,
    (5) is finite,
    (6) is infinite,
    (7) is both,
    (8) is neither,
    (9) has one mode of consciousness,
  (10) has various modes of consciousness,
  (11) has limited consciousness,
  (12) has infinite consciousness,
  (13) is altogether happy,
  (14) is altogether miserable,
  (15) is both,
  (16) is neither.[22]

The above-noted formula expresses misgivings and uncertainties. The speculators were not sure of the true conditions of the soul after death. Therefore, all the possibilities, both the positive and negative qualifying aspects, are included. It is a sort of guessing exercise at the best. Pakudha Kaccāyana, one of the six religious teachers who propounded the doctrine of Seven Elements, viz., earth, water, fire, air, ease, pain, and the soul, was regarded as an Eternalist. On a certain occasion he declared to Ajātasattu, king of Magadha, that the seven things are neither created nor caused to be created, they are steadfast as a mountain peak,

as a pillar firmly fixed. They are immovable and
unchangeable.[23] Possibly his doctrine could
have influenced others on the eternality of the
soul. Besides, there were other religious re-
cluses who held the doctrine of an unconscious existence after death, declaring, "The soul after
death is not subject to decay, and unconscious."
There were still others who held the view that the
soul after death is neither conscious nor unconscious.[24] However, they were all Eternalists in
regard to the theory of the soul.

In contrast to the Eternalist point of view
is the doctrine of Annihilation. This was represented by Ajita of the garment of hair. He
stressed the futility of making offerings to the
dead, because when one expires all his physical
elements and faculties will return to the four
elements, viz., earth, fire, water and space.
There is no such thing as "existence after death."
He summed up his position as follows:

Fools and wise alike, on the dissolution
of the body, are cut off, annihilated,
and after death, they are not.[25]

There were, however, other Annihilationists who
believed that "the soul is not completely annihilated" as there is a further soul or whole
soul that resides in the various planes[26]:

(1) It is divine, having form, belonging
     to the sensuous plane, feeding on
     solid food.

(2) It is divine, having form, made of mind,
     with all its major and minor parts
     complete, and not deficient in any
     organ.

(3) It reaches up to the plane of the
     infinity of space by passing beyond
     ideas of form and by paying no heed
     to ideas of difference.

124

(4)   It reaches up to the plane of infinity
      of consciousness by passing beyond
      the plane of the infinity of space.

(5)   It reaches up to the plane of no
      obstruction by passing quite beyond
      the plane of the infinity of conscious-
      ness.

(6)   It reaches up to the plane of neither
      idea nor the absence of idea by passing
      quite beyond the plane of no obstruction.

The statement in (1) and (2) does not differ very
much from the Eternalist position. It is a sort
of a replica of man or his counterpart after
death. That being the case, it is rather difficult for us to comprehend how it could consume
solid food and at the same time it is made of
mind. From (3) to (6) it is a description of the
various states of consciousness associated with
the practice of meditation. They are known as
the four formless dhyānas (caturārūpya brahma-
lokas). Gautama Buddha is said to have attained
to them while he was temporarily a pupil under
Ālāra Kālāma and Uddaka.[27] To connect the soul
with the mysterious states of meditation seems to
indicate that the activities of the soul penetrate
the regions of the living and the invisible.
It is ubiquitous in character. One drawback for
the Annihilationists under review is that instead
of being opponents of the Eternalists, the majority
of them are actually supporters of the Eternalist
theory. In other words, the doctrine of the
Eternalists became victorious over the opposition
of the Annihilationists.

     The foregoing categories illustrate the
general interest shown by the religious or philosophical schools in India in the sixth century.
It is evident that the interpretations are
intermingled with fantasy, skepticism, uncertainty,
confusion and bewilderment. As this is within
the arena of metaphysics, one is free to make an
interpretation. But one wonders what is the real

125

value in these speculations in relation to the
ultimate truth. In contrast to the speculative
rhetoric, there arose a great teacher in India
who discovered a new vista of rationality, righteousness and the middle path instead of the animistic
beliefs. We shall now assess the Buddhist attitude
toward the theory of the soul.

The Doctrine of Non-Soul
in Early Buddhism

The Eternalist and Annihilationist theories
of the soul generated unusual interest among
the populace in India, including the disciples
of the Buddha, as evidenced in the following
instances. In Sutta 63 of the <u>Majjhima-Nikāya</u>[28]
Māluṅkyāputta is described as having demonstrated
his dissatisfaction with the Buddha's indifference
toward the metaphysical speculations. The point
at issue was in regard to whether or not the
world is eternal, whether or not the soul and
the body are identical, whether or not the saint
exists after death, or that the saint both exists
and does not exist after death, or that the saint
neither exists nor does not exist after death. He
threatened that if the Buddha did not elucidate
these problems to him, he would abandon the
religious training and return to the ordinary life
of a layman.[29] In remonstration, the Buddha
stated that they had never entered into an agreement that the exposition of the above-noted topics
was a condition for his being accepted as a disciple
of the Buddha.[30] Then he explained the reason
for taking such a position:

And why, Māluṅkyāputta, have I not
elucidated this? Because Maluṅkyāputta,
this profits not, nor has to do with the
fundamentals of religion, nor tends to
aversion, absence of passion, cessation,
quiescence, the supernatural faculties,
supreme wisdom, and Nirvāṇa; therefore
have I not elucidated it.[31]

In the process of reasoning with Māluṅkyāputta, the Buddha made this analogy:[32] There was a man who was wounded by a poisonous arrow, and his friends rushed him to a hospital. However, the patient insisted that the arrow should not be removed unless he had learned of the causes, the circumstances, the various descriptions of the assassin, the materials with which the arrow was made of, and many other details which brought about the incident. The moral drawn here is that man would die soon without ever having learned all he wanted to know. Similarly a man would expire before he receives a satisfactory answer or solution to those metaphysical speculations. Moreover, the Buddha emphasized that the religious life does not depend on the dogma of whether or not the world and the soul are eternal, or whether the soul and the body are identical. Even if one obtains an answer to these queries, "there still remain birth, old age, death, sorrow, lamentation, misery, grief, and despair."[33] This illustrates that the Buddha's main concern was to find a solution for the cessation of suffering. That is the target at which he was aiming, and consequently it is the excellence and strength of Buddhism.

On another occasion, a wandering ascetic by the name of Vaccha put to the Buddha the same questions as Māluṅkyāputta did. Instead of making a reply, he challenged the ascetic with a counter question, viz., to which of the four directions would the fire go, once the fire had become extinct? As no suitable answer was forthcoming, the Buddha compared it with the unknown existence of a saint after death:

> To say that he is reborn would not fit the case. To say that he is not born. . .he is both reborn and not reborn. . .he is neither reborn nor not reborn would not fit the case.[34]

It appears that the Buddha was suggesting an indeterminate or agnostic state of a saint. He

did not align himself either with the Eternalist
or the Annihilationist position. He seemed to
stress that there are many more worthwhile pur-
suits to be undertaken rather than wasting time
on these speculations which tend not to edification.

The Buddhist constructive interpretation of
the five aggregates (skandhas) as the constitu-
ents of a being in place of the Hindu concept of
a soul (ātman) is a great contribution to Indian
thought. This is known as the doctrine of non-
soul (anattā). Together with the doctrine of
suffering (dukkha) and impermanence (anicca) they
are called the three characteristics of phenomenal
existence. We shall endeavor to examine the non-
soul theory in detail in order to bring out the
contrast in relation to the notion of immortality
of the soul in Chinese Buddhism.

The fundamental differences between the
Hindu concept of a soul and the Buddhist doctrine
of non-soul is based on their different interpretations of a living being. The Upaniṣadic
seers believed that there is a permanent entity,
a soul that will be born again and again in
various existences. The Buddhist approach is just
opposite to this. According to Theravāda Buddhism,
a living being consists of physical components
(rūpa) and mental faculties (nāma). In the
material aspect there are six sense organs: the
eye, ear, nose, tongue, body,and mind, and the
six objects of the senses: sight, sound, odor,
taste, touch, and non-sensuous objects.[35] For
the two parties to get into active operation,
a consciousness of specific function is attached
to each of the six sense organs, namely, the consciousness of the eye, the ear, and so forth.
They are called the six consciousnesses.

Collectively the first two groups are known
as the twleve places (āyatanas), or elements
(dharmas). When the third group of six consciousnesses is added to them, it is generally
termed the eighteen spheres (dhātus). In the
case of mental faculties they are: sensation

(vedanā), perception (saññā), predisposition
(saṅkārā), and consciousness (viññāna). At a
given situation in conjunction with the material
elements (rūpa), one is able to exercise his intellectual manipulation, such as feeling, perceiving,
making decisions, and the awareness of being. The
mental faculties cannot function without the
material foundation of sense organs and their objects. When rūpa and nāma (matter and mind) are
joined, they are known as the five aggregates
(skandhas), or elements of being. Erroneously
the traditional Hindu thinkers regard this compo-
nent as a soul, ego, self, individuality, personali-
ty and permanent entity. The Buddha and his
following emphatically and absolutely denied such
a theory and put forth the doctrine of non-soul
(anattā) instead. They are of the opinion that
what is called "soul" is nothing but

> a convenient designation for the single
> stream of elements constituting a living
> being at a given moment of time, though
> neither the stream itself, nor any single
> element, nor any combination of elements
> in the stream is a "soul," or contains
> a soul. Thus the term "soul" is but
> a name, and not a reality.36

To clarify this point further, Buddhaghoṣa, a
great Buddhist scholar and commentator of the
fifth century, made this observation in his
Visuddhi-magga (The Path of Purification, ch.
xviii):37

> Just as the word "chariot" is but
> a mode of expression for axle, wheels,
> chariot-body, pole, and other consti-
> tuent members, placed in a certain rela-
> tion to each other, but when we come to
> examine the members one by one, we dis-
> cover that in the absolute sense there
> is no chariot. . . in exactly the same
> way the words "living entity" and "ego"
> are but a mode of expression for the
> presence of the five attachment groups,

but when we come to examine the elements
of being one by one, we discover that
in the absolute sense there is no living
entity there to form a basis for such
figments as "I am," or "I"; in other
words, that in the absolute sense there
is only name and form./38/ The insight
of him who perceives this is called
knowledge of truth.

This comment was made on a discussion concerning
the soul or ego between King Milinda and Nāgasena,
a learned Buddhist scholar of the first century
B.C. It argued convincingly in support of the
doctrine of non-soul. In contrast to the notion
that the soul is a permanent entity, the Buddhists
hold the view that the units of the five aggregates, especially the "nāma" elements, are constantly changing, transitory and impermanent.
They are not stationary even for one fraction of
a second. They are compared to a powerful water-
fall that rushes downstream with millions of
gallons of water per second. One may say that
it remains "still" or even "permanent" in appearance, but actually it is an illusion. Likewise
the popular notion identifying the sensation,
perception, or consciousness to be the soul or
ego is illusive and erroneous. It is because there
is no continuous personal identity or the so-called
soul. The functioning of the mental faculty such
as sensation or consciousness is subject to
causation and circumstances.[39] They rise and
disappear. One may experience a certain sensation at a certain time. Once that is over, it
is gone forever. A similar sensation may occur
at a subsequent date, but it is a new and different one. Such being the case, one should not
identify sensation or consciousness to be the soul.

In terms of impermanence, "the duration of
the life of a living being is exceedingly brief,
lasting only while a thought lasts." Buddhaghosa
made this observation on sentient existence in
his Visuddhi-magga, ch. viii. To elucidate his
thesis further, he classified the condition of a

living being into three periods, the past, present, and future. Apparently there is no interrelation between them, as the following formula shows:

> The being of the past moment of thought has lived, but does not live, nor will it live.
> The being of a future moment of thought will live, but has not lived, nor does it live.
> The being of the present moment of thought does live, but has not lived, nor will it live.[40]

This may be regarded as an academician's way of arguing, cold, logical, and precise, with which many may disagree. As humans, most of us feel that what we are now must have some connection with our past as well as with the future. The thinking consciousness of an individual could not possibly be contained in three separate "time zone" capsules without any communication between them. However, the Buddhist message as demonstrated by Buddhaghosa is clear enough to indicate that the soul as a permanent entity is illogical and unacceptable. As the mental faculties are fleeting and transitory from moment to moment, the theory of the inner essence of a living being as a soul is rejected.

The Question of Immortality of the Soul in Chinese Buddhism

With reference to the Buddhist position concerning the doctrine of non-soul, we would expect to find the same trend in Chinese Buddhism. But unfortunately the opposite occurs. The Chinese Buddhists were defenders of the "immortality of the soul"; the Buddhists were regarded as superstitious, involved in the services for the spirits, while the Confucianists were looked upon as scientific, progressive and "modern." This may sound strange. As there is a great complexity lying under the surface, it requires careful investigation. We propose to examine objectively the factors which brought about this situation, so that a solution may be obtained.

One of the things which should be taken into consideration is that Buddhism was of Indian origin. When it was introduced into China in the first century A.C. many of its doctrines were presented to the public through the medium of translation. It is natural that the initial translations were imperfect, and many of the philosophical tenets were completely strange to the Chinese. It must have caused great bewilderment, confusion and possible misunderstanding. The adoption of ko-i (1A) (matching the meaning)[41] became a necessary tool in elucidating Buddhist teachings. However, even this device has its limitations and may have generated a more harmful than beneficial effect, due to its ambiguity and incorrect interpretation.

For instance, the Chinese word wu (without, none, not having, etc.) cannot convey the whole range of philosophical meaning and implication of śūnyatā. Likewise it was difficult for the early Buddhists in China to understand clearly the notion of saṁsāra, the effect of karma and rebirth, without being acquainted with the idea of the continuity of a permanent entity or a soul. The ideas of the ancestral or tree spirits,[42] of a soul in the form of hun and p'o (2A), and of ghosts[43] existing after death was recorded in the Shih-ching (3A) (The Book of Odes) and other historical works, such as the Tso chuan (4A). These beliefs were well known to the Chinese people. In the Book of Odes (3:1,1) there is a poem illustrating the after-life existence of King Wên, co-founder of the Chou[44] dynasty. It states that his soul was active in heaven, he "ascends and descends accompanying Ti (6A) to the sacrifices."[45] The pre-Buddhist belief in the existence of the soul, the worship of ancestral spirits based on filial piety, the misunderstanding of the process of rebirth, the salvation in the paradise of Amitābha Buddha,

132

and the theory of the transcendental body of the Buddha (dharmakāya) in Mahāyāna Buddhism are some of the factors which shaped the Chinese Buddhist attitude toward the concept of immortality of the soul. Further it was in response to a challenge offered by Confucian scholars who insisted on the destructibility of the soul. Thus the controversy became a heated topic in the sixth century. It is one of the interesting pages in Chinese intellectual history which concerns the conflict and synthesis of Chinese and Indian thought. Detailed considerations are given in the following sections:

(1)   Buddhism and Ancestral Worship

The worship of ancestors played an important role in Chinese political and social life. This is of great antiquity. The rulers of the Shang dynasty (1766-1154 B.C.) believed that Shang-ti (7A) (the Supreme Deity) was their primary ancestor.[46]   His will and instructions must be obeyed, otherwise the fortune of the dynasty would come to an end, and the mandate to govern would be transferred to someone else. The way to be in the grace of Shang-ti is to rule justly, behave righteously and make the appropriate sacrificial offerings at suitable times. The people of the Chou dynasty continued the practice of ancestor veneration. We are informed that "Sacrifices were offered to King Wên in the Ming-t'ang (8A) (Bright Hall), and he was paired to Shang-ti."[47]   However, there are evident differences between an ancestor-god and the ancestor who associated himself with God. When Confucius appeared on the scene in the fifth century B.C. he emphasized the ethical and social significance of filial piety. He taught that due respect must be shown to the parents while they are alive, a proper burial given them when they passed away, and sacrificial offerings made (after their death) in accordance with propriety.[48]   His disciple Ts'êng-tzŭ made the following statement in support of Confucius:

133

When one carefully fulfills his
obligation at the death of the parents,
and remembers those who had long gone,
the morality /virtue/ of the people will
be greatly strengthened.[49]

In spite of his skeptical attitude toward spirits
or phenomena of mysterious nature, Confucius did
not object to offerings made to the departed
ancestors. This practice reinforced the belief
in a soul after death. For centuries it had been
deeply rooted in the minds of the people. It is
obvious that religious beliefs took precedence
over Confucian ethics. Thus it paved the way for
popular Buddhism to play a significant part in
the religious rituals of service to the dead.
In the Taishō Issaikyō we come across several
works[50] dealing with rituals and distribution of
food and drinks to the spirits burning with
hunger (10A). They were translated by Pu-k'ung
(11A) (Amoghavajra) and Shih-ch'a-nan-t'o (12A)
(Sikṣānanda) of the T'ang dynasty. Religious
services based on some of them are still being observed in Taiwan. On the basis of another text[51]
entitled, Yu-lan-p'en ching (13A) (Avalambana
sūtra) translated by Dharmarakṣa (ca. 265-313)
a popular religious festival[52] was recorded in
538 A.C. during the reign of Emperor Wu of the
Liang dynasty (14A). Normally this festival
is held annually on the fifteenth of the seventh
month. On this day offerings of food were made
to the spirits, especially to those who had no
offspring to depend on. This is popularly known
as the "All Souls Day."

Of penetrating influence on Chinese masses
is the story concerning filial piety carried out
by a chief disciple of the Buddha. He rescued
his mother from the Avīci purgatory (15A), where
she was condemned because of her evil deeds
committed in the previous existence. This refers
to the famous Mahā Maudgalyāyana (Mu-lien /16A/
in Chinese). Preserved in the Tun-huang caves
and uncovered at the turn of the century, there
were included in the Tun-huang pien-wên chi[53]

(A Collection of Pien-wên from Tun-huang) three
works concerning "The Great Mu-lien rescues his
mother from the land of darkness" (17A). One of
the versions, dated 921, amounts to forty pages.
It describes vividly how Mu-lien went in search
of his mother in the various regions of purgatory,
how terrible and painful torture with boiling
water, melting metal, cutting knife, burning fire,
and so forth, was inflicted on her, how the Buddha
rescued her from the Avīci hell at the request of
Mu-lien, how she went to the plane of "hungry
ghosts" where food and water turned into flames,
how later she was born as a dog in the city of
Rājagṛha, and ultimately through the various
religious services rendered by Mu-lien, she was
reborn in the Trayastriṁśa (18A) heaven to enjoy
the heavenly bliss.[54]

As "pien-wên" is a "rewritten piece" of the
original story, and as it used to be dramatically
transmitted to an attentive audience by a
story-teller, the effect of filial piety in the
Buddhist fashion should be tremendous. Comparing
this to the Confucian counterpart, the latter
would appear somewhat superficial and unimpres-
sive. If we take the purport and intent of the
Buddhist works and rituals seriously, it would
mean that after death the individual would not be
deemed to be in a state of emptiness.

(2)   The Misinterpretation of Rebirth

The Buddhist doctrine of rebirth appears
in certain ways similar to the Hindu concept
of reincarnation. Thus it causes great confusion and misunderstanding, especially to those
who believe in animistic traditions. To our
surprise, we notice that early Chinese Buddhists
tended to interpret the term in that direction.
We refer to the writings of Mou-tzǔ,[55] who
flourished during and after the demise of Emperor
Lin (19A) (168-189) of the later Han dynasty.
He was one of the first Chinese intellectuals
to be converted to Buddhism, and his composition
entitled, Li-huo lun (20A) (Essays on the Settling

135

of Doubts) was in defense of Buddhist doctrines and practices. His understanding of rebirth illustrates the extent to which it goes against the doctrine of anattā. Below is a quotation from his work:

> When a man is about to die, members of his family ascend atop of the roof and call his name. As he is already dead, whom are they calling? Someone said, "Calling his hun and p'o (soul)." When the soul returns /21A/ that man will be born again. If not, where will it go to? Well, it will either become a spirit or a ghost. If that is so, it means that the soul, indeed is indestructible /22A/, although the body may perish. It may be compared to the roots and leaves of the five grains. The soul is like the seed of the plants. The roots and leaves will die, but the seed will live for ever.

> The soul of those who have realized the religion (Tao) will return to the Paradise of Bliss /23A/, while the soul of the evil-doers will suffer the consequence of retribution.56

Mou-tzǔ was evidently aware of the traditional Chinese belief in the soul and the practice of calling it to return after someone had passed away. When it responds to the call and returns, one will be born again as man, otherwise a ghost. Further, he was aware of the theory of karma and its effect. The performance of good or evil deeds will result in being born in paradise or in the planes of suffering. The agent in either case that will reap the consequences is the soul. This is the point where he differed sharply from the early Buddhist doctrine of non-soul. Possibly he misunderstood the original meaning and hence interpreted rebirth in the light of animistic beliefs with which he was familiar. Let us examine the doctrine of rebirth and karma in Theravāda Buddhism:

136

Early Buddhism denied the existence of a permanent entity or soul, but accepted the theory of rebirth. This may appear contradictory. The Buddhist explanation for this is that "rebirth" differs from "transmigration." In transmigration there must be a soul that is being transmigrated from one being to another, whereas in rebirth, the notion of a permanent entity is disallowed. The factors which bring about rebirth consist of karma, good or wicked action, and in turn, it depends on the five aggregates. This is to say that no action can take place without the combined effort of the mental and physical components, and through them rebirth becomes possible. One may ask, "What is it that is born into the next existence?" In reply to this question Nāgasena said, "It is name and form that is born into the next existence."[57] This statement denies the notion of a soul that is being transferred from the past existence to a future life. An oft-quoted example illustrating the process of rebirth and the positive stand on "Rebirth takes place without anything transmigrating," is a simile of lighting a candle from another candle.[58] In doing so the light of the first candle does not transmigrate to the second one, although there is interrelation between the two. Similarly the Buddhists regard the karmic force[59] to be the source that causes the materialization of rebirth.

Thus Mou-tzǔ misinterpreted the doctrine of non-soul by stating that the soul is the agent for rebirth. One wonders whether he was aware of committing an error of misrepresentation, although he worked enthusiastically as a defender of Buddhism.

(3)   Salvation by Faith and the Pure Land

The belief in the compassionate Amitābha Buddha who resides in the Sukhāvatī, the land of Bliss or the Pure Land (26A), and welcomes persons passing away from this world, is a new trend and religious movement in Mahāyāna Buddhism.

This has exerted a strong influence on the philosophical outlook of life, and has been very popular among the masses. Instead of attaining enlightenment through one's own effort ("Be ye lamps unto yourselves, be ye a refuge unto yourselves,"[60] the Buddha used to urge his disciples), it emphasizes reliance on the powers of Amitābha Buddha to effect salvation. This is known as "salvation by faith." Anyone, including the worst evil-doers, will be born into this paradise. He will enjoy the heavenly blessing of infinite happiness and be freed from evil modes of existence, such as animals, ghosts and purgatory. The only requirements for eligibility is that the dying individual should think of Amitābha for even a brief time. This land of Joy possesses many beautiful mansions, parks, lakes, rivers, flowers and trees, which are made of seven precious gems. The huge lotuses of various colors issue forth sweet fragrance and birds sing sweetly, praising the achievement of the Buddha and his disciples.[61]

An ideal paradise of this nature, it is bound to be attractive and flooded with aspirants. It is a goal that is within the reach of everybody, if anyone cares to go there. The earliest record of keen interest in the Pure Land is found in the biography[62] of Hui-yüan /27A/. It states that in 402 A.C. Hui-yüan, along with a group of 123 persons, the intellectual elite of the day, gathered in front of the statue of Amitābha Buddha in Mt. Lu-shan, and vowed solemnly that they would expect to be born in the Western Paradise /28A/. An essay was written by Liu I-min /29A/ in order to commemorate the occasion. Tradition has it that a "Lotus Society" was formed and Hui-yüan was regarded as the first patriarch of the Pure Land School. Later this school gained great popularity in China and Japan. The Jōdo and the Jōdo Shinshū are some of the leading Buddhist sects in modern Japan.

Regarding birth in the Pure Land, one may question what is it that is born there? It suggests that some sort of living entity that dies

here and is born there. It should be something
similar to the "soul," although the word "soul"
is hardly mentioned, but it is understood. This
belief should have reinforced the theory of indestructibility of the soul.

(4) The Theory of Dharmakāya

The term "dharmakāya" in the initial stage
means the body of the dharma or truth as preached
by Gautama Buddha. Later when Mahāyāna Buddhism
was firmly established, its meaning was drastically
changed. According to the Mādhyamika school it
is the true reality of everything, the void, the
immaterial, the ground of all phenomena and suchness (bhūtatathatā). Along with the body of enjoyment (saṁbhogakāya) with which the Buddha enjoys
the fruits of his past saving labors, and the
body of transformation (nirmāṇakāya) which indicates that he has the power to transform himself
at will to any shape for omnipresent salvation
for those who need him (the historical Śākyamuni
Buddha is regarded as one of the transformations),
the concept of trikāya (three bodies) was originated. This may have been an attempt to extend
the "Hīnayāna idealization of the earthly Buddha
with his thirty-two signs, eighty physical marks,
clairvoyance, clairaudience, holiness, purity,
wisdom. . ." but with additional attributes such
as   "the Buddha as the universal, the All,
with infinity of forms, yet above all our concepts of unity or diversity."[63] The mystical
aspect of dharmakāya compared favorably with the
Tao, the primordial principle in Taoism, and
rta, the cosmic rhythm in the Vedas. As an un-
changing principle without any form or substance,
the dharmakāya, like the Tao, can be said to
exist eternally everywhere or nowhere. This is
because it is beyond and above the process of
birth and death, and beyond any description.

Owing to the traditional background and
philosophical Taoism the Chinese intellectuals
who upheld the theory of indestructibility of

the soul tended to classify the dharmakāya into the same category as that of the soul. They very well knew that there are differences between them, i.e., one is philosophical and the other animistic. A sampling of the writings on this topic will illustrate the point:

When there is no birth, there will not be a body. However, the dharmakāya /Fa-shên, 32A/ is without a body, but it has a soul /shên, 33A/.64

The so-called "Doing nothing and everything is done," is similar in character to the dharmakāya, it is contained in everything /34A/ although it is without any form.65

Commenting on a statement from the Book of Changes, "Yin and yang is the Tao; when the operation of yin and yang is inscrutable, it is called shên /spirit or soul/," Tsung Pin /35A/, author of Shên pu-mei lun66 (On the Indestructibility of the Soul) had this to say:

The ultimate non-being is the Tao. . . descending from the Tao, there enters the Spirit /ching shên, 36A/. . . However, the soul of living beings may be equal in the Ultimate, its consciousness may be subtle or coarse owing to the transformation and process of causation. It /consciousness/ will not be destroyed in relation to its original source. . .As its origin was established before birth, it signifies that it will not be subjected to destruction after death.67

All the above-noted quotations are taken from Tsung's essay On the Indestructibility of the Soul. He endeavored to identify the dharmakāya with the Tao; it has a soul, and the soul may be of a refined or coarse quality due to the effect of one's karma (causation). Thus he came

140

to the conclusion that the soul is indestructible
because it exists before birth. We feel that his
analogy is somewhat inappropriate and uncon-
vincing. Soul, according to the Upaniṣadic sources,
is partially materialistic in nature. To pair
it with the dharmakāya, the true reality of the
universe, or the Tao, the primordial principle
is to classify the fluorescence of a glow-worm
and the bright sunshine in the same category.
This similarity is extremely superficial. However,
he was not alone; a very learned scholar of our
time echoed this expression by saying: "Dharmakāya is the spirit and intelligence /shên ming,
37A/ of a sage who had attained to the Path."[68]

The reason the Chinese Buddhist scholars
could make use of this simile is the ambiguity
of the term "shên" (38A). It may mean a spirit,
a god, a soul, a spiritual being, the divine,
the supernatural, the wonderful, and the mind.[69]
As the dharmakāya and the soul are not exactly
identical, the result is confusion, miscomprehension,
and misinterpretation.

The Central Focus of the Controversy

From ancient times Chinese philosophers
showed keen interest in the speculation that the
soul exists after death. This could be traced
to the writings of Mo-tzŭ (39A), Lao Tzŭ, and
Chuangtzŭ.[70] In the fourth and fifth centuries
prominent Buddhist scholars like Hui-yüan and
Chêng Tao-tzŭ (40A) endeavored to write treatises
explaining that the soul is not destroyed at
death. The former wrote Hsing chin shên pu-mei
lun (41A) (On the Indestructibility of the Soul
after the Dissolution of the Body[71]) and the
latter wrote Shên pu-mei lun (42A) (On the
Indestructibility of the Soul).[72] The purpose
of the treatises was to explain the Buddhist
doctrine of karma and rebirth. It was not
intended, at least at this time, as a refutation
of the opposite view, which became a heated topic
in the later part of the fifth and early sixth

centuries. The actual controversy was generated by
an essay entitled, Shěn mei lun (44A) (An Essay on
the Destructibility of the Soul). It was written
by Fan Chěn, who was born in 450 A.C. and passed
away ca. 507.[73] It was a rude shock to the Buddhist circles when the treatise was widely circu-
lated. The participants who responded and
challenged him in refutation were numerous, including an emperor and a prince. The government
aristocracy did not abuse its power by suppressing
Fan's thesis. This indicates that the intellectuals were allowed the freedom of speech, and the
cultural tradition of free discussion in terms of
"ch'ing-t'an" (45A) (pure conversation) was maintained in the Southern dynasties. Before dealing
with the essential contents of Fan's composition,
we would like to discover the purpose and motive
of his taking such a stand.

According to his biography in the Nan-shih
(46A) (History of the Southern Dynasties),[74] it is
stated that he was atheistic in outlook and did
not believe in the existence of spirits, nor the
effect of karma. He openly declared that there
was no such thing as the Buddha or the possibility
of becoming one. His treatise was aimed at the
uprooting of the foundation of Buddhism. He insisted that everything comes to an end at death,
and the soul does not exist. He earnestly hoped
that it would undermine the doctrine of rebirth,
karma, and its effect. In addition to his
iconoclastic operations[75] in the form of prohi-
biting sacrifices being made to folk religious
shrines, his principal purpose was to bring home
to the public the harmful influence of Buddhism
on society in the social, religious and political
spheres. Some of the injurious effects cited
by him were the renunciation of the family in
order to become mendicants, as it would lead
to the elimination of human population; the exces-
sive wealth of Buddhist monasteries and monks,
when the needs of the poor and the destitute
were never provided for--not even a handful of
grain was given; the deceptive teachings of
rebirth in heaven by performance of meritorious

deeds, and damnation forever in purgatory due to
evil acts. All these amounted to false promises
and imaginary fears in the minds of the people.
Thus Buddhism hindered the progress of governmental
administration, military service, and caused economic bankruptcy. He felt sorry for those who had
been deceived and desired to rescue them as well
as the country from the false religion, so that
the true facts would be revealed. The means for
carrying out this mission was through the wide
circulation of his treatise. However, most of his
criticisms were biased and exaggerated out of
proportion. For instance, not only did the
Chinese population not diminish, but over the
centuries it has grown constantly. Now it stands
at the astonishing figure of over 800 million
souls! He seemed to have inherited the traditional
Chinese character of national pride which despises
the religious practices of a foreign religion.

It can be inferred that Fan's anti-Buddhist
attacks concentrated more on popular Buddhist
practices prevailing at the time than on Buddhist
philosophy. But as the doctrines of karma and
rebirth constituted the essence of the religion,
they became a prime target. Apparently he was
not aware of the fact that Gautama Buddha was a
staunch denouncer of the theory of the soul. In
a way, he and the Buddha stood on the same platform
fighting against animistic speculations. It was
an irony of fate that brought about such a comic
situation. This tragic-comedy may be seen as a
product of historical comparison.

Now we shall proceed to examine the essentials
of Shên mei lun. It is included in the Hung-ming
chi (A Collection of Works on the Promotion of
Buddhism), and the History of the Liang Dynasty,
consisting of thirty-one dialogues (questions
and answers). The "question" part represents
the views of his opponent, while the "answers"
are the opinion of the author. This was the
literary style in vogue at that time. The few
dialogues at the beginning and the one at the end
are more important than the other sections, which

143

are explanatory in nature, trying to elucidate the relationship between the soul and the body. For the purpose of our discussion we shall translate only the relevant portions:

> The soul is identical with the body, and the body is identical with the soul. Therefore, when the body exists, the soul exists; when the body perishes, the soul, too, is destroyed.

> The body is the substance of the soul, and the soul the functioning of the body. Hence when we speak of the body, we mean its substance; when we speak of the soul, we imply its function. These two /soul and body/ cannot be differentiated from each other.

> The soul is to the substance what sharpness is to the knife; the body is to functioning what the knife is to sharpness. However, the designation "sharpness" is not the knife, the designation "knife" is not sharpness. But when sharpness is taken away, there is no knife, and when knife is taken away, there is no sharpness. We have never heard of a destroyed knife being able to preserve its sharpness. How can the soul still exist when the body is dissolved?[76]

From the materialistic point of view Fan equated the soul with the body. The soul will not exist independently without the body. Therefore, when an individual dies, his soul perishes at death. To the Chinese Buddhists this was a great threat to the fundamentals of Buddhism, and to the Confucians it was blasphemous in terms of ancestral veneration. In response to the call of Emperor Wu (502-549) of the Liang dynasty for refutations to Fan's thesis, there were sixty-three persons[77] who replied in writing in regard to the subject. In general they are brief and appreciative of the Emperor's concern and his

144

disapproval of Fan's proposition. Among them the
refutations of Hsiao Ch'ên (47A) and Ts'ao Ssǔ-wên
(48A) deserve further consideration in order to
learn the views of the opposition.

The treatise of Hsiao Ch'ên was entitled,
Nan shên-mei lun (49A) (Refuting the Thesis on the
Destructibility of the Soul).[78] In the first
place Hsiao pointed out that the statement regarding the identity between the soul and the body is
logically unsound. He argued that when one is
in a dream, his soul travels thousands of miles
flying in the sky (50A), while the body lying in
bed like a log is devoid of any consciousness,
viz., "it does not respond when it is called, nor
does it feel when it is touched." Under these
circumstances the equation of the soul and the
body seems unacceptable. Regarding the analogy
that the relation of the soul to the body is like
that of sharpness to the knife, Hsiao argued
that that, too, was wrong, because the sharpness
of the knife is owing to the effects of the
whetstone. Once the edge of a knife turns blunt,
it loses its sharpness, and its usefulness as a
knife comes to an end, but the knife itself still
remains. Therefore, it is not possible to say,
when the sharpness is lost, there is no knife.
This shows that "sharpness and knife are not lost
at the same time, the same is true regarding
the soul and the body."

Hsiao's refutation appears to be convincing
and well-organzied. Being a learned Buddhist, he
was a supporter of the indestructibility of the
soul. But he did not enlighten us on how the
soul exists without the body. By the way, he
was a brother-in-law of Fan[79] (he married Fan's
sister). Apparently he felt somewhat upset
that such a controversy should have been initiated
by one of his relatives. Altogether Hsiao refuted
six major points of Fan's thesis. In this context
he exerted himself more than anyone else. Through
his rebuttal the complete text of Shên-mei lun
has been preserved in Buddhist literature, as the
original sections and their refutations are dis-
played side by side.

Next to Hsiao's effort, Ts'ao Ssǔ-wên was
another contemporary scholar who defended Buddhism
and rebutted Fan's theory on the destructibility
of the soul. He concentrated his challenge on two
points, and his essay was much shorter in length
than that of Hsiao's. On the equation of the soul
and the body, he argued that if they have any
functioning, it is due to their combined effort;
as such they are not identical:

> When one is alive, they are united
> to produce a functioning; when one dies
> the soul goes away while the body remains
> behind.

To substantiate this point he quoted a statement
of Yen Lin (51A) on the occasion of burying his
child, "The bone and flesh will return to the
earth, but the soul can go anywhere."[80] He took
this to mean that the body may perish, but the
soul is indestructible. The other point of refutation is in regard to Fan's denial of existence
of spirits. Fan made the remark that the sacrificial offerings placed at the ancestral temples
were merely formalities in accordance with the
teachings of the sages. By so doing it satisfies
the sentiment of a filial son and serves as a
reminder (52A) so that he may not become ungrateful.[81] Disagreeing with this proposition Ts'ao
quoted an instance of Duke Chou (54A) who paired
Hou Chi (55A), an ancestor of the Chou people,
with T'ien (heaven), and King Wên with Shang-ti
(56A) (the Heavenly Emperor) at the various sacrificial offerings from the Book of Filial Piety,
which does not necessarily prove that the soul
of the Chou ancestors really existed. The Confucian explanation of sacrifice on ethical
grounds which was echoed by Fan apparently scored
a point (57A).[82]

On receiving Ts'ao's refutation, Fan Chên
made a suitable reply to most of the points.
However, Ts'ao wrote a "re-rebuttal" to Fan's
response. A fresh point he stressed in the
second communication was in regard to the analogy

of the sharpness of a knife. He correctly pointed out that the concept about the sharpness of a knife concerns two designations of the same thing (58A). As such no more sharpness will be there, if the knife is lost. The soul and the body, however, are in the category of two things being combined together (59A) to produce a function. It is substantially different from the simile of a knife and its sharpness. Therefore, he concluded that the body might be annihilated, but the soul could travel to other places.[83]

The foregoing passages represent the arguments set forth by participants from the camps for or against the notion of the indestructibility of the soul. From the materialistic point of view Fan Chên may assert that after the dissolution of the body, the soul could not possibly continue to exist, because these two are interdependent—if one is lost, the other cannot function. However, there is no way to prove or disprove that the soul does not exist after death. As this is in the area of metaphysical speculation or superstition, the best way out is to leave the question open for further investigation.

It is my opinion that Fan's analogy in comparing the sharpness of a knife to the mental intelligence related to the body is unfortunately a mistake. The mental and intellectual aspects of a sentient being are vastly complex, and cannot be equated with the sharpness of a knife. A blunt knife may be sharpened again and again, whereas the faculties and consciousness cannot be restored to the dead, not even once. On the other hand, a knife may become blunt, but we can say the knife is still "existing." This analogy cannot be applied to a dead body that is devoid of consciousness, because death means dissolution and destruction. The more we ponder the matter, the more inappropriate his analogy becomes. This may actually shake the foundation of his theory on logical grounds. At any rate the simile seems to have created more misgivings and little meaningfulness.

147

By the way, it may be mentioned that Fan's treatise attracted the attention of Marxist scholars in modern China. A translation of the Shên mei lun into spoken Chinese[84] was made by Jên Chi-yü (60A) and published in Peking in 1973. Jên praised Fan as the most powerful philosopher who opposed the Buddhist doctrine of karma and its effect. The oft-quoted example in this connection is his reply to a question put to him by Hsiao Tzŭ-liang, prince of Chin-lin (61A):

> If you do not believe in the cause and its effect, how is it that some are born rich and in high position, while others poor, lowly and despised?

Fan compared human fortune or misfortune to the blossoming flowers on a tree. Blown by the wind, some petals of the flowers may fall on a silk cushion in the palace, while others may land on a manure pile. Then he compared the prince to the lucky petal that fell on a silk cushion, and himself to the unlucky one that settled on a manure pile.[85] He insisted that everything happened by mere chance, "There is no such thing as cause and its effect" (62A). Commenting on this, Jên said that that was a very clever reply. However, he was criticized for not being able to understand the Marxist principle of class exploitation-- the root cause for being rich or poor. Further he was blamed for being a representative of a small-scale landlord class. His concept of Fortuitism as suggested in the reply was also rejected by Jên.[86]

In my view, Fan's denouncing the significance of cause and effect is unwise, and in a way he seemed to have misunderstood the doctrine of causation (Pratītya-samutpāda). The law of causation governs action and its results on an individual, a society or nations in the world. Events will not emerge by mere accident--there must be a cause behind the manifested phenomena. A millionaire may become a pauper if he dissipates his wealth in gambling or other extravagant operations; on the other hand, a poor and humble person like Abraham Lincoln may rise to the high office of president of the U.S. if he strives and works zealously for it. The case of becoming either a pauper or a president indicates unequivocally the consequences, based on causes and factors which in turn are related to one's actions. The law of causation is rational, scientific, easy to understand and devoid of any fortuitous occurrence. This is just the opposite of Fan's theory of accidental emergency. He may be against Buddhism. But to reject something that is right in the judgment of intelligent persons is a demonstration of his biased stubbornness, and his obstinate insistence on misunderstanding Buddhist doctrines.

Other Theories in Support of the Indestructibility of the Soul

This study would appear incomplete if we did not include some of the early expositions on this subject. They are not associated directly with the controversy initiated by Fan Chên, but they had great relevance to it. One may say that they had anticipated this, and were prepared for it in advance. In this context, Hui-yüan (344-416), one of the most learned Buddhist scholars of his time, was very qualified to write on this topic. As he was well-versed in the philosophy of śunyata and Taoism, his interpretations are generally philosophically oriented, and at times they may be metaphysical in appearance. He was of the opinion that the soul is nameless and extremely mysterious. It responds to things and functions in individual destinies. As it is not a thing, it will not be subject to dissolution, although the things may undergo transformation (63A). The soul has the power of moving imperceptibly and transcends the limitation of ordinary subjects. As such one cannot insist that both the "subtle" and the "coarse" aspects (soul and body) of a living being perish at the same time. To expound this theory, he gave an illustration of firewood and its relation to fire:

The transmission of fire to firewood
is like that of the soul to the body.
The transmission of fire to another piece
of firewood is like that of the soul to
another new body. The former body is
not the latter body. . .A deluded person,
seeing the body perish in one existence,
assumes that the soul and feelings also are
destroyed with it, as if fire would be
extinct for ever when a piece of wood
is burnt.[87]

The analogy here has a metaphysical significance. The Hindu philosophers regard fire as
one of the four or seven elements which constitute an aspect of a human being. At death the
heat in man returns to the fire,[88] so also the
other elements will go back to their respective
places where they belong. A man may die, but
the elements will remain active eternally. As
Hui-yüan believed in rebirth and karma, it was
natural for him to assume that the soul should
be classified in this category, and it would
continue to exist as long as there exists an
inflammable substance like firewood. A piece of
firewood may be burnt out, but it does not mean
that the fire as an element is destroyed. The
only difference between the soul and fire is
that fire is visible and can be tested, whereas
the soul is invisible and cannot be put to the
test. From the standpoint of a Theravādin
Buddhist, Hui-yüan might have erred in falling
into the view of an Eternalist. The Buddha used
to denounce both the Eternalist and the Annihilationist, maintaining a doctrine of the middle-
path, as demonstrated in his answer to the
question of whether or not a sage existed after
death:

I do not hold that the saint exists
after death. . .both exists and does not
exist after death. . .neither exists
nor does not exist after death.[89]

The reason being that none of the speculations

suits the case at hand, nor could such intellectual exercise lead anyone to the attainment of enlightenment and nirvāṇa. It appears that Hui-yüan tended to approach this problem from the concept of dharma-kāya and the fundamental essence of the Tao. It would be a serious error on our part to even suggest that he was interested in the superstitious belief of animism.

Following closely Hui-yüan's analogy of fire and firewood there was another scholar named Chêng Tao-tzǔ of the Sung dynasty of the House of Liu (420-479). His interpretation differs somewhat from that of Hui-yüan, although both attempted to color it with a metaphysical orientation. Here is Chêng's statement:

> There is fire on account of firewood, without the latter, the former will not come into being; firewood is not the primary cause of fire, although it produces fire. The primordial cause of fire is self-existence /64A/, through firewood, its function is materialised. . . Therefore, firewood is a shelter of fire, but not the primary cause. The interdependence between the soul and the body is in the same manner. . .How can one claim that the soul exists only because of the body, and the soul perishes when the body is destroyed?[90]

He seemed to assert that firewood is merely an agent through which the fire burns, likewise is the soul and the body. Being associated with a mysterious primordial principle, the soul and fire can exist independently and eternally, even if the body and firewood are destroyed. The concept of a primordial cause or cosmological principle behind the soul or fire reinforces the argument set forth by Hui-yüan. This simile appears to be much better than that of the knife and its sharpness, because, as an element, fire is potentially and eternally existing in any inflammable substance or in the form of heat. In the area of metaphysical sophistication, the soul

151

may be even more mysterious than fire, although
it is still beyond our knowledge to adequately
unearth its mystery. Perhaps someone will be able
to give a more satisfactory answer to this extremely fascinating question in time to come.

Conclusion

In conclusion, we may say that the discussion
on whether or not the soul exists after death is
extremely interesting and inspiring. It has been
noted that the seers in India and China had their
different views and interpretations. Actually
they took opposite positions; some were for the
notion, while others were against it. The no-
ticeably unique feature in the Chinese controversy
is that the Buddhists were defenders of the indestructibility of the soul, while some Confucians
were supporters of the doctrine of non-soul. In
other words, the Chinese Buddhists were opposing
Gautama Buddha in this regard. In this paper, I
have endeavored to explain the complex causes which
brought about this abnormal situation. It was
ironic fate that caused this unhappy episode.

In my impartial judgement, if soul is interpreted as a universal intelligence, immaterial
and self-existent like the Tao or the dharmakāya,
it may not be subjected to destruction at death.
Thus, it may exist eternally. Actually, Hui-yüan
and other defenders tended to move toward that
direction. That being the case, they may not be
accused of intentionally breaking away from early
Buddhist traditions. Moreover, it should be
borne in mind that China had the privilege of
receiving both the Mahāyāna and Hīnayāna teachings.
As contradictions do exist in these Buddhist
schools, the blame should not be ascribed to their
followers. Under these circumstances the view
held by the defenders of the indestructibility
of the soul is understandable and therefore,
excusable.

If freedom of speech is available to everyone,

152

Fan Chên should have the right to speak freely
in regard to the destructibility of the soul.
However, he misinterpreted the doctrine of causation. His analogy concerning the sharpness of
a knife is inappropriate and inaccurate. This
demonstrates that he was superficial and shallow
in learning, although he created controversy in
the intellectual history of China.

Finally we hope that this study may serve
as a reminder to those scholars who are interested
in Buddhism and Chinese religion. Our message
is that there are similar intricate issues which
await their early attention.

NOTES

1. S. Radhakrishnan, _Indian Philosophy_ (London:
George Allen & Unwin, 1941), I, p. 151.

2. T.W. Rhys Davids, trans., _Dialogues of the
Buddha_ (London: Luzac & Co., 1959), I, p. xxv.

3. Radhakrishnan, op.cit., p. 152.

4. Ibid.

5. Ibid., p. 153.

6. Ibid., pp. 154-57.

7. Ibid., p. 157.

8. Ibid., p. 158.

9. Ibid., p. 250; Kenneth K.S. Ch'en, _Buddhism,
the Light of Asia_ (Woodbury, NY: Barron's
Education Series, 1968), p. 6.

10. Radhakrishnan, op.cit., p. 136.

11. Max Müller, ed., <u>The Sacred Books of the East</u> (Oxford: Clarendon Press, 1884), XV, pp. 23-24.

12. Ibid., p. 11.

13. T.W. Rhys Davids, <u>Buddhist India</u> (Calcutta: Susil Gupta, 1903), p. 165.

14. <u>Dialogues of the Buddha</u>, III, p. 54.

15. Ibid.

16. Ibid., I.188; <u>Buddhist India</u>, p. 167.

17. Radhakrishnan, op.cit., pp. 134, 249, 251, 253.

18. Ibid., p. 252.

19. Ibid., pp. 252-53.

20. Ibid., p. 253.

21. Ibid., pp. 136, 255.

22. <u>Dialogues of the Buddha</u>, I, p. 44.

23. Ibid., I, p. 74.

24. Ibid., pp. 45, 46, 53.

25. Ibid., I, p. 74.

26. Ibid., pp. 46-48.

27. H.C. Warren, trans., <u>Buddhism in Translation</u> (New York: Atheneum, 1968), p. 69; E.J. Thomas, <u>The Life of the Buddha, as Legend and History</u> (London: Routledge & Kegan Paul, 1952), pp. 62-63.

28. Warren, op.cit., p. 117.

29. Ibid., p. 118.

30. Ibid., p. 119.

31. Ibid., p. 122.

32. Ibid., pp. 120-21.

33. Ibid. p. 121.

34. Ibid., pp. 123-25.

35. C.H.S. Ward, Buddhism: Hīnayāna (London: The Epworth Press, 1947), pp. 72-73.

36. Ibid., p. 66.

37. Warren, op.cit., pp. 133-34.

38. This is a literal translation of "nāma" and "rūpa." The more generally accepted translation is "mind" and "matter" which are the components of the five aggregates.

39. Warren, op.cit., p. 151.

40. Ibid., p. 150.

41. Sêng-yu, Kao-sêng chuan /The Biography of Eminent Monks/, in Taishō, ch. 6, vol. 50, p. 358A. The term "ko-i" may also mean to borrow Chinese or Taoist ideas to explain certain Buddhist concepts, such as "wu" (non-being) was equated with "sūnyatā."

42. Wang Chih-hsin, Chung-kuo tsung-chiao ssŭ-hsiang shih ta-kang (5A) (Outline of a History of Chinese Religious Thought) (Taiwan, Taipei: Chung-hwa Book Co., 1960), pp. 13, 26.

43. Ibid., pp. 26-27, 34-36.

44. The Chou dynasty lasted for 867 years, from 1122 to 255 B.C.

45. D. Howard Smith, Chinese Religions (New York: Holt, Rinehart and Winston, 1968), p. 18.

46. Smith, op.cit., p. 14; Wang Chih-hsin, op.cit., p. 35.

47.   Ibid., p. 44.

48.   Cf. James Legge, trans., Confucian Analects
in Hua-yin ssŭ-shu (9A) (The Four Books in Chinese
and English) (Shanghai: Commercial Press, n.d.),
p. 11.

49.   Cf. ibid., p. 5.

50.   The numbers in the Taishō are: 1313, 1314,
1318, 1319, 1320, and 1321.

51.   Taishō, No. 685.

52.   Charles Elliot, Japanese Buddhism (London:
Edward Arnold, 1935), p. 216. In Japan it is
known as 'Urabon-e'. Empress Saimei observed
this festival for the first time on the 15th of
the seventh month in 606 on behalf of her ancestors for seven generations. The 'Bon' festival
is still observed in Japan in July or August
according to the lunar calendar.

53.   Wang Chung-min et al., eds., Tun-huang pien-
wên chi ,   (A Collection of Pien-wên from
Tun-huang) (Peking: The People's Literature
Publishing House, 1957), pp. 714-55. The other
two versions are entitled "Mu-lien yüan-chi"
(The story of Mu-lien), pp. 701-13, and "Mu-lien
pien-wên" (The pien-wên about Mu-lien), pp.
756-60. The first of the three is more complete
than the rest.

54.   Ibid., pp. 720-40.

55.   Sêng-yu, ed., Hung Ming chi (25A) (A
Collection of Works on the Promotion of Buddhism)
(Shanghai: Commercial Press, being a photostatic
copy of the Ssŭ-pu ts'ung-kan tsu-pien /24A/
of the Ming edition), ch. 1, p. 8; Taishō, 52,
pp. 1-96. Regarding the date for the composition
of this work, see Kenneth K.S. Ch'en, Buddhism
in China (Princeton: Princeton University Press,
1964), pp. 36-38.

56. Ibid., pp. 11-12.

57. Warren, op.cit., p. 234, under the heading "Rebirth is not transmigration."

58. Ibid.

59. Ibid., p. 235.

60. See "Mahā-parinibbāna-suttanta" in the Dialogues of the Buddha, II, p. 108.

61. Kumārajīva, trans., Sukhāvatī-amrta vyūha, Taishō, 12, pp. 346-47; Saṅghavarman, trans., Sukhāvatīvyūha, Taishō, 12, pp. 265-78   The Chinese titles are: Āh-mi-t'o-ching   30A (Sūtra of Amitābha), and Wu-liang-shou ching (31A) (Sūtra on the Limitless Life) respectively. For the English translation of the above, see F. Max Müller, trans., Sukhāvatī-vyūha Sūtra (larger), and Sukhāvatī-vyūha Sūtra (smaller) in the Sacred Books of the East (Oxford: Clarendon Press, 1894), vol. 49.

62. Kao-sêng chuan, ch. 6, Taishō, 50, pp. 358C-59A; T'ang Yung-t'ung, Han-Wei liang-tsin Nan-pei-Chao fo-Chiao-Shih (History of Buddhism in the Han, Wei, Eastern Tsin, Western Tsin, Southern and Northern Dynasties) (Shanghai: Chung Hwa Book Co., 1955), pp. 365-66; Ch'en, op.cit., pp. 106-108.

63. W.E. Soothill, A Dictionary of Chinese Buddhist Terms (London: Kegan Paul, 1937), pp. 77-78; D.T. Suzuki, Outlines of Mahāyāna Buddhism (New York: Schocken Books, 1973), pp. 242-62; B.L. Suzuki, Mahāyāna Buddhism (London: David Marlowe, 1948), pp. 36-47.

64. Hung-ming chi, ch. 2, p. 26A.

65. Ibid., p. 28B.

66. Ibid., pp. 23-36. It is also called "Ming-

157

fu lun" ("An Essay on the Understanding of the Buddha"). This is one of the best treatises in defense of the immortality of the soul.

67. Ibid., p. 24B.

68. T'ang Yung-t'ung, op.cit., p. 364.

69. R.H. Mathews, A Chinese-English Dictionary (Shanghai: China Inland Mission and Presbyterian Mission Press, 1931), pp. 791-92.

70. Wang Chih-hsin, op.cit., pp. 107-108.

71. Hung-ming chi, ch. 5, pp. 65-67. This is the fifth essay being included under the title, "A Buddhist śramana should not show veneration to the King" (43A).

72. Ibid., ch. 5, pp. 58-61.

73. Jên Chi-yü, Han-t'ang fu-chiao ssŭ-hsiang lun chi (A Collection of Essays on Buddhist Thought in the Han and T'ang Dynasties) (Peking: The Peoples' Publishing House, 1973), p. 303.

74. For the cultural traditions in the Southern dynasties, see T'ang Yung-tung's book, op.cit., pp. 415-86; Nan-shih (History of the Southern Dynasties), being the photostatic copy of the Ta-teh edition of the Yüan dynasty (China: Publishing House of the Twenty-five Dynasty Histories, n.d.), ch. 57, pp. 18-20; Liang shu (History of the Liang Dynasty) (China: Publishing House of the Twenty-five Dynasty Histories, n.d.), ch. 42, pp. 5-13.

75. T'ang Yung-tung, op.cit., pp. 470-71; Nan-Shih, ch. 57, p. 20.

76. Hung-ming chi, ch. 9, pp. 110-11; T'ang Yung-tung, op.cit., p. 471; Jên Chi-yü, op.cit., pp. 307-309.

77. Hung-ming chi, ch. 10, pp. 120-34.

78. Ibid., ch. 9, p. 111.

79. Ibid., ch. 9, p. 110.

80. Ibid., p. 115.

81. Ibid., p. 116; Jên Chi-yü, op.cit., p. 321, has "t'ou-po" (53A) (to steal laziness and be light-hearted). The correct reading should be "yü-po" (negligent and ungrateful). See 52A for the Chinese characters.

82. Hung-ming chi, ch. 9, p. 116.

83. Ibid., p. 118; there are many instances concerning reincarnation in recent times; some took place in Asia, especially in India and Ceylon, while others were associated with the West. For further information on this topic, see Francis Story, The Case for Rebirth (Kandy, Ceylon: Buddhist Publication Society, 1959), pp. 14-34. The case concerning Edgar Cayce of Kentucky is of great interest, p. 18.

84. Jên Chi-yü, op.cit., pp. 303-25.

85. T'ang Yung-tung, op.cit., p. 473.

86. Jên Chi-yü, op.cit., pp. 303-306.

87. Hung ming chi, ch. 5, pp. 65-66. For further information about Hui-yüan, see Kenneth K.S. Ch'en, Buddhism in China (Princeton: Princeton University Press, 1964), pp. 110-12.

88. Dialogues of the Buddha, I, pp. 73-74.

89. Warren, op.cit., pp. 122, 123-25.

90. Hung-ming chi, ch. 5, pp. 59-60.

GLOSSARY

1A 格義

2A 魂魄

3A 詩經

4A 左傳

5A 中國宗教思想史大綱

6A 帝

7A 上帝

8A 宗祀文王於明堂以配上帝

9A 華英四書

10A 焰口餓鬼

11A 不空

12A 實义難陀

13A 盂蘭盆經

14A 梁武帝

15A 阿鼻地獄

16A 目連

17A 大目乾連冥間救母變文

18A 忉利天

19A 是時灵帝崩後天下大乱

20A 牟子：理惑論

21A 神

22A 魂神固不滅矣

23A 有道雖死神歸福堂

24A 四部从刊初編

25A 弘明集

26A 淨土

27A 慧遠

28A 共期西方

29A 劉遺民

30A 阿彌陀經

31A 無量寿經

32A 法身

33A 無身而有神

34A 法身無形普入一切

35A 宗炳：神不滅論

36A 精神

37A 神明

38A 神

39A 墨子

40A 鄭道子

41A 形尽神不滅論

42A 神不滅論

43A 沙門不敬王者論

44A 范縝：神滅論

45A 清談

46A 南史

47A 蕭琛

48A 曹思文

49A 難神滅論

50A 或夢上騰玄虛遠適万里

51A 延陵窒子

52A 渝薄

53A 偷薄

54A 周公

55A 后櫻

56A 上帝

161

IX

A STUDY OF THE PHILOSOPHICAL

AND RELIGIOUS ELEMENTS IN

THE RED CHAMBER DREAM

It has been claimed that Hung-lou mêng (1A) or the Red Chamber Dream[1] by Ts'ao Hsüeh-ch'in (2A) is one of the most outstanding novels in China. This claim is made on merit, with no exaggeration. For nearly a century a host of scholars devoted themselves to the research and investigation of this work, with special reference to its author. They penetrated the sphere of ideology, life and times of Ts'ao Hsüeh-ch'in. They also surmised much, with the intention of identifying some of the characters mentioned in the novel with leading Chinese personalities of the eighteenth century. As a consequence, the term Redology[2] was coined, and those engaged in this type of research were called Redologists. From this one can get an inkling of its importance and popularity.

Regarding the merit of this work, scholars and critics hold quite different views. Some shower it with generous praise, saying that it is a great masterpiece, while others brand it as a debased publication publicizing obscenity and immorality.[3] Some say that it is a work representing the humanistic and democratic spirit which revolts against the feudalistic system[4] and institutions of the Manchu dynasty, while others say that it is merely a biographical reminiscence of the author which may be realistic in outlook, but includes imaginary fantasies. Yet another school of scholars says that its ideals and inner significance are very complicated, and so, it is rather difficult for

163

people to comprehend them. These divergent views are a little puzzling. An impartial judgement with regard to the merits and demerits of this great novel would be welcome.

The purpose of the present article is not to match the leading characters to known personalities, nor to study the life of the author. I wish, however, to investigate two important aspects: 1) the pessimistic philosophical outlook on life which influenced the thought of the author, and 2) the religious institutions and practices which formed a part of Chinese social life in the eighteenth century. The first is directly concerned with the author's philosophy of life, and the second is a study on the social life of Ch'ing China based on the descriptions and reflections of this book. Our aim, as defined above, is absolutely objective in nature. It is hoped, therefore, that it may not cause any unnecessary controversy which a Redologist, normally, would not like to miss.

The Philosophical Outlook on Life

Anyone who has read the Red Chamber Dream will form the impression that human existence consists of two aspects, the bright side and the dark side. On the bright side, there is love, joy, laughter, glory, wealth, fame, high position and fortune; and on the dark side, there is hatred, sorrow, misery, low status and misfortune. Most of us, at a certain stage during our lifetime, must have experienced some of the items mentioned above. A few fortunate ones may enjoy a longer period of sunshine in life, whereas the unfortunate may be suffering all the time. However, as human beings are mortal and subject to change, the happiness they enjoy is transitory and impermanent. Anything that is impermanent causes sorrow. Therefore, the fortunate, who are happy, are in fact not very much better off than the unfortunate, who are unhappy; although there seem to be differences between

164

them. The whole trouble is that nobody can live
forever, and inevitably everything is subject to
the law of change. This is an eternal truth,
however little we may like it. Well then, have
we ever felt that human life is like a "dream"?
It appears to be real, but at the same time it is
elusive, nebulous, and intangible, and finally
it will fade away. It is very likely that when
Ts'ao Hsüeh-ch'in wrote the Red Chamber Dream, he
had already collected a rich harvest of experience
in life. He knew love and luxury, especially
since he was born with a silver spoon in his
mouth. On the other hand he also knew very well
the suffering caused by hardship and poverty.
In his case, the contrast of the two extremes
was very great. Therefore, the pain experienced
by him was exceptionally severe. The fruition of
such an experience is the birth of the Red Chamber
Dream--a great drama woven with the threads of
laughter and tears. Beyond any shadow of doubt,
this novel is one of the masterpieces of world
literature.

1.   The Life-sketch of Ts'ao Hsüeh-ch'in

     It may not be out of place here to trace the
circumstances under which Ts'ao Hsüeh-ch'in, the
author, wrote this work. He belonged to the
family of a high-ranking official of the Ch'ing
dynasty (1616-1911 A.C.), and some members of
that family held important government positions
successively for about a century, from 1650 to
1745. From 1663 onwards, Ts'ao Hsi (3A), his
great-grandfather, Ts'ao Yin (4A), his grandfather, Ts'ao Yu (5A), his uncle, and Ts'ao Fu
(6A), his father, were successive Commissioners
of Textiles stationed at Nanking (7A). His
grandfather had the unique honor of being
commissioned to receive Emperor K'ang-hsi (1662-
1722) (8A) during his several Imperial tours
to southern China. This indicates the great
confidence the Manchu emperor had in his grandfather, and indirectly it signifies how
influential this family was.   However, when

Emperor Yung-chếng (1723-1735) (9A), the second
ruler of the Ch'ing dynasty, ascended the throne
in 1723, misfortune began to strike this family.
About 1724 his father was dismissed from the
office of Commissioner of Textiles. The official
accusation was that he had committed embezzlement
of public funds. In the following year their
palatial mansion, along with other property in
Nanking, was confiscated, with the exception of
the estate that was left in Peking. Consequently
they had to return to northern China after a
period of over sixty-five years. This unfortunate
event seems to have been closely associated with
a political involvement. Some twelve years
later, when Ch'ien-nung (1736-1795) (10A), the
third emperor, succeeded to the throne in 1736,
the Ts'ao family was pardoned, and his father was
reinstated as a Secretary to the Board of Civil
Affairs (11A). This welcome opportunity gave
this family a new lease on life. But, unfortunately
this did not last very long. In approximately
1745, when the author was about twenty-two years
of age, the Ts'ao family received another blow
of misfortune, the cause of which is still a
mystery. Thence the glory of that distinguished
house, which had lasted for a century, began to
crumple to dust, and finally moved to oblivion.

The Red Chamber Dream was written after the
final crash. At that time, the destitute author
lived in a dilapidated hut in the western suburb
of Peking. As he could not afford the cost of
rice for his meals, he was forced to take gruel
as a staple diet throughout the years. In
addition, he was occasionally humiliated under
unavoidable circumstances. Compared to the
comfort and luxury he used to enjoy, this indeed
was a shocking experience to him. Being sensi-
tive in nature, the author obviously could not
bear all the suffering, whenever he recalled
to mind the past glory of the old days. To add
sorrow to misery, his only son, after a pro-
tracted illness, passed away in 1763. He was
deeply shocked. The grief that struck him was
so intense that within a short time, he, too,

fell seriously ill. On a dreary wintry day of
the same year, he peacefully bid good-bye to his
miserable existence of forty years (ca. 1724-
1763).[5]

Such was the sad and pathetic tale of the
personal life of Ts'ao Hsüeh-ch'in. Undoubtedly
his experience of bitter struggle must have
influenced his philosophical outlook on life.
The very title, in the form of Red Chamber Dream,
reflects the illusion of worldly phenomena. One
can imagine his frame of mind when he wrote the
book, and naturally he was very bitter about the
whole affair. His introductory verse,[6] to the
Record on the Stone, otherwise known as the Red
Chamber Dream, is ample evidence to this inference. It runs as follows:

These pages are full of non-sensical tales,
And a handful of sorrow-soaked tears.
All say that the author is devoid of his
    senses,
But who understands the inner significance?

Having undergone all the hardship and suffering,
he might have asked himself: What is the meaning of life? Is it not a dream and impermanence?
We do not know what the answer was. However,
this much is clear, that his view on life was
very pessimistic. To substantiate this statement, we may cite a few instances from the
novel itself. First of all, let us see briefly
the life-sketch of Pao-yü.

2. The Life-sketch of Pao-yü

We all know that Chia Pao-yü (12A), the hero
of the Red Chamber Dream, was born with a piece
of "Precious Jade"[7] and hence was named after
it. He lived a life of great luxury, and was
always in the company of beautiful young girls.
He was intelligent, talented and well-versed in
literary works, except the Confucian classics.
This is because he did not like the idea of

getting a government job by means of passing
the civil service examinations. He was well
looked after and protected by his mother, grandmother and elder sister Yüan-ch'ün (13A), who
was an Imperial secondary consort, and others.
On account of this, he was soft and thoroughly
spoilt. As these well-wishers like to see him
happily settled down, Pao-yü was married to Pao-
ch'ai (14A), a cousin of his, through conspiracy.
Actually, he preferred to marry Tai-yü (15A),
another cousin of his, and the heroine of the
book. On the other hand, this beautiful young
lady of delicate health was in love with Pao-yü.
They thought secretly to themselves that they
would make an ideal couple. However, Fate did
not favor them in their plans. Lying on her
sickbed, one day she learnt that Pao-yü was getting married to her rival. She was shocked beyond
words. Having burnt a handkerchief, which was
given to her by Pao-yü as a token of love, and
the manuscripts of her poems, she breathed her
last. It is suggested that while she went through
all the agonies of death, she might have faintly
heard the marching band which led Pao-yü's
wedding procession.[8]

Not long after this, Pao-yü, accompanied
by Chia Lan (16A), his nephew, set out for the
provincial examination. On the last day of the
examination, he was lost in the crowd, and could
not be traced.[9] Many months later, his father
Chia Chêng (17A), while visiting a place called
Pi-lin-i (18A), saw a young Buddhist novice
who had a close resemblance to Pao-yü. Having
kowtowed to him four times, this young novice
went away in the company of a Buddhist monk and
a Taoist priest, without uttering a word.[10]

Thus, Pao-yü's life-sketch comes to an end,
and along with it the novel itself. One would
like to ask: What is the substance and achievement of Pao-yü's life? Practically speaking it
achieved nothing, except for the fact that the
hero had a glorious time and a tragic end. In
general, this is the very essence which constitutes

168

human existence, i.e., happiness and sorrow, laughter and tears, and then, finally, death comes along.

3. The Philosophy of Impermanence

The concept of impermanence and the unreality of life has occupied a very prominent place in this book. In his introductory note, the author has made this point very clear. He says: "I have frequently used the words such as 'dream,' 'illusion' and so forth in the various chapters. This is the objective of my book. But it may also serve the purpose of making my readers be aware of this idea."[11]

Among the names of persons and places we come across the follwoing: 1) K'ung-k'ung tao-jên (19A), or the Taoist of Emptiness; 2) Mang-mang ta-shih (20A), or the Great Scholar of Boundless-ness; 3) Miao-miao chên-jên (21A), or the Perfect Man of Non-substantiality,[12]; 4) Ching-hüan-hsien-tzǔ (22A), or The Fairy Queen-of-Warning-the-Illusive[13] of the Phantom Realm of the Great Void (T'ai-hsü hüan-chin) (23A)[14]; 5) Chao-ti ssǔ (24A), or the Department of Morning Tears; 6) Mo-k'u ssǔ (25A), or the Department of Night Sobbing, and 7) Po-min ssǔ (26A), or the Depart-ment of Misfortune in Life.[15] Of considerable philosophical interest is a note which explains the meaning of the Phantom Realm of the Great Void. It runs thus: "When unreal is taken to be real, the real is unreal; and when non-existence is taken for existence, that existence is non-existent."

The above-mentioned names suggest a tinge of sadness. It is obvious that the mind of the author can be read through these hints.

Dwelling on the theme of impermanence, unreality and sorrow, the author writes excellent poems using melancholic expressions. Take for instance: ". . .one is the moon reflected in the

169

water, and the other a flower in the mirror. As
for tears, how much more are there in the eyes?
How could they flow endlessly, from Autumn to
Winter, and from Spring to Summer?"[16]

His Song of Hao-liao (27A), and the poem
called Ku-hua-shih (28A) or Lamenting over the
Flowers and other lyrics point to the same trend.
The contents of the Song of Hao-liao may be
summed up as follows:

An ordinary man knows very well the importance
of becoming an Immortal (Shên-hsien) (29A). But
he is attached to 1) worldly interest such as high
positions in the civil and military services;
2) wealth and property; 3) beautiful spouse;
and 4) lovely children and other family ties. To
each of these categories, the author makes the
following comment:

1)   Where are the generals and prime
ministers of ancient and recent times now? Well,
they are in the shapeless heaps of graves which
are covered with weeds.

2)   Day in and day out he regrets that he
has not been able to collect much money. And
when he has earned enough, he breathes his last,
and his eyes are closed forever!

3)   While you live, your wife every day talks
of her love for you. But after your death, she
goes to other men.

4)   From time immemorial, there are parents
who show undivided parental love to their
children. But has anybody ever seen filial devotion in his offspring?[17]

The facts mentioned in (1) and (2) are
absolutely true, though they are unpalatable
to most of us. The generalization as found in
(3) and (4) may not be applicable in certain
cases. Still, one can never be sure what the
wife would do, when the husband is no more. It

is such attachment that hinders man from becoming
an Immortal. In other words, it means that man is
mortal and impermanent.

The poem of Lamenting Over the Flowers is
attributed to Tai-yü, the young heroine. It makes
one feel very sad when she says:

Now you are dead, I am burying you.
I know not when I shall die.
People laugh at me for burying the flowers
And say that I am mad.
How do I know who will bury me in the future?[18]

It is, indeed, a moment of joy when we see
flowers bloom. But we cannot expect the flowers
to stay blooming forever. They will fade away
in the course of time. Similarly, we cannot
expect human beings to remain young and
beautiful forever. They will become old and
finally pass away. Obviously there is hardly
anything that is truly permanent.

Other titles[19] of his poetical compositions
such as 1) Hen wu-chang (30A) or Regrets of
Impermanence; 2) Fên ku-ju (31A) or Separation
from One's Dear Ones; 3) Lo-chung-pei (32A)
or Sorrow in Happiness; 4) Hsü-hua wu (33A)
or Realization of the Flower of Unreality; and
5) Hao-shih chung (34A) or The End of Good
Fortune and so forth, point to the same concept
of pessimism. As Ts'ao Hsüeh-ch'in was one of
the pioneers in realistic writing, the stress on
sorrow and impermanence would intensify the
dramatic effect. He was very successful in this
respect. However, one should not forget the
fact that his bitter experience must have influenced his philosophical outlook on life to a
great extent. Of course, one cannot deny that
there were occasional outbursts of happiness
as mentioned in the book. But "Sorrow in
Hapiness," as his poem suggests, is a
dominant[20] feature in his philosophical concept.

If we trace the sources by which the author

171

was influenced and thereby became so pessimistic,
it becomes very clear that the Buddhist philosophy
of śūnyatā and anitya (unreality and impermanence)
the Taoist concept of mutation and immortality,
and the Nineteen Ancient Poems (Ku-shih shih-chiu
shou) (35A) and so forth should form the chief
sources.   In one of these poems which begins with
the words, "Driving the chariot to the eastern
gate," a description is given of the dreary conditions of a graveyard.   It runs as follows:

> The dead lie there quietly and never
>   to awake from sleep; slowly the
>   time passes by.
> Alas! Man's life is like a drop of
>   morning dew.

The statements made by two other famous poets
points to the same direction.   Poet Li Po
(36A) says in one of his essays:[21] "Life is
like a dream, how much could any one enjoy?"

Ts'ao Ts'ao (37A), an earlier poet, expressed
the same sentiment by saying:

> How long could a person live?
> Let us sing while we enjoy a drink.[22]

All the quotations cited above indicate that
there is a feeling of helplessness regarding
the existence of human life.   It is natural that
every individual wishes to live as long as
possible, and hates the very thought of death.
It is on account of this that the Taoist wishes
to attain immortality by means of the so-called
elixir of life.   Having this idea in mind, Ts'ao
Hsüeh-ch'in did not wish his hero to be a world-
ling forever, but made him a Buddhist mendicant.
In this way he might "realize śūnyatā from the
foundation of Rūpya" (38A).[23] He might also
attain nirvāna, which is a state of eternal
bliss, free from impermanence.   Undoubtedly this
is an ideal objective.   At least, it gives the
consolation that there is a way to overcome the
endless sorrow in the world.

The Popular Buddhist and Taoist
Religious Elements

The popular religious aspects as featured
in the Red Chamber Dream do not seem to be important from the standpoint of the author. But
they do form an essential part of social life in
the eighteenth-century Chinese society, especially
among the upper-class Chinese. Even today, some
of these practices and beliefs may still be observed on the mainland, or else in Taiwan and
Hong Kong. In general, they are associated with
Taoism and Buddhism, though there are exceptions.
They may be partly due to Confucian influence,
and partly connected with local superstitions.
A striking feature concerning the leading religions during this period is the unusual degree of
harmony between the Taoist and the Buddhist. It
is noted that members of the same family may have
the option of becoming a follower of either
Buddhism or Taoism. This is illustrated in the
case of the Princess Ancestress[24] (Chia mu; 39A)
or Lao tsu-tsung (40A) who was a Buddhist, while
Chia Ching (41A) the (Prince Hermit), her nephew,
was a Taoist.[25] On account of this, the members
of the Chia House observed Taoist and Buddhist
ceremonies. For the convenience of this study,
I shall examine separately these religious elements
and practices.

A.   The Buddhist Elements

The author has a good knowledge of Buddhist
literature, especially the popular literary
works. He knows the story 1) of Tripitaka[26]
of the Great T'ang dynasty (T'ang San-tsang)
(42A), who went to India, accompanied by Sun
Wu-k'ung (43A), or the Monkey, and other
disciples in search of Buddhist scriptures;
2) of Bodhidharma's[27] practice of meditating in
front of a blank wall, and his miraculous crossing
of a river; 3) of Hui-nêng (44A),[28] the sixth
patriarch of the Ch'an school, who was actually
an illiterate, but was nominated to the high
office of patriarch owing to a stanza composed

by him; 4) of the work called Wu-têng hui-yüan
(45A), or The five lamps traced back to the
common source,[29] and many other instances of
intuitional outburst concerning Zen practice and
terminology. It may be interesting to examine
this topic a little further.

On various occasions when Pao-yü was annoyed
by, or angry with, somebody, he would sit alone
with closed eyes and legs practicing Zen, or hold
conversations with his associates, or compose
short stanzas similar to the sayings of famous
Zen masters. One of the stanzas[30] is cited below:

> You realize, I realize,
> And the mind realizes.
> There is no realization at all.
> Thus, it may be said that one has realized
> When there is nothing that can be
>   called realization.
> Then it is the ground on which one may
>   put his feet.

At a glance, this appears to be "mystifying"
enough. However, Tai-yü, the young heroine,
tried to make an improvement on it by adding
the following:

> When there is no ground on which to put
>   one's feet,
> Then, it will be perfect and complete.

On the same occasion, Tai-yü put the following
questions[31] to Pao-yü, after the style of Zen
masters:

> Pao-yü, I wish to question you,
> The most valuable is the precious,
> And the most hard substance is jade,
> What value have you and
> What firmness have you?

It is amusing to note that Pao-yü failed to give
a suitable reply. And accordingly he acknowledged
his defeat.

174

Some two years later, Pao-yü said that the world would be free from trouble, if he had not been born. Commenting[32] on this, Tai-yü said: "It is because of the self, there are others and because of others, the innumerable evil dispositions such as fear, distortion and day-dreaming are arisen, in addition to many other obstructions. . . .All these are due to your confused imagination, and you have entered the path of Māra."

Noticing that Pao-yü was convinced, Tai-yü pushed the matter further by putting to him the following questions:

What will you do, if sister Pao is friendly
    with you?
What will you do, if she is not friendly
    with you?
What will you do, if she was friendly
    with you in the past, but not now?
What will you do, if she is friendly
    with you now,
But not in the future?
What will you do, if you wish to be
    friendly with her,
But she does not like to be friendly
    with you?
And what will you do, if you are not
    friendly with her,
But insistently she wants to be friendly
    with you?

For quite a while Pao-yü could not give any reply. Perhaps Pao-yü had not reached the higher stages of Zen attainment. If he were a great Zen master, he would have given a blow to that fair lady, and that would have been the correct answer. It is possible that most of us, at one time or another, might have experienced some of the unhappy situations. Well, "What will you do?" I wonder whether the reader is prepared to solve this type of Zen puzzle?

B. Popular Buddhism and Society

Regarding the practical and institutional aspects, the Chia House was closely associated with many Buddhist monasteries and nunneries, such as Lung-ts'ui an (46A) or the Purple-tinted Convent,[33] Pan-hsiang ssŭ (47A) or the Dragon-incense Monastery,[34] Sui-yüeh an (48A) or the Moon-in-water Convent,[35] Chih-t'ung ssŭ (49A) or the Wisdom-comprehension Monastery,[36] Hu-lu miao (50A) or the Bottle-gourd Temple,[37] Pu-t'ung ssŭ (51A) or the Eastern Pu Monastery[38] and Ti-tsang an (52A) or the Kṣitigarbha Convent,[39] and others. It was the practice with this House that Taoist and Buddhist priests were maintained in its family temples. For the occasion of the homecoming of Yüan-chün, who was the secondary Imperial consort and a sister of Pao-yü, young Buddhist and Taoist nuns were specially trained to recite sūtras,[40] so that they would be able to attend on her when she was praying in the Grand View Garden (53A). Further, when the funeral rites of Ch'in K'o-ch'ing (54A) were to be performed, leading Buddhist and Taoist high priests were invited to perform a religious service for forty-nine days. They had their religious platforms erected side by side at the Ning-kuo Palace (55A).[41] On another occasion, when Yu Erh-chieh (56A), a second wife of Chia Lien (57A), committed suicide, Buddhist and Taoist monks were invited to say prayers[42] in order to save the soul of the dead. In addition, there were family temples maintained by other high officials. In these places Buddhist nuns used to reside, devoting themselves to religious practices.[43]

Moreover, the Buddhist priests played another important part when there were birthday celebrations for persons in high positions. This was the case for the Princess Ancestress's eightieth birthday.[44] On this occasion several Buddhist monasteries were requested to recite the Sūtra on safety and longevity (Pao-an yen-shou ching) (58A), and Pao-yü was sent to kneel down before the shrines while the recitation took

place. At the same time two Buddhist nuns were
invited to her Palace to bless a good measure of
beans by chanting Buddhist stanzas. These beans
were called "Fu-tou" (59A) or Buddhist beans,[45]
and they were distributed free to people at a
crossroad, so that they, too, might reach a
grand age of eighty. The copying of Buddhist
texts such as the Vajracchedikā-prajñāpāramitā-
Sūtra (Chin-kang Ching) (60A) for free distribution, the recitation of the names of the Buddhas,
and the practice of occasionally confining oneself
to a vegetarian diet, were observed by the
Princess Ancestress, though she confessed that [46]
she had not taken up those matters very seriously.

From the foregoing instances, it is clear
that Buddhism exerted a profound influence on
society at that time. The fact that Pao-yü and
Hsi-chün (61A), two well-known members of the
Chia House, joined the Buddhist Order, the former
as a monk and the latter as a nun, is ample evidence indicating the powerful impact of Buddhism.
In addition, Miao-yü (62A), who was a close
associate of the inmates of the Grand View Garden,
and famed for her learning, artistic way of
living and unusual temperament, was also a Buddhist
nun. Pao-yü and other young ladies showed her
great respect, thinking that she was far superior
to them in every way. Judging by this, one may
say that the attitude of the eighteenth-century
Chinese society towards Buddhism and Buddhist
institutions was favorable.

C. The Taoist Elements

In this novel, the two most mysterious
figures who are closely associated with the
jade of Pao-yü, until his renunciation of the
world, are K'ung-K'ung Tao-jên or the Taoist of
Emptiness, and Mang-mang ta-shih or the Great
Scholar of Boundlessness. The former is a
Taoist and the latter a Buddhist. The strange
thing about them is that they are always
together. It may be argued that they are fictitious characters. Even so, one cannot deny

177

the fact that the Buddhists and Taoists were, in general, friendly toward one another at that time. This is stated earlier, in the case of Ch'in K'o-ch'ing's funeral, when the leading Buddhist and Taoist priests performed religious services for her on the same platform.[47]

The Fairy Queen-of-warning-the-Illusive of-the-Phantom-Realm-of-the-Great-Void[48] is an imaginary creature, undoubtedly influenced by Taoist thought and literature such as the Immortal of Miao-ku-shê Mountain (63A)[49], the Song of Eternal Regret[50] by Po Chü-i (64A), the Record of Eternal Regret[51] by Ch'ên Hung (65A), and the Unofficial Biography[52] of Yang T'ai-ch'ên by Yüeh Shih (66A). These works describe in detail the heavenly paradise of Yang T'ai-chên, who was the most favorite secondary Queen of Emperor Hsüan-tsung (67A), but died under tragic circumstances. The description of the Phantom Realm is very similar to Yang T'ai-Ch'ên's Dream-land. Of course, neither of them exists on this earth. If there is any difference between them, it is only this, that the Dream-land of Yang T'ai-ch'ên was discovered by a Taoist through his magic powers, whereas the Phantom Realm was supposed to have been seen by Pao-yü in his dream.

Among the more important Taoist scriptures, the following works are mentioned, 1) Ts'an tung-ch'i or the Meditational Communion (68A)[53]; 2) Yüan-min pao (69A)[54] or the Bud of original life; 3) Kan-ying pien (70a)[55] or On the Spiritual Response; and 4) Nan-hua ching (71a) or Chuang-tzǔ.[56] It seems that Pao-yü was keenly interested in some of the philosophical ideas of Chuang-tzǔ. Not only did he fully approve of his scheme of preventing crimes which might be committed by robbers and thieves, but he imitated his style and composed an essay on how one might escape from the snares and entanglements of the fair sex. Apparently Pao-yü was not serious about what he had written. Nevertheless, the Taoist idea of leading a life free from family attachment must have imprinted itself deep on his subconscious.

D. Popular Taoism and Society

Regarding the institutional aspect we come across many names of Taoist monasteries, such as Ch'ing-hsü kuan (72A) or the Pure Void Monastery,[57] T'ien-ch'i miao (73A) or the Skyscraping Temple,[58] and Yüan-chên kuan (74A) or the Primordial Truth Monastery,[59] and so forth. It is clear that the Taoists, too, played an important part at that time, in regard to their contributions to society. They participated in the funeral[60] rites of noble persons (as seen in the case of Ch'in K'o-ch'ing), performed a thanksgiving service for peace (P'ing-an chiao) (75A) at the request of a member of the imperial household. Such occasions provided great opportunities for the rich families to offer and accept gifts, to make pleasure trips into the country, and to convert the monastery apartments into a temporary hotel. In addition, a chief Taoist priest even made proposals[61] of marriage to Pao-yü. They used to issue charms[62] to the children of wealthy families. Some of them were experts in divination by interpreting the positions of the eight diagrams (Pa-kua) (76A) based on the Book of Changes,[63] or the verses obtained through planchette.[64] They were also locally trained physicians and pharmacists. One of them prepared a medicated plaster (77A) which could cure any ailment as soon as it was stuck on, and there was no necessity to use it again. Therefore, the manufacturer of this plaster earned the nickname of Wang, the-stick-it-only-once (78A).[65]

Further, the same Taoist wrote a prescription for the cure of jealousy which was a concoction consisting of crystallized sugar, candied peel and pieces of pear. However, he was frank, and confessed that he had been a quack; if he really knew the secret, he would have attained the high rank of an Immortal.[66] It is believed that the Taoists possessed magical powers which could command spirits and invoke divine generals[67] (Chü-shên chao-chiang) (79A), although no concrete

179

example was given. The preparing of horoscopes[68] and fortune-telling were also some of the functions of the Taoists. On the occasion of birthday celebrations of a distinguished person, the Taoists as well as the Buddhists would give him presents consisting of the following items:[69] protective charm, an image of the God of Longevity (Shou-hsin) (80A), the name of his zodiacal patron deity for a particular year, and so forth. These, in short, are some of the contributions made by the Taoists towards society in eighteenth-century China. They appear to be magnificent.

The Traditional Chinese Religious Elements

As this novel reflects the way of life prevailing in eighteenth-century society of China, it is natural that many references occur to the moral and ethical ideals of Confucianism. This is well illustrated in chapter thirty-three when Pao-yü was severely punished by his father because of his inexcusable misdeeds. Chia Chêng (81A), his father, felt that it was his duty and responsibility to bring up his son properly, so that Pao-yü might bring honor and glory (kuang-tsung yao-tsu) (82A) to the ancestors[70] of the Chia House. This is based on the teaching of Confucian filial piety. As Pao-yü was brought up very badly and was spoiled by the members of his family, he blamed himself for having violated the ethics of filial piety. This incident also refers to the teaching of Confucius that a father should behave like a father,[71] and a son like a son. In this way, we do find many instances of moral and ethical teachings of Confucianism, but not so much of philosophical influence as in the case of Buddhism and Taoism. We shall, therefore, confine ourselves to the popular Chinese religious elements which may, or may not, necessarily be associated with Confucianism.

1. Ancestor Worship

This type of worship has a very ancient origin, and we could not possibly fix a definite date for its early beginning. It is, however, obvious that during the time of Confucius, the practice of making offerings to the ancestral temple was very popular. This could be inferred from the statement[72] made by Ts'êng-tzŭ (83A): "The respectful performance of funeral rites to parents and which is followed when long gone with the ceremonies of sacrifice--will improve the virtue of the people," on the one hand, and the saying[73] of Confucius himself, i.e., "That parents, when alive, should be served according to propriety; and when dead, they should be buried according to propriety; and that they should be sacrificed to according to propriety," on the other. It is possible that through the teachings of Confucius and his disciples, especially Ts'êng-tzŭ, the cult of ancestor worship became all the more popular, and penetrated deeply into the hearts of the Chinese people. This has a lasting effect which can be seen from the description given in the Red Chamber Dream.

The author has devoted almost an entire chapter to the details[74] of worship at the ancestor shrine of the Chia House. On the day the Spring offering was made at the ancestor shrine, all members of the Chia House, from the Princess Ancestress downward, were present there. They made offerings to the tablets and the portraits of the ancestors, some of which were specially exhibited for the occasion. During the ceremony, they bowed down to them, offered them cups of wine with various dishes, and burnt paper money and incense to the accompaniment of traditional music. This ceremony took place on New Year's Eve. It was customary at that time for the junior members of the family to pay their respects to the elders by kowtowing to them. In return, the elders would give them presents which might include money. After that, they sat at the table to enjoy the annual lunch of various delicacies, or engaged themselves in traditional festivities.

As a gesture of religious piety, cooked foods and incense were offered on that eve at the shrines of the Buddha, and to the God of the Stove (Fu-t'ang, Chao-wang) (84A). To do this on the occasion of worshipping the ancestors indicates that the veneration[75] of the Buddha was an integral part of the national life of the Chinese. It may be mentioned in passing that some of the officials of the Ch'ing Court were unable to make the annual offering to their ancestral temples. To them, as well as to the well-to-do families, an allowance was given by the Court for that purpose. This achieves two ends, one being encouragement in practicing filial piety, and the other an indirect hint that subjects should be loyal to the Emperor,[76] in accordance with the Confucian teachings.

Associated with this cult are seasonal offerings made to the ancestral tombs,[77] especially on the occasion of Ch'ing-min (85A)[78] (about the beginning of April). This is a very ancient custom which was mentioned in the Mencius. It is stated that a man from Ch'i (Ch'i-jen) (86A) used to beg and enjoy the leftovers of sacrificial offerings which were offered to the ancestral graves[79] in a country cemetery.

One of the items used at these sacrificial offerings was the burning of paper money (not currency notes). They believed that by doing so, the departed ancestors would be greatly relieved of their financial difficulties. However, this type of remittance does not confine itself to the ancestors, but applies also to departed friends or beloved ones, as seen in the case of Ou-kuan's[80] remittance to Yo-kuan (87A).

Thus, we see the profound influence of this cult. Owing to its ethical and social value, it may continue to occupy an important place in human society, especially in the East.

2. The Practice of Black Magic

Of sociological and psychological interest
is a terrible event which occurred to two leading
figures of the Chia House, i.e., Pao-yü and
Wang Hsi-fêng (88A), a cousin sister-in-law, of
Pao-yü and one of the most brilliant female
characters in the Red Chamber Dream. It happened in this way. One day, all of a sudden,
Pao-yü felt a severe headache as if someone had
hit his head with a huge club. He also felt as
if his head had been tightened with several iron
clamps. He gave a heart-rending cry of pain,
and leaped up about four feet from the ground.
He was delirious and wanted to commit suicide.
While this took place, Wang Hsi-fêng carried a
sharp knife rushing to the Grand View Garden.[81]
She attempted to kill everyone within her reach,
be it a fowl, a dog or a human being. She felt
as if she had been possessed, and was ordered
to kill all the living beings. She had no control of herself and did not know what she was
doing. The members of the Chia House were
greatly worried. They tried almost every available
means at their command. Among the remedies suggested were 1) to get a sorcerer to drive away
the evil spirits (Sung-sui) (89A); 2) to perform
a devil dance for appeasing the spirits and
deities; 3) to enlist the help of a Taoist for
catching the bogies; 4) to get charmed water; and
5) to send for doctors and get medical aid.[82]
Apparently all these did not improve the serious
condition of Pao-yü and Wang Hsi-fêng; finally
a Taoist and a Buddhist monk paid them a visit
and purified Pao-yü's jade. Later, they re-
covered from their temporary insanity, due chiefly
to the effect of this purification.[83]

Well, one may ask the question: What was
the cause of this incident? From what we have
gathered, it was due to the effect of black
magic performed by a woman called Ma Tao-p'o
(90A) or Ma, the Taoist Grandmother. This witch
used to frequent the houses of officials and
of the wealthy. She made people fall sick and

then claimed that she could cure the illness.
By this process, a huge amount of money was ex-
tracted from the victims. At times she acted
at the request of someone, and naturally she was
paid a handsome sum for the job done. Here are
some of the tools[84] of her trade: she had a
seven-starred-lamp. Under the lamp there were
several figures made of straw: one wore an iron
clamp, one's chest was penetrated by a big nail,
and another's neck was tied to a lock. In addition, she had a box of naked male and female
figures made of ivory, seven red fine needles
and scented medicinal pills. By comparing the
tools with the description of Pao-yü's severe
headache, one may understand the cause of his
trouble. However, the practice of such magic was
against the law. Therefore, she was arrested by
the Imperial Security Bureau (Chin-i-fu) (91A)
and put into prison. Probably she was sentenced
to death.[85] This served as a warning that the
practice of black magic is immoral and anti-social,
and should not be permitted in a civilized society.

Another case of practicing black magic was
connected with Chin-kuei (92A), wife of Hsüeh
P'an (93A). It is said that a figure cut out
of paper[86] was placed in Chin-kuei's pillowcase
along with a description of her horoscope. Five
needles were pinned down at the points of heart,
ribs, limbs, and other places on the paper figure.
Actually, this was a false case, being cleverly
designed by Chin-kuei in order to involve
Hsiang-lin (94A), a maid of her husband. For
the purpose of this study, it is clear that in
addition to figures made of straw as mentioned
earlier, human figures cut out of paper were
sometimes used for performing black magic.

3. The Belief in Ghosts

The question concerning the existence of
ghosts and spirits is a controversial one. Some
are in favor[87] of this theory, while others
are against it. The author of the Red Chamber

Dream seems quite uncertain about it. On the positive side, he has given us the following interesting cases: 1) He believes that the soul of a departed individual could appear in a dream or in the form of a ghost in order to give certain advice, as in the case of Ch'in K'o-ch'ing.[88] 2) Before her death, Wang Hsi-fêng saw in broad daylight the ghost of Yu Erh-chieh (95A),[89] a co-wife of her husband and for whose death she was fully responsible. Later, she realized that she had come to demand repayment for her life. 3) King Yama (Yen-lo wang) (96A), lord of the Kingdom of Death, administers justice and punishes those who have committed sins during their lifetime. This is illustrated in the case of Chao I-liang (97A),[90] a concubine of Chia Chêng. It seems she was punished and tortured to death by order of King Yama, because she caused suffering to Pao-yü and Wang Hsi-fêng by means of Ma Tao-p'o's black magic. And 4) There is a possibility that the soul of a dead person, especially those who passed away under tragic circumstances, may possess a person, and make that person confess his or her misdeeds. It was suggested by some that Chao I-liang had been possessed by Yüan-yang (98A),[91] a maid of the Princess Ancestress, although this was merely a guess.

On the other hand, the author appears to be sarcastic about some of the ghost stories which had originated from the Grand View Garden. For instance, he ridicules the unnecessary worry and confusion created in the mind of the members of Chia House, when Yu Shih (99A), a wife of Chia Chên, and her husband fell sick after a visit to the Grand View Garden on two separate occasions. During her illness, soothsayers were called upon to predict its outcome by means of divination based on the Book of Changes and by other methods. Taoist priests were also invited to perform religious services in grand style. Besides the highest Taoist officials, heavenly generals were invoked and devils or evil spirits were supposed to have been caught.[92] One may be curious about the cause of all the trouble.

185

Ultimately it was revealed by one of the servants who was an eyewitness to the incident. He said that it was a big cock pheasant which leaped forward and passed along the path when they visited the Grand View Garden. Being frightened, they deliberately maintained the lie uttered by Shuan-êrh (100A) that they had seen a bogey with a yellow face and a red beard, dressed in green.[93]

If that was the truth which the members of the Chia House had believed, we may say that it was really a big farce.

4. The Belief in Spirits

There was a faint idea in early China that life does not end with death. It may undergo a process of change, even though we may not be able to understand the mysterious changes. According to this theory, the author of the Red Chamber Dream seems to suggest, though at times jokingly, that living beings and inanimate things may continue to live in different forms, some of which may be invisible. The following instances will illustrate this trend:

i) Before the death of Ch'ing-wên (101A), a clever and beautiful maid of Pao-yü, two of her friends went to see her. She told one of them that she would become a fairy in heaven looking after the flowers, especially hibiscus.[94] This was a deliberate lie manufactured by a maid with the motive of pleasing Pao-yü. The hero of the novel accepted the whole story as true. He wrote a poetical composition entitled, "A Condolence to the Young Lady of Hibiscus[95] (Fu-yung nü-êrh)" (102A) in excellent classic style.

ii) According to ancient Chinese custom, the day of Mang-chung (103A) (the twenty-sixth of the fourth Moon on this particular occasion) is reserved for young girls to bid farewell

to the Fairy of Flowers (Hua-shên) (104A).
It is said that after this day the flowers will
fade away, therefore, she should pack up and go
home.[96] Further, Pao-yü believed that there was
a fairy in charge of apricot flowers (105A).[97]
This points out that people believed in the
existence of such fairies.

iii) Aside from the above-mentioned beliefs,
the author seems to think that there existed
a sort of flower-devil[98] (Hua-yao) (106A). This
is based on a report that a number of pryus
spectabilis (Hai-tang) (107A) flowers in the
private garden of Pao-yü had withered for quite
some time, but suddenly bloomed out of season
in winter. Therefore, a section of the Chia
House thought it to be an inauspicious portent.
Possibly it was the creation of a devil.

iv) The belief that there were deities
in charge of fatal disease such as the God of
Plague (Wên-shên) (108A) and Goddess of Smallpox[99]
(Tou-chên liang-liang) (109A), seems to have
been fairly popular at that time. The God of
Plague is described as having a green face and
a red beard.[100] The motive of worshipping them
might have been fear, as it is a matter of one's
life and death should anyone be assailed by such
a dreadful disease.

v) Finally, one of the most popular beliefs
in early China is that an animal in the form of
a Fairy-Fox (Hu-li ching) (110A)[101] may be able
to transform itself into a beautiful woman and
bewitch the young men of the area. This belief
is also applicable to a statue made of clay which
was erected in memory of a young lady who died
as a teen-ager. However, this was fabricated[102]
by Liu Lao-lao (111A), an old country woman, for
the purpose of amusing the elite of the Grand
View Garden. Naturally one should not take it
seriously. But the comic aspect of it was that
Pao-yü faithfully believed it to be true. He
sent his boy Pei-ming (112A) to make a search
for the statue, and worship it on his behalf.

187

Later, the boy returned and complained to him that he had experienced great difficulty in locating the place where the statue was enshrined. Finally he did come across one, but he was frightened to death, because instead of the image of a beautiful young lady, he saw the statue of the God of Plague with a horrible appearance.[103]

The foregoing passage gives some idea regarding the more popular elements of religious practices and beliefs prevailing at the time the Red Chamber Dream was written. Of course, it is not for us to state the extent to which the truth of these stories could be proven. If we do, it would be beyond our scope of studies.

Regarding the philosophical aspect, the general outlook on life, as illustrated in the novel, is very pessimistic. This is partly due to the author's bitter experience in life which he could not easily forget, and partly due to the deep influence of the Buddhist philosophy of impermanence, and the Taoist doctrine of mutation. From this standpoint, one may be permitted to say that Ts'ao Hsüeh-ch'in's views could be traced to the sources of ancient Chinese culture and philosophies.

It may be stressed in passing that the Red Chamber Dream is really an outstanding work. Apart from its most excellent literary merit, it provides a mine of information concerning various aspects of Chinese society and culture of the Ch'ing period. It is hoped that Sinologists will pay more attention to the study of this great novel.

NOTES

1. The other titles for this work are 1) Shih-t'ou chi (113A) (A Record on a Stone); 2) Chin-ling shih-êrh ch'ai (114A) (The Twelve Beauties

of Nanking); 3) Fêng-yüeh pao-chien (115A) (A Precious Mirror for Romantic Life); 4) Ch'ing-sêng lu (116A) (Memoirs of a Passionate Monk); and 5) Chin-yü yüan (117A) (A Marriage Between the Gold and the Jade). Cf. Wu Shih-ch'ang, On the Red Chamber Dream (Oxford, 1961), p. 1.

2. Ibid., pp. 4-5; Chiang Shui-tsao, Hsiao-shuo k'ao-chêng (118A) (The Verification of Chinese Novels) (Shanghai, 1957), p. 558.

3. Wên Chi, Chung-kuo ku-tien hsiao-shuo chiang-hua (119A) (Talks on Classical Chinese Novels) (Hong Kong, 1958), p. 3.

4. Ibid., p. 23.

5. See Wu En-yü, Yu-kuan Ts'ao Hsüeh-ch'in pa-chung (120A) (The Eight Works Concerning Ts'ao Hsüeh-ch'in) (Shanghai, 1958), pp. 28, 30, 100; Lu Hsün is of the opinion that Ts'ao Hsüeh-ch'in's son died in 1762. See A Brief History of Chinese Fiction (Peking, 1959), pp. 313-14; see the "Introductory Notes about the Author," Hung-lou mêng (The Author's Publishing House, Peking, 1953), pp. 5-6. This edition, on which the study of the present paper is based, consists of 120 chapters. It is generally accepted that the first eighty chapters were written by Ts'ao Hsüeh-ch'in and the remaining forty chapters by Kao Ngo (121A) in 1791.

6. Hung-lou mêng, ch. 1, p. 3.

7. Ibid., ch. 2, p. 17.

8. Ibid., ch. 97, pp. 1102-14.

9. Ibid., ch. 119, pp. 1346-48.

10. Ibid., ch. 120, p. 1354.

11. Ibid., ch. 1, p. 1.

12. I id., ch. 1, p. 3.

13.   Ibid., ch. 1, p. 4.

14.   Ibid., ch. 5, p. 48.

15.   Ibid., ch. 5, p. 48.

16.   Ibid., ch. 5, p. 53.

17.   Ibid., ch. 1, p. 10.

18.   Ibid., ch. 27, pp. 280-81.

19.   Ibid., ch. 5, pp. 53-55.

20.   Ibid., ch. 5, p. 54.

21.   Li Po, "Ch'un-yeh an tao-li-yüan hsü"
(122A) or "On a Party held at the Peach-Plum
Garden in a Spring Night."

22.   Cf. Ku-shih yüan (123A).

23.   Hung-lou mêng, ch. 1, p. 3. The character
"sê" (124A), in the traditional Chinese usage,
has the meaning of "color, beauty, appearance
and of the fair sex." However, in the Chinese
Buddhist terminology, it means "form, matter,
substance, etc.," because this was translated
from the Sanskrit "Rūpya." When Ts'ao Hsüeh-
ch'in uses the phrase "Sê-k'ung" (125A), the
word "sê" has the meaning of "woman, beauty,
fair sex, etc." The original Sanskrit meaning
is not indicated here.

24.   Ibid., ch. 106, p. 1202; ch. 39, p. 411.

25.   Ibid., ch. 11, p. 110; ch. 53, p. 584.

26.   Ibid., ch. 54, p. 596; ch. 73, p. 822.
Also see Arthur Waley's translation entitled,
The Monkey.

27.   Ibid., ch. 85, p. 979; ch. 64, p. 716. Also
see Taishō, vol. 51, pp. 219-20.

28.   Ibid., ch. 22, p. 223; also see the S̄utra of Wei Lang (London, 1953), pp. 11-26.

29.   This is a collection of sayings of the Chinese Zen Masters. Ibid., ch. 118, p. 1335.

30.   Hung-lou mêng, ch. 22, p. 222.

31.   Ibid., ch. 22, p. 223.

32.   Ibid., ch. 91, p. 1043.

33.   Ibid., ch. 41, p. 439.

34.   Ibid., ch. 41, p. 441.

35.   Ibid., ch. 93, p. 1061.

36.   Ibid., ch. 2, p. 15.

37.   Ibid., ch. 1, p. 9.

38.   Ibid., ch. 51, p. 552.

39.   Ibid., ch. 71, p. 802.

40.   Ibid., ch. 18, pp. 174-82.

41.   Ibid., ch. 13, p. 129.

42.   Ibid., ch. 69, p. 787.

43.   Ibid., ch. 58, p. 643.

44.   Ibid., ch. 71, p. 800.

45.   Ibid., ch. 71, p. 807.

46.   Ibid., ch. 109, p. 1241.

47.   Ibid., ch. 12, p. 129.

48.   Ibid., ch. 5, p. 14.

49. Kuo Ch'ing-fan, ed., Chuang-tzǔ chi-shih (126A) or A Collective Commentary on Chuang-tzǔ (Peking, 1961), vol. 1, p. 28.

50. Lu Hsün, ed., T'ang-sung chuan-ch'i chi (127A) (A Collection of Well-Known Stories of the T'ang and Sung Dynasties), pp. 106-108.

51. Ibid., pp. 103-106.

52. Ibid., pp. 232-49.

53. Hung-lou mêng, ch. 21, p. 210.

54. Ibid., ch. 118, p. 1335.

55. Ibid., ch. 73, p. 831.

56. Ibid., ch. 21, pp. 210-11.

57. Ibid., ch. 28, p. 294.

58. Ibid., ch. 80, pp. 916-18.

59. Ibid., ch. 63, p. 710.

60. Ibid., ch. 13, p. 129.

61. Ibid., ch. 28, pp. 294-305.

62. Ibid., ch. 28, p. 302.

63. Ibid., ch. 102, pp. 1160-62.

64. Ibid., ch. 91, p. 1081. However, it should be noted that this was performed by Miao-yü, a Buddhist nun.

65. Ibid., ch. 80, p. 917.

66. Ibid., ch. 80, p. 918.

67. Ibid., ch. 73, p. 830.

68. Ibid., ch. 69, p. 785.

69.   Ibid., ch. 62, p. 682.

70.   Ibid., ch. 33, p. 347.

71.   Confucian Analects, Book xii, ch. 11.

72.   Ibid., Book i, ch. 9.

73.   Ibid., Book ii, ch. 5.

74.   Hung-lou mêng, ch. 53, p. 579.

75.   Ibid., ch. 53, pp. 581-84.

76.   Ibid., ch. 53, pp. 576-77.

77.   Ibid., ch. 13, p. 124.

78.   Ibid., ch. 58, p. 644.

79.   The Work of Mencius, Book iv, ch. 33.

80.   Hung-lou mêng, ch. 58, pp. 645-49.

81.   Ibid., ch. 25, pp. 256-59; ch. 81, pp. 926-27.

82.   Ibid., ch. 25, p. 256.

83.   Ibid., ch. 25, p. 259.

84.   Ibid., ch. 81, p. 927.

85.   Ibid., ch. 81, p. 926.

86.   Ibid., ch. 80, p. 913.

87.   Joe Hyams, "Our Haunted House," Reader's Digest (December, 1966), pp. 118-22.

88.   Hung-lou mêng, ch. 13, pp. 124-25; ch. 101, p. 1148.

89.   Ibid., ch. 113, p. 1274; ch. 69, pp. 781-86.

90.   Ibid., ch. 112, pp. 1270-73.

91.   Ibid., ch. 112, p. 1270.

92.   Ibid., ch. 102, pp. 1160-65.

93.   Ibid., ch. 102, p. 1165.

94.   Ibid., ch. 78, pp. 891-92.

95.   Ibid., ch. 78, pp. 898-900.

96.   Ibid., ch. 27, pp. 272-73.

97.   Ibid., ch. 58, p. 645.

98.   Ibid., ch. 94, pp. 1070-72.

99.   Ibid., ch. 39, p. 419; ch. 21, p. 212.

100. Ibid., ch. 39, p. 419.

101. Ibid., ch. 64, p. 716.

102. Ibid., ch. 39, pp. 416-18.

103. Ibid., ch. 39, p. 419.

GLOSSARY

1Ａ紅樓夢	2Ａ曹雪芹	3Ａ曹　璽
4Ａ曹　寅	5Ａ曹　顒	6Ａ曹　頫
7Ａ江寧織造	8Ａ康熙，清聖祖	9Ａ雍正，清世宗
10Ａ乾隆，清高宗	11Ａ內務府員外郎	12Ａ賈寶玉
13Ａ元　春	14Ａ寶　釵	15Ａ黛　玉
16Ａ賈　蘭	17Ａ賈　政	18Ａ毘陵驛
19Ａ空空道人	20Ａ茫茫大士	21Ａ渺渺真人
22Ａ警幻仙子	23Ａ太虛幻境	24Ａ朝啼司
25Ａ暮哭司	26Ａ薄命司	27Ａ好了歌
28Ａ哭花詩	29Ａ神　仙	30Ａ恨無常
31Ａ分骨肉	32Ａ樂中悲	33Ａ虛花悟
34Ａ好事終	35Ａ古詩十九首	36Ａ李　白
37Ａ曹　操	38Ａ自色悟空	39Ａ賈　母
40Ａ老祖宗	41Ａ賈　敬	42Ａ唐三藏
43Ａ孫悟空	44Ａ惠　能	45Ａ五燈會元
46Ａ櫳翠菴	47Ａ蟠香寺	48Ａ水月菴
49Ａ智通寺	50Ａ葫蘆廟	51Ａ蒲東寺
52Ａ地藏菴	53Ａ大觀園	54Ａ秦可卿
55Ａ寧國府	56Ａ尤二姐	57Ａ賈　璉
58Ａ保安延壽經	59Ａ佛　豆	60Ａ金剛經
61Ａ惜　春	62Ａ妙　玉	63Ａ藐姑射之山有神人焉
64Ａ白居易：長恨歌	65Ａ陳鴻：長恨傳	66Ａ樂史：太真外傳
67Ａ玄　宗	68Ａ紅同契	69Ａ元命苞
70Ａ感應篇	71Ａ南華經	72Ａ清虛觀
73Ａ天齊廟	74Ａ元真觀	75Ａ平安醮
76Ａ八　卦	77Ａ膏　藥	78Ａ王一貼
79Ａ驅神招將	80Ａ壽　星	81Ａ賈　政
82Ａ光宗耀祖	83Ａ曾　子	84Ａ佛堂灶王
85Ａ清　明	86Ａ齊　人	87Ａ萬官藥官

X

ANCIENT CULTURAL RELATIONS

BETWEEN CEYLON AND CHINA

> Missions were constantly despatched
> charged with an interchange of courtesies
> between their sovereigns; theologians
> and officers of state arrived in Ceylon
> empowered to collect information regarding
> the doctrine of the Buddha; and envoys
> were sent in return bearing royal dona-
> tions of relics and sacred books.[1]

This remark made by J.E. Tennent, a recognized authority on Ceylon history, aptly shows
the cordial and intimate cultural relationship
that existed between Ceylon and China in ancient
times. Indeed, the ancient Chinese travellers
to the shores of the Indian Ocean and Laṅkā Dvīpa
were not attracted by treasure or riches but
prompted by religious devotion in search of the
True Dharma. The common link which brought
China and Ceylon together was obviously Buddhism.
Through Buddhism there came into existence a
cordial friendship between these two countries
for over 1,500 years. The very fact of this
lengthy duration indicates that there must have
been something extraordinary in this relationship
which stood the test of time. I shall, in the
following sections, endeavor to illustrate the
historical factors which cemented the cultural
ties between the two countries.

The Visit of Fa-hsien

Buddhism was formally introduced into China
in 67 A.C. From that time onward a chain of
Indian Buddhist sages and scholars continued

197

to pour into that country for the spread of
Buddhist doctrines and the translation of
canonical literature. It might appear to have
been a "one-way traffic" had Fa-hsien (1A)
not been able to pay a return visit to India on
behalf of the Buddhists in China. He was
prompted to undertake this journey because, as is
stated in his famous work The Travels of Fa-hsien,
he had felt the imperfect condition of the Vinaya
Pitaka in China. Desiring to improve it, he had
agreed with his friends to go to India for the
purpose of seeking the original Vinaya texts.[2]
This noble mission in quest of truth had far-
reaching consequences. He was the first Chinese
person who visited India and Ceylon as early as
401 A.C., and left behind him an invaluable
record concerning not only his journey, but the
social, political, religious and other conditions
of the countries he had visited as well. This
record of his inspired hundreds of Chinese
Buddhists, including Hsüan-tsang and I-tsing (2A)
who at a later period (in the seventh century
A.C.) also went to India and wrote Travels, which
also received universal recognition as a documen-
tary on the general conditions in ancient India
and Ceylon.

Having spent over thirteen years in India
Fa-hsien came to Ceylon in the winter of 413 A.C.
by sea. The last port where he boarded the ship
was Tamralipti in Bengal. He stayed on the
Island for over two years, searching for Buddhist
texts and paying homage to the sacred places,
including Adam's Peak, Anuradhapura and other
Buddhist sanctuaries. Among the Scriptures he
acquired from the monasteries in Ceylon were a
copy each of the Mahīśāsaka Vinaya, the
Dīrghāgama, the Samyuktāgama, and a collection of
the Miscellaneous Pitaka (Sannipāta).[3] All
these were introduced into China for the first
time and some of them were later translated
into Chinese. Probably these were the original
texts which constitute the Hīnayāna section of
the Chinese Tripitaka.

Regarding the general condition, both religious and secular, in Ceylon at that time, he informs us in detail about the exposition of the Tooth Relic of the Buddha, the ceremony of cremating an arhat, the donation of land to the Saṅgha by the Ruler, the magnificent ornamentation of the Abhayagiri Saṅghārāma, the deep veneration shown to the bhiksus and the blooming prosperity of the people who were wealthy and free from famine and starvation, and other particulars.[4]

The Ceylonese Bhiksuṇīs Visited China

It appears that both the bhiksu and bhiksuṇī Saṅghas were well established from the time Buddhism was first introduced into Ceylon, because we know that these orders had been represented by Mahendra and Saṅghamitrā. Comparatively, China was not so fortunate as Laṅkā with regard to the bhiksuṇī Saṅgha and that is why it was necessary to invite Ceylonese bhiksuṇīs to China. According to the Biography of the Bhiksuṇīs, in the year 429 A.C. there was a captain of a foreign ship, Nandi by name, who brought bhiksuṇīs from the Simhala-Country (Shih-tzŭ-kuo) to the capital of the early Sung dynasty (420-477 A.C.) at Nanking.[5] They were staying in the Chin-fu monastery, and they came to China to form a bhiksuṇī Saṅgha so that under this body the higher ordination would be given to the nuns as hitherto they had been ordained by the bhiksu Saṅgha. It seems that the first group of Sinhalese bhiksuṇīs was small in number and that eleven more, led by Therī Trisāraṇa (Tieh-sa-ra) (3A) had to be invited. The new arrivals landed in China in 433 A.C. and consequently over 300 nuns were ordained by them under the able guidance of Saṅghavarman, a prominent Indian Sramana who came from India in the same year.

This event took place just thirteen years after Fa-hsien's visit to Ceylon (he went back to China in 416 A.C.). As he took up residence in Nanking and devoted himself to the translation

of Sanskrit manuscripts into Chinese, especially
Vinaya literature, we think he had a large part
in bringing about this mission of Sinhalese nuns
to renovate the bhiksunī Saṅgha there, although
his biographers have been silent on this point.

With regard to Nandi, the captain of the
foreign vessel, we presume that he might be
Ceylonese. Tennent stated, "The Sinhalese,
though most expert as fishers and boatmen, never
embark in foreign vessels";[6] how far this is
justifiable, we cannot say yet. But in this case
it might be a Sinhalese captain. If he were an
Indian, why should he not bring bhiksunīs to China
from India on both occasions?

The Visit of Amoghavajra
and Tantrism in Ceylon

Buddhism in the eighth century A.C. began
to drift toward Tantrism. This is proven by
the practices among the Buddhists in India in
general, and the Tantric works of that period
translated into Chinese in particular. Among the
prominent teachers of the Tantric cult who went
to China from India in the eighth century A.C.,
the names of Vajrabodhi, a graduate of Nālandā
University, and Amoghavajra may be specially
mentioned. The relation between these two is
that of a guru and his pupil and both had been
to Ceylon. While in Ceylon Vajrabodhi climbed
Adam's Peak, and from there he went to China
sometime after 713 A.C.[7] The case with Amoghavajra
is a little different. He was a brahmin from
northern India and had become a disciple of
Vajrabodhi when he was fifteen years of age. In
all probability he proceeded with his teacher
to China. And at the time Vajrabodhi died in
733 A.C. he had been instructed to pay a visit
to Ceylon and India for the purpose of collecting
Tantric scriptures.

Amoghavajra reached the Simhala-Kingdom in
742 A.C. and was accorded a royal reception,

including a guard of honor by the royal forces.
The King, Śilamegha by name,[8] saluted him by touch-
ing his feet, and invited him to stay in the palace
for seven days. To express his deep veneration,
the king bathed Amoghavajra every day with scented
water pouring from a golden hu or can.[9] From the
crown prince on down--namely the queen, the ladies
in the harem, and the ministers--all showered him
with great respect in exactly the same degree as
the king did.[10]

During his sojourn in Ceylon, Amoghavajra met
for the first time Samantabhadra Ācārya, a great
master of the Tantric cult. He requested this
master to perform the ceremony of the two mandalas,
the vajradhātu and garbhadhātu, which consist of
the eighteen central objects of worship. When the
request was granted he gave permission to two of
his Chinese disciples, Han-kuang and Hui-pien (4A),
to join him in learning the secrets of the five
abhisecani baptisms from the great ācārya. Later,
he collected more than 500 volumes of Tantric texts,
sūtras and śāstras, in addition to the detailed information concerning the mudras, images, colors,
and flags of the guardian deities in a maṇḍala.
To prove his mastery over the esoteric art he gave
a demonstration of his power by subduing a number
of mad elephants in the presence of the king. He
also visited India and returned to China in 746 A.C.
He presented to the emperor the official message
sent by King Śilamegha of Ceylon, along with jewels,
pearls, white fine muslin, Sanskrit manuscripts,
and other valuable presents.[11]

We find in the Nikāya Saṅgraha, a book
written in the fourteenth century A.C. dealing
with the history of the Buddhist Saṅgha, a
reference to the introduction of Tantric Buddhism
in Ceylon in the form of Vajiriya Vāda or
Vajrayāna in the tenth century A.C. by King
Matvala Sena.[12] However, judging by the above-
mentioned evidence and the Dhāraṇī "Om tare,
tu tare, ture svāhah" discovered near the
Vijayārāma monastery at Anuradhapura[13] as well
as the Tisā Veva lithic diagram which was also

found in that ancient capital,[14] we have reason
to believe that Tantrism was introduced to Ceylon
in eighth century A.C., if not earlier. Moreover, the names known as Nīlapaṭa, or Nīla Sādhana
and Vajravāna or Vajiriya Vāda mentioned in the
Nikāya Saṅgraha invariably indicate that Tantrism
was popular and prevalent on the Island in its
various forms.[15] We are sure that it had some
influence on Chinese Buddhism when Amoghavajra
returned to China.

The Mission of Chêng Ho and
Its Political Consequence
in Ceylon

        Judging by the fact that Fa-hsien went home
by sea from Ceylon via Java, we may assume that
sea communication between different countries
in Southeast Asia and the Far East in ancient
times must have been well established. Presumably
the regular service was maintained by merchants
for their commercial purposes. An official
expedition armed by marine corps from China was
never heard of until the Ming dynasty (1368-
1628 A.C.). General Chêng Ho (5A), at the
command of Emperor Ch'êng-tsu (6A), led expedition
forces to the ports in the region of the South
Seas and the Indian Ocean, including Ceylon,
on several occasions.[16] The motive behind this
was threefold: First, it served as a goodwill
mission from the emperor so that friendship and
closer contact between China and her neighboring
countries might be brought about. Of course,
this did not mean ambitious imperialism. Second,
Emperor Ch'êng-tsu suspected that his opponent
Hui-ti (ex-emperor) from whom he had snatched
the throne had escaped and taken asylum in one
of the countries in these regions.[17] To satisfy
himself, he directed Chêng Ho to keep this matter
in mind during his missions abroad. Third--
probably this is a more reasonable explanation--
the founder of the Ming dynasty, i.e., the father
of Emperor Ch'êng-tsu, had cherished the idea of
developing sea communications and making contact

202

with foreign nations. This is consequently
proven by the fact that he had established a
Royal Institute for Foreign Languages and had
ordered government agents to collect materials
for shipbuilding, including a large-scale plan-
tation of tung-oil trees, the oil of which is
usually used for varnishing.[18] He could not
realize this dream during his lifetime. What
Ch'êng-tsu did was just to pick up the thread where
his father had left it. These were the essential
factors which prompted Chêng Ho to undertake the
journey abroad.

The official position of Chêng Ho, according
to Ming-Shih, or the History of the Ming Dynasty,
was that of a eunuch in the palace.[19] This does
not sound attractive, but he was the righthand
man of the emperor. Through his ability, sagacity,
courage, and judgment he helped his master to
the throne and achieved great success in his
hazardous missions abroad. From 1405 to 1430
A.C. he was credited with seven voyages. On his
second voyage in 1408 he landed in Ceylon and
shortly afterwards an encounter took place
between Alagakikonāra (A-lee-ku-nai-erh) or
Vijaya Bāhu VI, the Ruler of Ceylon, and his
armed forces.[20] The cause for this unpleasant
incident according to one version was that
earlier in 1405 A.C. there was a group of Chinese
Buddhist pilgrims who went to Ceylon to pay homage
to the Tooth-Relic of the Buddha. They were ill-
treated by King Vijaya Bāhu VI. Taking it to be
an insult and desirous of righting the wrong,
the expedition force was sent.[21]

The other version[22] was that earlier during
his first voyage in 1405 Chêng Ho brought with
him incense and flowers to be offered to the
Buddhist shrines in Ceylon and called on the king
requesting him to show respect to Buddhism and
its followers. The King was apparently a Hindu.[23]
He not merely rejected the visitor's advice but
threatened him with dire consequences. Chêng Ho
had 27,000 well-equipped soldiers with him who
were conveyed by forty-eight big vessels. Being

aware of the fact that he was discourteous to the Chinese envoy on his previous visit he feared that the visitor's army might bring him destruction. Therefore, he conspired with his ministers to entrap Chêng Ho by trickery. This is how it worked out.

In the beginning, the king pretended to be friendly with him, and his party was decoyed to the interior. While the envoy and his party were well on their way to the capital, the King secretly dispatched an army of 50,000 strong to welcome the main body of Chinese forces at the port with a surprise attack, and at the same time stockades were thrown up with a view to their capture so that a ransom might be obtained from them. This plan was, however, revealed to the envoy, and by a dexterous movement, Chêng Ho led an infantry of 2,000 strong and captured the capital. After the fall of the city, the king was made a prisoner, and the members of his family, including officials, were taken to China. Later on they were released and sent back to their homeland.[24]

From 1410 to 1459 A.C. the relationship between China and Ceylon was very cordial.[25] The reason for this is that King Parākrama Bāhu VI, known in Chinese as Seay-pa-nai-na, was recommended for the throne by the Chinese emperor.[26] As a sequel, the new king sent envoys and gifts to China on three occasions, in 1433, 1435, and 1459 A.C. After 1459 there was no official communication between the two countries because King Parākrama Bāhu VI passed away in 1462, and because the Portuguese appeared on the scene by showing their presence in Goa in 1496. Finally they had the monopoly of sea trade and the eastern nations were no longer able to maintain their former contact.

Regarding the hostility between Chêng Ho and King Vijaya Bāhu VI, we would like to quote a passage from the Rājāvali, a Sinhalese historical record which presents a different picture.[27] The relevant passage runs as follows: "In the reign of King Vijaya Bāhu, the King of Mahā Chīna landed in Ceylon with an army pretending that he was bringing tribute; King Vijaya Bāhu, believing his professions, acted incautiously, and he was treacherously taken prisoner by the foreign king. His four brothers were killed, and with them fell many people, and the King himself was carried captive to China."[28]

This is another version of the story. Of course it is not our intention to investigate the original cause of the unhappy event and deliver a judgment on who was right or wrong. From the standpoint of history, this piece of information is very important because it confirms that this event really occurred, as historical annals of both the countries agree.[29]

Other Interchange of Arts and Culture

Ever since the beginning of the first century A.C. Chinese ships and merchants have been calling on the ports of Ceylon, especially Galle, where, it is said, "Ships anchor and people land."[30] It is obvious that the relation-ship between the two countries in the initial stage was commercial and gradually rose to a diplomatic level. Envoys were sent to China by the rulers of Ceylon and return visits were paid by the Chinese ambassadors. According to Chinese historical annals, from 97 to 762 A.C. there were altogether sixteen trips of Ceylonese mis-sions to China carrying with them presents and commercial commodities for trade.[31] Among the articles known to have been imported from Ceylon were: gold ornaments, jewelry, pearls, coral, crystal, rubies, sapphires, amethysts, car-buncles, topazes of four distinct tints, models of the shrines in which were deposited the sacred relics of the Buddha and other valuables.[32] In return, the Chinese merchants brought to the shores of Laṅkā silk, variegated lute strings, blue porcelain, enamelled dishes and cups, and large quantities of copper cash wanted for adjusting the balance of trade.[33] As of particular interest it should be mentioned here that a Ceylonese artist of the highest rank was deputed to produce a Buddha-image in China. It is recorded in the History of the Wei Dynasty, 386-556 A.C., that kings in Central Asia were requested to send sculptors to China to make images of the Buddha. Many artists came from that region but none could rival the productions of Nandi, a bhiksu from Laṅkā in 456 A.C. His unique skill waś exhibited by the fact that the images made by him appeared truly brilliant when placed at a distance of about ten paces, but the lineaments gradually disappeared on a closer approach.[34] On another occasion, we are told by Liang-Shu, or the History of the Liang Dynasty, 502-556 A.C., that the king of Ceylon sent an ambassador to China carrying a jade image of Buddha which was unique in workmanship and appeared to be a work of super-human skill.[35] Thus the art of image-making in Ceylon seems to have reached a very high standard by the fifth century A.C. It is no wonder that the Chinese historians paid glowing tributes to the creators of this art.

Later in the early part of the Yüan dynasty, 1260-1341 A.C., we are informed that Kublai Khan sent three successive envoys to Ceylon who were empowered to negotiate the purchase of the sacred alms bowl of the Buddha. This was confirmed by Marco Polo in his Travels.[36] The compliment paid to the craftsmanship of that piece of art is as follows: "In front of the image of the Buddha is a sacred bowl which is neither made of jade, nor copper, nor iron; it is of a purple color and glossy, and when struck it sounds like glass" (Tao-yi chih-lüeh).[37]

The Grand Khan's desire to obtain the bowl may have been inspired by religious sentiments. If that article was also produced in Ceylon (though we are not sure), then it is further proof of the great achievement attained by Ceylonese artists.

However, besides commercial exports, China made certain contributions to the cultural life of the people on the Island, namely, in 1266 A.C. Chinese musical instruments were imported into Ceylon and some Chinese soldiers took service in the army of Parākrama III. A description concerning this point is found in Kāvya-Sekara, a work in Sinhalese written about 1410 A.C.[38]

The details enumerated in the foregoing paragraphs would convince one of the close cultural relationship which China and Ceylon have had for over 1,500 years, since the beginning of the first century A.C. The cultural ambassadors of both countries came and went not so much for material gain as to carry incense and offerings to the shrines of the Tooth-Relic, paying homage to the Buddhist sanctuaries and copying the Sanskrit sūtras for the sake of propagating the religion of the Blessed One. This cultural interchange naturally pivoted around Buddhism. It is because of co-religionist feelings that the Buddhists in China, from the emperor on down, used to send greetings to the Buddhists on this Island. They have sincerely regarded Laṅka as sacred a sanctum as that of Buddha-gaya or Sarnath in India. This crystallization of cordial friendship and sympathetic sentiments between these two countries is a phenomenon which had no antecedent except perhaps in the ancient Sino-Indian relations.

NOTES

1. James Emerson Tennent, Ceylon (Longmans, Green, Longman, and Roberts, 1860), vol. I, p. 400.

2. Cf. Samuel Beal, trans. and ed., Buddhist Records of the Western World (Calcutta: Susil Gupta, 1957), p. 11.

3. Ibid., p. 51; Fa-hsien, The Travels of Fa-hsien, in Taishō, vol. 51, pp. 857-65.

4. Fa-hsien, op.cit.

5. Pao Chang, Pi-ch'iu-ni chuan (Biographies of the Bhiksunīs), in Taishō, vol. 50, pp. 934ff.

6. Tennent, op.cit., p. 441.

7. Tsan-ning, Sung kao-sêng chuan (Biographies of Eminent Buddhist Teachers of the Sung Dynasty), in Taishō, vol. 50, pp. 709ff.

8. There is no mention of a king bearing this name in the Sinhalese Chronicles. From 729 to 769 A.C., the king who ruled the island was Agrabodhi III or Akbo, whose capital was at Pollonaruwa. See Tennent, op.cit., p. 322. In Culavaṃsaṁ, Chapter 44, v. 63, we have "Śilameghavanna," who was king of Ceylon with Anuradhapura as his capital, though the author is silent on this point.

9. "Hu," a Chinese corn measure, nominally holding ten pecks. In this case, it may be a kind of large can for pouring water.

10. Tsan-ning, op.cit., pp. 712-14.

11. Ibid.

12. Martin Wickramasinghe, "Tantrism in Ceylon and Tisa Veva Lithic Diagram," Ceylon Historical Journal, vol. I, no. 4 (1951), p. 288.

13. B.C. Law, ed., The Buddhist Studies (Calcutta: Thacker, Spink, and Co., 1931), p. 486.

14. Wickramasinghe, op.cit., p. 287.

15. Ibid., p. 289.

16. Visva Bharati Annals, vol. I, p. 103.

17. Chang T'ing-yü, et al., <u>Ming-Shih</u> (<u>History of the Ming Dynasty</u>) (Peking: Chang Hwa Book Co., 1974), pp. 8444-45.

18. Ibid.

19. Ibid.

20. Tennent, op.cit., p. 599.

21. Henry Yule, <u>Cathay</u>, vol. I (London: Hakluyt Society, 1866), p. 76.

22. A later insertion printed at the end of the eleventh chapter of Hsüan-tsang's <u>Si-yu ki</u> in the Chinese <u>Tripitaka</u>.

23. This is proven by the following evidence:
   a) At the beginning of the fifteenth century A.C., "the glory of Buddhism had declined and the political ascendancy of the Tamil had enabled the Brahmans to taint the national worship by an infusion of Hindu observances." See Tennent, op.cit., p. 598.

   b) According to <u>Se-yih-ke-foo-choo</u> or <u>Description of Western Countries</u>, Vijaya Bahu VI was a native of Sollee (Soli) in South India and an adherent of the heterodox faith who tyrannized his followers.

   c) In Ma Huan, <u>Ying-ya shêng-lan</u> (7A) or <u>Description of the Coasts of the Oceans</u> (Taiwan: Commercial Press, 1962), pp. 34-37, it is said that Vijaya Bāhu VI used to burn cow dung and smear his body with it. All these sources indicate that he was a Hindu and not very friendly towards Buddhism.

24. Tennent, op.cit., p. 599.

25.   The view expressed by J.E. Tennent in Vol. I
of his work Ceylon, pp. 600-601, appears to be
misleading and partial, because the exchange of
gifts between China and other countries does not
necessarily mean humiliation to a country which
is less powerful. It was the policy of the
Chinese emperors to maintain close contact by
meeting or sending envoys from or to other lands
and exchange presents with them.

26.   Tennent, op.cit., p. 600.

27.   The 1459 mission was sent by "Ko-li-sheng-
hsia-lu-hsi-li-pa-hu-ra-ja"; the original form
of this name may be "Kulina Simhala Sri Bāhu
Rāja."

28.   B. Gunasekara, trans., The Rājāvali: A
Historical Narrative of Sinhalese Kings from
Vijaya to Vimala Dharma Suriya III (Colombo:
Government Press, 1900), pp. 104-105.

29.   According to the statement of Fei Hsin in
Hsin-chia shêng-lan (8A) or An Excellent View of
the Star Raft (Taiwan: Commercial Press, 1962),
pp. 29-31, in 1409 Chêng Ho set up an inscription in Ceylon. In 1912, this inscription was
found in Galle. It is inscribed in three
languages--Chinese, Tamil, and Persian--and
records the event of Chêng Ho's second visit
to Ceylon. See the Journal of the Royal Asiatic
Society, hereafter cited as JRAS, North China
Branch, 1914, pp. 171-72.

30.   Shu wên-hsien t'ung-k'ao (9A) (Second Series
of General Investigations of Literary Documents)
(Taipei, Taiwan: Hsin Hsin Book Co., 1958),
p. 19.

31.   B.J. Perera, "Ancient Ceylon's Trade with
the Empires of the Eastern and the Western
Worlds," Ceylon Historical Journal, vol. I, no.
4, pp. 306-307; JRAS, Ceylon Branch, vol. XXIV,
no. 68 (1915-1961), pp. 106ff.

32. Tennent, op.cit., pp. 590-91.

33. Shen Yüeh, Sung-Shu (History of the Sung Dynasty) (Peking: Chung Hwa Book Co., 1974), p. 2384.

34. Wei Shou, Wei Shu (History of the Wei Dynasty) (Peking: Chung Hwa Book Co., 1974), p. 2384.

35. Lee Ssŭ-ching, ed., Tse-fu yüan-kuei (10A) (The Great Deposit of National Archives) (Taiwan: Chung Hwa Book Co., 1972), p. 7; Wei Shou, op.cit.

36. Yao Ssŭ-lien, Liang Shu (History of the Liang Dynasty) (Peking: Chung Hwa Book Co., 1973), p. 800.

37. Henry Yule, trans. and ed., The Book of Sir Marco Polo, vol. I (London: J. Murray, 1929), pp. 319-20.

38. This means A Brief Record of the Island People. See Tennent, op.cit., p. 598.

GLOSSARY

1A 法顯

2A 玄奘, 義淨

3A 鉄薩羅

4A 含光. 慧辯

5A 鄭和

6A 明成祖

7A 瀛涯勝覽

8A 星槎勝覽

9A 續文献通考

10A 册府元龜

XI

THE VOYAGE OF BUDDHIST MISSIONS

TO SOUTHEAST ASIA AND THE FAR EAST

Central Asia, stretching from the northwestern boundaries of China to the northern
territories of ancient India (including modern
Afghanistan), was considered to be the lifeline
of international trade and cultural exchange.
It was also known as the silk route through
which silk, spice and other commodities were
offered for commercial exchange with countries in
the West. We are not sure of the actual date
when this international route first came to be
used. The earliest historical record written
in Chinese indicates that as early as the second
century B.C. textile and bamboo products manufactured in China were sold in the market of
Bactriana in the Oxus valley. This was personally seen by Chang Ch'ien (1A), the envoy
sent by Emperor Wu-ti of the Han dynasty in
129 B.C. to negotiate with the Yüeh-chi rulers
in Bactriana in order to form a military alliance.
Further he was reported to have said that these
commodities were brought to Bactriana via
India.[1]

This presupposes the existence of this international route between China and Central Asian
countries, including India. Therefore, it
appears to be very natural that most of the Indian
and Central Asian Buddhist teachers who travelled
to China followed the trail of this caravan route
through Central Asia or modern Chinese Turkestan.
This particular route served a useful purpose
for over 1,000 years, from the beginning of the
third century B.C. Besides the Indian teachers,
who were prompted by missionary zeal, Chinese
Buddhist pilgrims like Fa-hsien and Hsüan-tsang

took the same route to India. It is from the records of these travellers that we understand that the land route via Central Asia was chiefly responsible for the spread of Buddhism to China. Of course the importance of this route cannot be denied. However, the sea route, too, played an equally important role in the international, commercial, and cultural exchange.

The fact that Fa-hsien in the early fifth century A.C. returned to China by the sea route indicates that the sea communication between China and India was fairly popular at that time. It is beyond our knowledge to trace the date of the actual beginning of this route. Han-Shu, one of the earliest Chinese historical sources of the Han dynasty (206 B.C. - 25 A.C.) gives us a list of names of countries in Southeast Asia and India.[2] Most of the countries could not be identified except Huang-chi (2A) (Kānci or Conjeevaram). It appears that Conjeevaram was on friendly terms with the Chinese Imperial Court, for during the reign of Emperor P'ing-ti (1-5 A.C.), the powerful minister Wang Mang (3A) presented to the king of Conjeevaram valuable gifts with the request that the latter should dispatch to China a live rhinoceros.[3] Later the annals of the later Han dynasty (25-220 A.C.) say that several embassies were sent to China by India in 159 and 161 A.C. It also mentions that an ambassador was sent to China by "King Antonius" of Rome in 166 A.C. This particular mission reached China through the outskirt districts called Jih-nan in southern China.[4] These are the clear bits of evidence that sea communication between the Indian Ocean and the China Sea was established at least in the beginning of the first century A.C. Moreover, this route was not used by India alone, but other countries like Rome and Parthia as well. This shows that the sea route to China has an early beginning, and it has been proven to be as popular as the land route via Central Asia.

It is my intention to trace and discuss the Buddhist missions which proceeded to the South

Seas and the Far East through the sea route. I
will also point out the extent of the contributions made by these missions toward the spread
of Buddhism in these regions. Therefore, a study
of the following Buddhist teachers regarding their
mode of travel, missionary activities and their
achievement and so forth is essential.

An Shih-kao (Pārthamaśrī)

One of the earliest Buddhist missions to
China which has been accepted as trustworthy is
the one led by An Shih-kao (4A). It is said that
before taking the Buddhist vow he was the son of King
Pakor and crown prince of Parthia.[5] He reached
China in the beginning of the reign of King
Huan-ti (146-167 A.C.) and from 148 to 168 A.C.
he devoted himself to the task of translating
more than thirty Buddhist texts which deal with
the practice of meditation and other types of
early Buddhist literature. His biographer does
not state precisely whether he reached China by
the land or the sea route. However, there are
certain indications that possibly he went there
by sea.

For instance, it is said in his biography
that at the end of the reign of King Ling-ti
(168-189 A.C.), because of a national uprising,
he left Lo-yang and went to southern China when
he had completed the task of translating
Buddhist works.[6] This would mean that he spent
most of his time (over twenty years) in northern
China. He had a lengthy stay at Lo-yang because
that was the capital of the Han dynasty. Thus
he would get ample assistance from the government
to facilitate his task of translation. However,
there is a very significant episode presented
in the form of a legend in his biography. The
gist of the legend is, according to the statement
made by An Shih-kao himself, that in his previous
birth he had been a Buddhist monk of Parthia.
Owing to the effect of karma he went to Canton in
South China and was slain by a youth there.

215

After his death his "consciousness returned to Parthia and he was born again as the crown prince to the king of Parthia--and that was the present life of An Shih-kao."[7]

The story itself may not carry much weight, but judging by the places in southern China with which he was closely associated,[8] it would appear that he came to China by the sea route and Canton was probably the port where he disembarked. If we interpret the legend in this way, it would give us some meaning which is probably closer to the truth.

K'ang Sêng-hui (5A)

The spread of Buddhism to southern China along the lower Yangtse valley in the early part of the third century A.C. chiefly depended on the enthusiasm shown by a few foreign missionaries who had close connection with central Asia and Indo-China. Among them K'ang Sêng-hui's endeavor was unique. His ancestors were of Sogdian origin, but for generations they had been residing in India. Later his father migrated from India to Tonkin in Indo-China (it was called Chiao-chih at that time) for the purpose of trade. During his childhood his parents died and he took the vow of a Buddhist monk in one of the monasteries there. This must have taken place many years before 247 A.C. (because he reached Nanking in the tenth year of Tz'ŭ-wu, viz., 247 A.C. of the Wu Kingdom). No mention is made of his voyage from Indo-China to Nanking except for a sentence indicating the direction of his journey: "Taking his monk's staff he travelled towards the East."[9] We presume he took the sea route from Indo-China and reached Nanking via Canton. That is the most convenient and direct route through which one could easily reach south China. Moreover, Canton is in the eastern direction judging by the standpoint of Indo-China. There is the other alternative route via Yünnan, Szechwan, Hupei and Chiangshi provinces to reach Nanking. This is

certainly circuitous and full of obstructions.
For instance, during the reign of the second
ruler, Hou-chu (223-263 A.C.) of the Shu Kingdom
(in modern Szechwan province), K'ung Ming, the
prime minister of this kingdom, waged war constantly against the native tribes of Yünnan.[10]
Under such circumstances, it is not quite certain
whether one could pass through Yünnan at that
time. It is very unlikely that K'ang Sêng-hui
ventured himself to take this risky and roundabout
route instead of the safe and comfortable sea
voyage to China.

His contribution to Buddhism in southern
China consists of converting Sun Ch'üan, the
founder of the Wu Kingdom (222-251 A.C.),
causing the miraculous power of the relics of
the Buddha to be exhibited, thereby gaining a
large following, the building of the first Buddhist
monastery (Chien-t'zŭ ssŭ) and stūpa and the
establishment of the Buddha's Village (Fu-t'o-li).
Thenceforward Buddhism was firmly established
on the soil of southern China and a large number
of people became Buddhists. Comparing this with
the early beginning of Buddhism in that area, the
contrast is rather shocking. It is said that
when he arrived at Nanking in 247 A.C., the officials of the Wu Kingdom were suspicious of his
strange appearance and the monk's costume. He
was officially interrogated and put to incon-
venience.[11] The whole trouble lies in the fact
that he was the first Buddhist śramaṇa to enter
that territory in southern China. However,
Buddhist works like the Dhammapada and Vimalakīrti Nirdeśa were known to a section of the
people of the Wu Kingdom at that time, through
the effort of Chih Ch'ien, a lay disciple of
Yüeh-ch'i origin. He might have exercised some
influence on the intelligentsia, but the credit
in showing Buddhism to be a popular religion
should go to K'ang Sêng-hui. Besides, in the
existing Chinese Tripitaka two works are said
to be the translation of K'ang Sêng-hui. They
are the Shatpāramitāsannipāta-sūtra and the
Samyuktāvadāna-sūtra.

Dharmayaśas and Buddhabhadra

Dharmayaśas

Among the Kashmirian teachers who went to China, Dharmayaśas and Buddhabhadra may be said to have set up a record in finding a circuitous way to reach that country. Dharmayaśas was a native of Kashmir and an expert on the Vibhāsā Vinaya of the Sarvāstivādin school. He arrived at Canton in southern China during the period of Lung-an (397-401 A.C.) of the eastern Tsin dynasty. Later he proceeded to Ch'ang-an in northern China during the I-hsü period (405-418 A.C.), and together with Dharma-gupta he translated two works, namely, the Strīvivarta-vyākaraṇa-sūtra and the Sāriputrābhidharma-śāstra.

His biographer does not state the details of his journey but simply says: "He travelled many well-known countries and passed through a number of kingdoms and districts."[12] As he disembarked at Canton, we presume he must have, first of all, travelled from Kashmir to Bengal and embarked on a ship at Tāmralipti for the South Seas and thence to southern China. This assumption may not be too far from fact if the case of Fa-hsien could be cited. Fa-hsien sailed from Tāmralipti for Ceylon, Java, and China sometime in 413 or 414 A.C.[13] If, twelve years later, the voyage could be easily undertaken by Fa-hsien, it was also possible for Dharmayaśas to have travelled the same route.

It is mentioned in his biography that he returned to the Western Regions (India) during the Yüan-chia period (424-451 A.C.).[14] This time we are at a loss to know how he returned to India.

Buddhabhadra

Another interesting route through which an Indian teacher found his way to China has

been recorded in the life of Buddhabhadra. This
teacher originally belonged to Kapilavastu. Later
he went to Kashmir to study dhyāna of Kashmir.
He was highly praised by his teacher (Buddhasena)
for his mastery in meditation and <u>Vinaya</u> observance. The arrival of Buddhabhadra in Kashmir
must have taken place sometime before 401 A.C.
This is calculated on the fact that Chih-yen
(6A), one of the companions of Fa-hsien, started
his journey from China to India in 399 A.C. It
took him two to three years to reach Kashmir
(ca. 401-402 A.C.).[15] As Chih-yen was very keen
on inviting a renowned teacher to go to China to
teach dhyāna practices in the proper way, the
burden fell on the shoulders of Buddhabhadra,
though in the beginning he was rather hesitant
to accept the offer.[16] In this regard we see
how he travelled to China: "Having crossed over
the Pamirs (Ts'ong-ling, the Onion Ranges), he
passed through six countries. The rulers of
these kingdoms were sympathetic to his missionary
zeal in going to distant lands. They provided
him with abundant requisites. Having reached
Chiao-chih (Tonkin), he boarded a ship. . .
after sometime he reached the Tung-lai pre-
fecture of Ch'ing-chow./17/ When he learned
that Kumārajīva was staying at Ch'ang-an, he
immediately proceeded thither to meet him."[18]

If we examine his itinerary carefully,
it gives us the impression that Buddhabhadra,
who was accompanied by Chih-yen, started his
journey from Kashmir and followed the trails
leading to the Pamirs.[19] When he was on the
tracks of Central Asia or Chinese Turkestan, he
passed through six countries. The names of these
countries are not given. It is quite likely
that some of the important places like Hashgar,
Yarkand, Khotan, Niya, and so forth, situated
on the southern route leading to the Chinese
frontier should be the kingdoms which he
passed through. Otherwise, if he took the
northern route along which the ancient kingdoms
such as Bharuka near Uch-Turfan, Kucī (modern
Kuchar), Karashar and Turfan were situated,[20]

219

he would have easily reached the northwestern
frontiers of China, and would not have taken the
sea route to reach the Shangtung province in
northern China. If our presumption be correct,
it poses the problem as to how he travelled from
Chinese Turkestan to Chiao-chih (Tonkin) in
Indo-China. We have never heard of any Buddhist
missionary or pilgrim who had taken that unusual
and circuitous route before. As his biographer
does not say anything about the journey from
Chinese Turkestan to Indo-China, we may suggest
that his journey from Central Asia might have
covered the territories of Tibet, Assam, Burma,
Thailand, and Indo-China. This possibility is
seen from the fact that the fourteenth Dalai
Lama, who ran away from Lhasa because of political
disturbance, reached Tezpur in Assam in 1959.
In the fifth century A.C. there might have existed
footpaths in the above-mentioned areas which
were used by caravans for trading purposes. If
that be the case, the possibility of Buddhabhadra's
travelling from Chinese Turkestan to Indo-China
cannot be ruled out. We must admit, however,
that the itinerary of Buddhabhadra is the most
strange and unique among the Buddhist missionaries
to the Far East.

While at Ch'ang-an Buddhabhadra met
Kumārajīva. The latter was glad to receive him,
and on many an occasion consulted him on
Buddhist doctrines. As Buddhabhadra devoted
himself to the teaching and practice of meditation as well as the observance of the Vinaya
rules, his way of life was quite different from
that of Kumārajīva. It is said that on account
of a prophecy made by Buddhabhadra, the disciples
of Kumārajīva took advantage of it and expelled
him from living among other members of the
Saṅgha at Ch'ang-an.[21]

During his stay in southern China, many
Sanskrit texts were translated into Chinese
by him. Among his translations the Avataṁsaka-
sūtra and the Mahāsaṅghika-vinaya are some
of the important works which have influenced

220

Buddhism in China to a large extent. He passed
away in 429 A.C. at the age of seventy-one.

Guṇavarman

Among the Kashmirian teachers who took the
sea route to China, Guṇavarman achieved greater
success as a Buddhist missionary than most of
his contemporaries. His missionary zeal took
him to propagate Buddhism in Southeast Asia and
the Far East, although his original plan was not
specifically directed toward China. If we accept the statement of his biographer, it appears
that he belonged to the ruling family of Kashmir.
As he was greatly interested in the study of
Buddhist literature and the practice of meditation he scorned the idea of being made the ruler
of Kashmir.[22] To avoid further trouble, he
decided to leave Kashmir, and in course of time
he reached Ceylon (Simhala country). According
to the verses he composed before his death, he
attained the Sakadāgamin Fruition at the Ka-po-li
(Kapārā or Kāpiri[23]) village in Ceylon.[24] It
appears that he lived in Ceylon for a very long
time, and his fame as a saint must have spread
far and wide, because he said: "Offerings
heaped up in large piles, but I regard them as
fire and poison. My mind was greatly distressed,
and to get rid of this disturbance I embarked
on a ship. . . .I went to Java and Champa. Owing
to the effects of karma, the wind sent me to the
territories of the Sung Dynasty (420-479 A.C.)
in China. And in these countries I propagated
Buddhism according to my ability. . . ."[25]

The few lines quoted above indicate to us
the causes and circumstances under which he
was forced to carry on his missionary activities.
He was essentially a dhyāna master of the Sarvāstivādin school, which was still popular in
Kashmir at that time. There is no record
available to us now regarding his missionary
activities in Ceylon and Champa, but fortunately
we have details about his success in Java and China.

221

Before the arrival of Gunavarman in Java,
the religion in that country was chiefly Brahmanic
and there was hardly any Buddhist influence.
This is clearly stated in the Travels of Fa-hsien.
We know that Fa-hsien reached Java from Ceylon
in 413 or 414 A.C. He was of the opinion that
the Buddhist religion there was not of sufficient
importance to mention.[26] Therefore, it is very
likely that Gunavarman converted P'o-to-chia
(Vadhaka?), the king of Java, and his mother to
Buddhism. In the beginning, both of them received the five precepts from him. However, the
king went a step further, expressing his intention to his ministers to renounce the throne
and become a member of the Sangha. His subjects
strongly objected to his intended departure, and
entreated him to continue to be their ruler.
Finally he yielded to their request, if they
could agree to the following conditions:

1. that the people throughout his kingdom
should show respect to the venerable Gunavarman;

2. that all the subjects in his kingdom
should completely stop the taking of life of
living beings; and

3. that the accumulated wealth in the
government treasury should be distributed
among the sick and the poor.

Needless to say, the people in Java
willingly agreed to all the conditions and
received the five precepts from Gunavarman.
Later the king erected a vihara for him. It is
said that the king carried timber personally
for the construction of the monastery.[27] This
indicates the tremendous success of the spread
of Buddhism in Java in the early part of the
fifth century A.C. Naturally the credit goes
to Gunavarman.

His journey from Java to China is also
of unusual interest. The news of Gunavarman's
missionary activities in Java reached China

sometime before 424 A.C. In 424 A.C. the Chinese
Buddhists in Nanking, headed by Hui-kuan (7A),
requested Emperor Wu-ti (424-452 A.C.) of the Sung
dynasty to write to Guṇavarman and the king of
Java (Vadhaka), with the intention of inviting
Guṇavarman to China. Later, the Emperor sent
Fa-chang and other Buddhist scholars to Java in
order to extend the Emperor's invitation to him
in person. However, before the arrival of these
messengers in Java, Gunavarman had already left
the country by boat and was going to a small
country. But fortunately the seasonal wind caused
him to reach the shores of Canton in southern
China. He stayed at a place called Shih-hsin
for quite a long time. It was only in the
eighth year of Yüan-chia (431 A.C.) that he reached
Nanking, at the repeated request of Emperor Wên-ti.
His advice to the Emperor on benevolent government was greatly appreciated by the ruler. Among
his propagation activities, he preached
Saddharmapuṇḍarīka-sūtra and the Daśabhūmi-sūtra
to a large audience and translated more than ten
works, of which the following five are still
extant:

1. Upāli-pariparicchā-sūtra;

2. Upāsaka-pañcaśīlarūpa-sūtra;

3. Dharmagupta-bhikṣuṇī-karma;

4. Śramaṇera-karmavāca;

5. Nāgārjuna-bodhisattva-suhrillekha.

Another important contribution of Guṇavarman
was the assistance he gave in conferring
higher ordination on the bhiksunīs in China in
accordance with the specifications of the Vinaya.
The normal practice was that bhikṣuṇīs received
their Upasampada ordination from both the bhikṣu
and the bhikṣunī Saṅghas. Otherwise it was
incomplete. The institution of bhikṣunīs
in China has an early beginning. The Chinese
historical annals inform us that toward the
end of the fourth century A.C. the rulers and

members of the royal family showed great respect
for both the Buddhist bhikṣus and bhikṣunīs.
Take, for instance, the Queen of Mu-ti (345-
361 A.C.) who built the Yung-an ssǔ nunnery
for bhikṣunī Tan-pi,[28] and Emperor Hsiao-wu-ti
(373-395 A.C.), who was a great patron of
bhiksunī Maio-yin, though the latter was unworthy
of the honor. This shows that by the middle of
the fourth century A.C. there existed a large
number of Buddhist nuns.[29]

However, the earliest translation of the
bhiksunī Prātimoksa was done by Fa-hsien and
Buddhabhadra in 414 A.C.[30] and the formal pro-
ceedings for the bhikṣunīs (Dharmagupta Bhikṣunī
Karman, Nanjio No. 1129), was translated by
Guṇavarman himself in 431 A.C. This being the
case, it is very doubtful that the bhikṣunīs
in China were properly ordained before the
arrival of Guṇavarman in 431 A.C. Therefore, it
became necessary (and a request was made to
him) for him to help the bhiksunīs perform the
rites for the higher ordination for the second
time. At this same time there came from Ceylon
to the capital of the Sung dynasty at Nanking,
a group of eight Sinhalese bhikṣunīs, intending
to confer higher ordination on the Chinese nuns.
As their number was less than ten and some of them
had not yet reached the required age after the
Upasampadā ordination,[31] Guṇavarman helped them
to invite an additional group of bhikṣunīs from
Ceylon (the leader of this new delegation was
Therī Triśārana).[32] As Guṇavarman had been in
Ceylon for a long time, he was possibly the most
suitable person to do it. But unfortunately
he could not live to see the fruit of his labor.
He passed away in 432 A.C. at the age of sixty-
five. This sad event took place just before
the arrival of the second group of bhikṣunīs
from Ceylon.[33] He left behind him a verse of
thirty-six stanzas regarding his views on meditation, his attainment and missionary career.

Guṇabhadra

Guṇabhadra was known as the Mahāyāna in
China. He belonged to a Brahmin family in
central India. Before his coming to China, he,
too, had spent sometime in Ceylon and other
countries in the South Seas. He reached Canton
in 435 A.C. and was accorded a warm welcome by
Emperor T'ai-tsu of the Sung dynasty (420-
479 A.C.) at Nanking.[34] During the period of
his voyage from Ceylon to China, he and his
companions experienced great difficulty owing
to the shortage of drinking water. Fortunately
Nature came to their rescue, and there was a rain
shower. This was said to be the effect of his
prayer to the merciful Avalokiteśvara Bodhisattva.[35]

He stayed in southern China for thirty-three
years and passed away in 468 A.C. at the age
of seventy-five. He translated more than twenty
works pertaining to both the Hīnayānic and Maha-
yānic forms of Buddhism. Among his translations,
the Śrīmala-devī-siṁhanāda (Nanjio, No. 59) and
Saṁyuktāgāma-sūtra (Nanjio, No. 544) are very
popular.

Saṅghapāla and Mandra

Both Saṅghapāla and Mandra (or Mandrasena)
belonged to Fu-nan or modern Cambodia. They
were probably the first Buddhist missionaries
to go to China from that country and undertake
the work of translation. Naturally they must
have gone to China by sea, because it is
said in the biography of Saṅghapāla that he
reached the capital (Nanking) of the Ch'i
dynasty (479-502 A.C.) by ship.[36] While at
Nanking he studied the Vaipulya Mahāyāna texts
(under Gunabhadra?[37]). From 506 A.C. onward
for over fifteen years he translated eleven
works including the Vimokshamārga-śāstra
(Taishō, No. 1648), which is supposed to be the
counterpart of the Visuddhimagga of Buddhaghoṣa
with slight variations.[38] The rest of his works

225

concern the Mahāyāna doctrines,[39] although it is stated in his biography that earlier he specialized in the Abhidharma-śastras.[40] He passed away in 524 A.C. at the age of sixty-five.

Mandra went to China at the beginning of the Liang dynasty (502-557 A.C.). He worked jointly with Saṅghapāla in translating Buddhist texts such as Ratnamegha-sutra (Taishō, No. 658), Saptaśatika-prajñā-pāramitā (Taishō, No. 232), and so forth. This indicates that Fu-nan at that time was very familiar with Mahāyānic literature. However, his translations were not satisfactory because he did not possess a good knowledge of Chinese.[41]

Paramārtha

Paramārtha or Gunaratna was one of the well-known Indian teachers in China who contributed extensively to the propagation of Mahāyāna Buddhism by translating many important Sanskrit texts into Chinese. However, the way of his going to China, and the several attempts made by him with the intention of returning to India, indicate that originally he had no idea of going to that country; and apparently he was not very happy there.

He belonged to Ujjayinī (Ujjain) of western India and was very enthusiastic in travelling to distant lands to propagate the teaching of the Buddha. We are not very clear as to how he went to Fu-nan (Cambodia) from India, but we know how he went to China from Fu-nan. While he was in Fu-nan, the Emperor Wu-ti of the Liang dynasty sent Chang Fan, his envoy, to Fu-nan, to pay a return visit during the period of Ta-t'ung (535-545 A.C.). This Emperor also requested the king of that country to collect Mahāyāna texts and invite eminent Buddhist teachers to go to China, so that his envoy would accompany them.[42] Paramārtha was chosen by the king of Fu-nan, and 240 bundles of Buddhist texts were

226

entrusted to him to be taken to China. He arrived at Nan-hai in southern China in 546 A.C.
and two years later he reached Nanking in 548 A.C.
Owing to the political upheaval in the country,
he could not settle down, and had hardly any time
to devote himself to the task of translating the
Buddhist works into Chinese. He had to move from
place to place in the regions of Kiangsi, Nanking,
and Canton. This upset his plan. Therefore, he
was rather disappointed and wanted to find more
fertile soil for the spread of Buddhism in the
South Seas--that is, he intended to go to Lankasuka
(now the northern part of the Malayan peninsula).
This happened in 558 A.C. However, both the
members of the Saṅgha and the laity earnestly requested him to stay on in China. Again, in 562 A.C.,
he embarked on an ocean-going ship at the port
of Liang-an, intending to return to India. This
time, he must have felt very happy that he was
finally going back to his homeland. But unfortunately, unfavorable winds brought his boat
back to the port of Canton in southern China!
Since then he thought it was useless to try to
escape from the effect of one's karma, and decided
to settle down in China for good. During his
twenty-three years' stay (from 546 to 569 A.C.)
in that country, he translated sixty-four works,
of which twenty-nine are still extant.[43] Among
his translations, the Madhyānta-vibhāga-śāstra
(Taishō, No. 1599), Mahāyāna-samparigraha-śāstra
(Taishō, No. 1596), Mahāyāna-śraddhotpādā-śāstra
(Taishō, No. 1666), and so forth, are very
popular.[44] It is obvious that most of the śāstras
translated by him formed a nucleus of the Yogācāra
doctrine of Asaṅga and Vasubandhu in China, and
on this foundation, we see the establishment of
the Dharmalakṣṇa school of Hsüan-tsang in the
seventh century A.C.

He passed away in 569 A.C. at the age of
seventy-one.

Puṇyopāya

Puṇyopāya was known in China as Nadi, the master of Tripiṭaka. He was comparatively less fortunate in his missionary endeavor in that country. He came from central India. Before his arrival in China in 655 A.C. he had been to the Laṅkā Mountains (The Adam's Peak) in Ceylon (the Siṁhala country), and visited the countries in the South Seas for the purpose of propagating Buddhist teaching. While in these regions he heard of the name of China; therefore, he collected over 500 bundles of both Mahāyāna and Hīnāyana texts, totalling 1,500 works. Later, he brought these texts along with him to the capital (Ch'ang-an) of the T'ang dynasty. He stayed in the Tz'ŭ-ên ssŭ (8A) monastery where Hsüan-tsang was engaged in the task of translating Buddhist works.

As the glory and fame of Hsüan-tsang at this juncture reached dazzling heights, Puṇyopāya was put into the shade. Moreover, they differed greatly in their learning. Hsüan-tsang laid emphasis on Dharmalakṣṇa or the doctrine of Consciousness, while Puṇyopāya followed the traditional teaching of Nāgārjuna and his accent was on Śūnya philosophy. To add fuel to this unhappy situation, in 656 A.C. Emperor Kao-tsung requested him to go to the Kun-lun regions (or the Pulo Condore Island in the China Sea) to gather some rare medicinal herbs for him.[45] This mission took him seven years. In 663 A.C., when he returned to the monastery, he found to his dismay that all the Sanskrit manuscripts he had brought with him were taken by Hsüan-tsang, and at that time the latter was staying in the Yü-hua Palace. Naturally he was at a loss and could not translate any work of importance except some minor texts.[46] Sometime in 663 A.C., the king of Chên-la (Cambodia) expressed the wish to the Chinese emperor that they would like to have Puṇyopāya, their old spiritual teacher, with them, and the request was duly granted. He went to Cambodia and never returned to China.[47]

Vajrabodhi and Amoghavajra

Vajrabodhi and his pupil Amoghavajra were chiefly responsible for the establishment of a separate Esoteric school of Buddhism in China in the early part of the eighth century A.C. Vajrabodhi belonged to a Brahmin family of the Malay region in South India, and his father was the preceptor of the king of Conjeevaram. He studied at the Nālandā University as well as in western India. He was famed for his mastery of the Tripiṭaka and of Tantric Buddhism. We have a clear record of his itinerary. He started his journey from his hometown in Malay heading toward the Laṅkā Mountain (the Adam's Peak) in Ceylon. Later, embarking on an ocean-going ship, he passed through the Nicobar Islands, Śrīvijaya (Palembang) and over twenty other countries in the South Seas. Then he proceeded to China and reached Canton in 719 A.C. Through his effort many religious performances used to take place, and Tantric mandalas were made in various regions in China. The Catalogue of Nanjiō lists eleven works as his translations, which pertain chiefly to the Tantric Dhāraṇīs. He passed away in 732 A.C. at the age of seventy-one.48

Amoghavajra was possibly the most successful disciple of Vajrabodhi. Not only did he succeed him in putting Tantric Buddhism on a firm footing by popularizing it among the members of the royal family and the general public, but the large number of Tantric texts translated by him, and the mission undertaken by him in search of the Buddhist texts in India and Ceylon, should be regarded as an important event in the history of Chinese Buddhism. According to his biographer, he belonged to a brahmin family in northern India,49 but according to Yüan-chao, author of Chên-yüan hsin-ting shih-chiao mu-lu (9A) or A Buddhist Catalogue of the Chên-yüan Period (785-804 A.C.), it is said that his native country was Ceylon (the Siṁhala country) in South India.50 Probably the former statement is more correct, because up to the time with which

229

we are dealing, Ceylon has never been a part of
India in the sense in which we understand the
expression. His biography states that after
the death of his parents, Amoghavajra went to
China with his uncle on a visit, and at the age
of fifteen became a disciple of Vajrabodhi.[51]
This part of his biography is rather complicated.
If he were really of a brahmin family, and had
nothing to do with trade, what was the purpose
of going so far on a tour to the Far East?
Granted that was so, then why should he become
a Buddhist novice at such an early age? These
are points yet to be answered.

To carry out the wishes of his late teacher,
who instructed him to go to India and Ceylon in
order to collect more Tantric works, he began his
journey in 741 A.C. with the assistance of
Chinese government officials. The route he followed was from Canton to Ceylon via Java (Ho-lin--
Kaliṅga, 10A), and then from Ceylon to India.
On his way to Java, he and his companions en-
countered a terrific storm at one stage, and
their boat was tossed about in the mountain-like
waves caused by a huge whale at another stage.
They managed to escape from these dangers
unharmed. While in Ceylon he was respected by
King Śīlamegha (Aggabodhi VI) to such an extent
that the king himself bathed him with scented
water every day during his stay in the king's
palace.[52] Later, he requested the well-known
Sinhalese Tantric Master Samantabhadra (P'u-hsien)
Ācārya to perform the ceremony of the two
maṇḍalas, the vajradhātu and garbhadhātu, and
initiate him as well as his Chinese disciples
into the profound mystery of Tantrism. It is
said that he collected over 500 volumes of
sūtras, śāstras and Tantric texts on the Island
of Ceylon. When he completed his work in that
country, he proceeded to India, and in 746 A.C.
he returned to China.[53] From that time on ,
until his death in 784 A.C. he engaged himself
in the performance of Tantric rites and ceremonies.
He was the spiritual teacher to three emperors
of the T'ang dynasty, i.e., Hsüan-tsung,

230

Shu-tsung, and Tai-tsung. It was under his influence that the Tantric practices dealing with
talismanic forms and the occasional exhibition of
supernatural powers gained currency in China.

According to his statement made in 771 A.C.
he translated seventy-seven works consisting
of over 120 fasciculi, but according to the
Catalogue of Nanjio there are 108 works ascribed
to him, and they are extant in most of the
editions of the Chinese Tripitaka. His translations chiefly deal with Tantras and Dhāranīs.[54]

Prajñā

This teacher may be regarded as one of the
unhappy travellers who went to China by the sea
route. He was a native of Kapiśā, and studied
the Hīnāyana, Mahāyāna and Tantric literature
in northern and southern India and at Nālandā.
While he was in south India he learned that
Mañjuśrī Bodhisattva had his abode in China, and
so he decided to embark on a ship sailing for
that country. It is said that when he was almost
to Canton, an unfavorable wind brought his boat
to the east of Ceylon (Simhala Kingdom).[55] No
clear indication is given with regard to the
actual position of his boat. It is very doubtful
that his boat was close to the shores of Ceylon.
It may be that his boat was somewhere close to
Indo-China or Cambodia. This is strengthened
by the fact that after some time he collected
funds and built a large boat, and then travelled
extensively all the countries in the region of
the South Seas. Later, when he was not very far
from Canton for the second time, there arose a
sudden storm and his boat was capsized, though
he managed to save himself from drowning and
salvaged his Sanskrit texts.[56] He reached the
city of Canton in 780 A.C., and six years later
he arrived at Ch'ang-an in 786 A.C. In 792 he
was under the patronage of Emperor Teh-tsung
(779-804 A.C.) who asked many Chinese Buddhist
scholars to help him in his task of translating
Sanskrit works.

In Taishō, there are four translations ascribed to him, among which the Mahāyanabhuddhi-shatpāramitā-sūtra is well known.[57]

He passed away at Lo-yang sometime after 792 A.C.

The foregoing passages point out some of the more well-known cases of Indian, Central Asian, and southeast Asian Buddhist teachers who undertook their journeys by the sea route to the South Seas and the Far East, especially China, for the propagation of Buddhism. However, this chiefly deals with those teachers who were connected with translation. A few others, like Bodhidharma, who was known as the founder of Zen Buddhism,[58] also went to China by the sea route in 480 A.C. He, first of all, reached the territories of the earlier Sung dynasty (421-479 A.C.) in southern China, and then proceeded to Lo-yang and other places in northern China.[59] Similarly, Pan-la-mi-ti (11A) (Pāramiti), a teacher from Central India, went to China by the same route. He reached Canton sometime before 705 A.C. and stayed at the Chih-chih ssŭ (12A) monastery in order to translate the Śuraṅgama-sūtra (Nanjio, No. 446) into Chinese. Later he returned to India by boat.[60] The cases here cover a period of over 600 years, from about 150 A.C. to the end of the eighth century A.C. The sea route leading to India was very popular, so much so that more than thirty Chinese and Korean monks undertook their journey by this route either to India, Siam, or the South Seas.[61] I-tsing tells us that he embarked on a Persian boat from Canton in 671 A.C. He stayed for six months in Palembang to learn Sanskrit or the Śabdavidyā, then passed through Malayu (Sumatra), Kedah, Nicobar Islands, and finally reached Tamralipti in eastern India. On his return journey, he stayed for sometime in Malayu in 689 A.C.[62]

All this shows that up to the middle of the eighth century A.C. the sea communication

between India and China was chiefly monopolized
by the Persians or other Western nationals,[63]
and the regions of Malaya. Sumatra and other
nearby places were to a large extent influenced
by Indian culture through the Indian colonists.
Otherwise I-tsing would not be able to learn
Sanskrit at Palembang.

Buddhism appeared in Java due to the effort
of Gunavarman, who introduced the Hīnayānic
form of Buddhism into that country in the early
part of the fifth century A.C. This school of
Buddhism must have existed until the end of the
seventh century A.C. The observation made by
I-tsing in this regard is very valuable. He was of
the opinion that most of the Islands, including
Java (Ho-lin), Malayu or Śrīvijaya, Borneo, etc.,
in the South Seas followed the Mūlasarvāstivādin
and Sammitīya schools.[64] There was not much of
Mahāyāna Buddhism there except to a certain
extent in Malayu (Sumatra). However, I-tsing
did not mention clearly what form of Buddhism
existed in Fu-nan (Cambodia) at that time, as
there were no monks in that country on account
of the persecution carried out by the evil
kings. From the fact that Saṅghapāla and Mandra
went to China from Fu-nan in the beginning of
the sixth century A.C. and translated many
Mahāyāna texts into Chinese and that later in
546 A.C. when Paramārtha went to China from
Fu-nan he took with him 240 bundles of Mahāyāna
works from that country, it would seem that
Fu-nan was an important center of Mahāyāna
literature. Moreover, in 539 A.C. the envoy
from Fu-nan to the court of the Liang dynasty
(502-557 A.C.) told the Emperor that in their
country there were hairs of the Buddha measuring
twelve feet in length.[65] All this indicates
that Buddhism in Fu-nan in the early part of
the sixth century A.C. was chiefly Mahāyānic
and the Buddhist texts were in Sanskrit. Till
then, the influence of Pali Buddhism had not
yet begun.

Thus, the voyage of Buddhist missions to

southeast Asian countries and to China gives us valuable evidence of the historical development of Buddhism in those regions. Further, it provides us with specific instances of the cultural relations of these countries between China on the one hand, and India on the other.

NOTES

1. Ssŭma Ch'ien, Shih-chi (A Historical Record) (Nanking: Ching-lin Book Co., 1878), ch. 123, pp. 2-3.

2. P'an Ku, Han-shu (Annal of the Former Han Dynasty) (Canton: Office of the Commissioner of Lin-tung, 1873), ch. 28, pt. 2, p. 27.

3. Fan Hua, Hou-han shu (Annal of the Later Han Dynasty) (Peking: Chung Hwa Book Co., 1973), pp. 2919-20.

4. Fung Ch'êng-chün, Les Moines Chinois et Étrangers qui ont Contribué à la Formation du Tripitaka Chinois (Shanghai: Commercial Press, 1931), p. 4.

5. Hui-chiao, Kao-sêng Chuan (Biographies of Eminent Buddhist Teachers), in Taishō, vol. 50, p. 323.

6. Ibid.

7. Ibid.

8. It is said that he converted the deity of the Tung-ting Lake which is situated at the Lower Yangtse valley in modern Chianghsi province. He also supposedly met the man who had killed him in his previous life at Canton. It is said in addition to this that he died an accidental death at Kúei-chi in modern Chechiang province.

9. Hui-chiao, op.cit., p. 325.

10. Lo Kuan-chung, San-kuo yen-i (Romance of the Three Kingdoms) (Hong Kong: Kuang Chih Book Co., n.d.), pp. 1159-61.

11. Hui-chiao, op.cit., p. 325.

12. Ibid., p. 329c.

13. Fa-hsien, The Travels of Fa-hsien, in Taishō, vol. 51, pp. 864-66.

14. Hui-chiao, op.cit., p. 339; Fa-hsien, op.cit., p. 857.

15. Hui-chiao, op.cit., p. 334.

16. Ibid.

17. Ch'ing-chow was one of the nine divisions of China under Yü the Great. It was situated in the eastern part of modern Shantung province.

18. Hui-chiao, op.cit., p. 334.

19. Ibid.

20. P.C. Bagchi, India and China (New York: Philsophical Library, 1951), pp. 12-14.

21. Hui-chiao, op.cit., p. 335.

22. Ibid., pp. 340-42.

23. In the eighth century A.C., there was a Kapārā Pativena (next to the Twin Pond) in Anuradhapura. See Epigraphia Zeylanica, vol. V, pt. 1. Of course there is a village Kāpirigama, now so-called. I am indebted to Mr. D.T. Devindra for this information.

24. Hui-chiao, op.cit., p. 342a.

25. Ibid., p. 342b.

26. Fa-hsien, op.cit., p. 866.

27. Hui-chiao, op.cit., p. 340.

28. Pao-chang, Pi-ch'iu-ni chuan (Biography of the Bhiksunīs), in Taishō, vol. 50, pp. 935-36.

29. Pao-chang, op.cit., pp. 936-37; T'ang Yung-t'ung, Han-wei liang-tsin nan-pei-ts'ao fu-chiao shih (History of Buddhism in the Han, Wei, Eastern and Western Tsin, and the Northern and Southern Dynasties) (Peking: Chung Hwa Book Co., 1972), pp. 349-50, 453-54.

30. See the Sarvāstivāda-bhiksunī-prātimoksa-sūtra, in Taishō, vol. 22, pp. 479-88.

31. Hui-chiao, op.cit., p. 341a, b.

32. See W. Pachow, "Ancient Cultural Relations Between Ceylon and China," University of Ceylon Review, vol. 12, no. 3 (1954); Tao-hsüan, op.cit., p. 341.

33. Hui-chiao, op.cit., p. 342.

34. Ibid., p. 344b.

35. Ibid.

36. Tao-hsüan, Hsü Kao-sêng Chuan (Second Series of Biographies of Eminent Buddhist Teachers), in Taishō, vol. 50, p. 426.

37. As Gurabhadra died in 468 A.C., he could not have been able to meet him (Sanghapala) in 497 A.C. at Nanking. It may be that Sanghapala was his disciple earlier.

38. See P.V. Bapat, Vimuttimagga and Visuddhimagga, a Comparative Study (Calcutta: J.C. Sarkhel, 1937).

39. See Wên-shu Shih-li So Shuo Mo-ho Pan-jo
Po-lo-mi Ching (The Prajñapāramitā Sūtra Spoken
by Mañjuśrī) in Taishō, vol. 8, pp. 732ff.;
Fu-shuo Ta-ch'êng Shih-fa Ching (The Sūtra on
the Ten Dharmas of Mahāyāna Spoken by the Buddha),
in Taishō, vol. 11, pp. 764ff.; Tu I-chieh Chu Fu
Ching-chiai Chih-Yen Ching (The Sūtra on the
Ornament of Wisdom for Passing the Realms of All
the Buddhas), in Taishō, vol. 12, pp. 250ff.;
Wên-shu Shih-li Wên Ching (The Question of
Mañjuśrī, in Taishō, vol. 14, pp. 492ff.

40. Tao-hsüan, op.cit., p. 426.

41. Ibid.

42. Ibid.

43. Ibid.

44. See Sylvain Levi, et al., eds., Hobogirin:
Fascicule Annexe; Tables du Taishō Issaikyo
(Tokyo: Maison Fransco-Japonaise, 1931),
p. 148.

45. Tao-hsüan, op.cit., pp. 458-59.

46. Ibid.; see Shih-tzǔ Chuang-yen Wang P'u-sha
Ch'ing-wên Ching (The Questions of Lion-Ornament-
King Bodhisattva), in Taishō, Vol. 14, pp.
297ff.; see also Li Kou Hui P'u-sha So Wên Li-fu
Fa Ching (The Questions of Vimala-jñanā Bodhisattva on the Method of Worshipping the Buddha),
in Taishō, vol. 14, pp. 698ff.

47. Tao-hsüan, op.cit., p. 459a.

48. Tsan-ning, Sung Kao-sêng Chuan (Biographies
of Eminent Buddhist Teachers of the Sung Dynasty),
in Taishō, vol. 50, pp. 711b-712a.

49. Ibid., pp. 712a-714a.

50. Yüan-chao, Chên-yüan hsin-ting shih-chiao mu-lu (Buddhist Catalogue of the Chên-yüan Period), in Taishō, vol. 55, pp. 771ff.

51. Tsan-ning, op.cit., p. 712a.

52. See W. Pachow, op.cit., pp. 184-85.

53. Nothing has been mentioned of his return trip.

54. Tsan-ning, op.cit., p. 713a.

55. Ibid., p. 716b.

56. Ibid.

57. See Taishō, no. 261.

58. See W. Pachow, "Zen Buddhism and Bodhidharma," Indian Historical Quarterly, vol. XXXII, nos. 2 and 3, pp. 329-37.

59. Tao-hsüan, op.cit., p. 551.

60. Tsan-ning, op.cit., p. 718.

61. I-tsing, Ta-t'ang Hsi-yu Ch'iu-fu Kao-sêng Chuan (Eminent Buddhist Teachers of the T'ang Dynasty Who Sought the Dharma in the Western Regions), in Taishō, vol. 51, pp. 1-12; Fung Ch'êng-chün, op.cit., pp. 85-87.

62. I-tsing, op.cit.

63. It is stated in the Life of Amoghavajra that in 741 A.C., before his departure for Ceylon, Liu Chu-lin, an important minister, told I-shi-pin (Ibrahmin?), chief of the foreigners residing at Canton, to instruct the captain of the boat by which Amoghavajra was travelling to look after Amoghavajra well. This would indicate that a large number of foreign merchants and shipping agents, chiefly from Persia or Arabia, were in the ports of China. See Tsan-ning, op.cit., p. 712b.

64. Cf. I-tsing, A Record of the Buddhist Religion as Practiced in India and the Malaya Archipelago, trans. J. Takakusu (Oxford: Clarendon Press, 1896).

65. See the chapter on Fu-nan in Yao Ssŭ-lien, Liang-Shu (Annal of the Liang Dynasty) (Peking: Chung Hwa Book Co., 1973).

GLOSSARY

1A 張騫

2A 黃岐

3A 王莽

4A 安世高

5A 康僧會

6A 智嚴

7A 慧觀

8A 慈恩寺

9A 圓照：貞元新定釋教目錄

10A 訶陵

11A 般剌密帝

12A 制止寺

INDEX

Ai-ti, Emperor, 58
Aiyer, Gopala, 69
Ajatasattu, King of Magadha, 123
Ajita of the garment of hair, 124
Akṣobhya Buddha, 50
Ālāra Kālāma, 125
Alchemy and Amulets, Taoist sects of, 90
Amoghavajra (Pu-k'ung), 107, 134, 200, 201, 202,
     229, 230
An Shih-kao, 5, 22, 56, 87, 102, 104, 215, 216
anattā, doctrine of (non-soul), 87, 128, 129, 136
ancestor worship, 132, 133, 134, 144, 181
ancestral spirits, 132, 181, 182
anicca, 128
anitya, 172
Annihilationists, 124, 125, 150
Annihilation, Doctrine of, 124, 125, 126, 128
Antonius, King of Rome, 214
anupadhiśeṣa-nirvāṇa, 49
arghya, 110
arhat, 14, 29
Ariṭṭha, 76, 77
Aryans, 122
asaṁskṛta dharmas, 37
Asaṅga, 227
Aśoka, King, 76
Aśvaghoṣa, 6
ātman, 10, 117, 118, 119, 120, 128
Avalokiteśvara Bodhisattva, 225
Avici hell, 134, 135

bhikṣu(s), 51, 199, 206, 224
bhikṣuṇī(s), 70, 199, 223, 224
bhūtatathatā (suchness), 39, 139
black magic, 183
La Bibliothèque Nationale, 11, 35
Bo-tree, 78
bodhi, 28, 29, 51

241

Ekayāna, 52
enlightenment, 28, 31, 150;
    gradual, 27;
    sudden, 14, 26, 27, 28, 29;
Esoteric school, 229
Eternalist doctrine(s), 123, 124, 125, 126, 128,
    150

Fa-chang, 223
Fa-hsien, 60, 78, 103, 106, 198, 199, 202, 213,
    218, 219, 222, 224
Fa-hu (Dharmaraksa) of Magadha, 107
Fan Chên, 117, 142, 143, 144, 145, 146, 147,
    148, 149, 153
Fa-t'ien (Dharmadeva), 107
Fei Chang-fang, 70, 71, 73, 76, 78, 80
five aggregates (skandhas), 128, 130, 137
Five-Bushels-of-Rice, Cult of, 90
Fleet, J.F., 69
Form, School of (Yu-hsiang-tsung), 3
Fortuitism, 148
four formless dhyānas, 125
Fu Chien, 105
Fu-nan, 79, 80, 81
Fu-ta-shêng-to (Buddhaśānta), 2
Fu Tu-têng, 87

garbhadhātu, 230
Geiger, Wilhelm, 69, 75, 80
Giles, L., 36
God of Plague (Wên-shên), 187, 188
God of the Stove (Chao-wang), 182
Goddess of smallpox (Tou-chên liang-liang), 187
Gunabhadra, 225
Guṇavarman, 221, 222, 223, 224, 233

Han-kuang, 201
Hīnayāna, 12, 25, 79, 102, 118, 139, 152, 225,
    228, 231, 233;
    practices of, 56
homa, 110
Hou Chi, 146

śabdavidyā, 232
Sakadāgāmin fruition, 221
Samādhi, 5, 46, 49;
    vajra-samādhi, 49
Samādhi and Prajñā, School of (Ting-hui-tsung), 3
Samantabhadra Ācārya, 201, 230
sambhogakāya (body of enjoyment), 139
sammitīya, sect, 233
saṁsāra, 122, 132
saṅgha, 26, 89, 92, 93, 94, 199, 201, 220, 222, 227;
    bhiksu, 199, 223;
    bhiksuni, 199, 200, 223
Saṅghabhadra (Sêng-ga-pa-t'o-lo), 70, 71, 72, 74,
    77, 78, 79, 81
Saṅghabhūti, 103
Saṅghamitra, 199
Saṅghapāla, 225, 226, 233
Saṅghavarman, 199
Sarvāstivādin School, 218, 221
sea route, 214, 215, 216, 217, 220, 231, 232
Sekiguchi, Shindai J., 11, 12
self, 44, 119, 120, 121, 175
Sêng-chao, 27
Sêng-fu, 8, 15
Sêng-ts'an, 16
Sêng-wei, 70, 72
Sêng-yu, 70, 73, 74, 78
Seven Elements, Doctrine of, 123
Shang-ti, 133, 146
Shao Ong, 88
shên (spirit or soul), 140, 141
Shên-hsiu, 27
Shih-ch'ao-nan-t'o (Siksānanda), 134
Shih-tsung, Emperor of the Later Chou dynasty, 89
Shun, 90
Shu-tsung, Emperor, 231
Siggava, 72, 76
śīla, 5
Śilamegha, King of Ceylon, 201, 230
Silence, School of (Chi-ching-tsung), 3
silk route, 213
Simha Bhiksu, 6, 7
skandhas, 38, 128
Smith, V.A., 69
Sonaka, 72, 76

unrecorded (neutral) mind (wu-chi), 47
Upāli, 71, 72, 76, 78
Upaniṣads, 141
upasampadā ordination, 223, 224

Vaccha, 127
Vaipulya Mahāyāna, 225
Vajiriya Vāda (Vajrayāna), 201, 202
Vajrabodhi, 200, 229, 230
vajradhātu, 230
Vasubandhu, 6, 227
Vattagāmini Abhaya, 103
Vedas, 139
Vedic literature, 119
Vijaya Bāhu VI (Alagakikonāra), 203, 205
Vinaya Practice, school of (Chiai-hsing-tsung), 3

Wang Fou, 61, 65
Wang Hsi-fêng, 183, 184, 185
Wang Mang, 214
Wei Po-yang, 90
Wên, King, 132, 133, 146
Western Paradise (pure land), 138
What-belongs-to-me, conception of, 41, 42, 44,
    46, 49
Wu, Emperor of the Liang dynasty, 2, 4, 7, 134,
    144
Wu-ti, Emperor of the Ch'i dynasty, 71
Wu-ti, Emperor of the Han dynasty, 213
Wu-ti, Emperor of Liang, 79, 226
Wu-ti, Emperor of the northern Chou dynasty, 14,
    89
Wu-ti, Emperor of the Sung dynasty, 223
Wu-ti, Emperor of the Tsin dynasty, 79
Wu-tsung, Emperor of the T'ang dynasty, 89
Wu-wang, King of the Chou dynasty, 62, 65

Yama (Yen-lo-wang), 185
Yang, 140
Yang Hsüan-chih, 1
Yang T'ai-chên, 178
Yao, 90

About the Author

Dr. W. Pachow is Professor of Asian Religions
and Buddhist Studies at The University of Iowa
School of Religion. Prior to his appointment there
in 1968, he studied in China and India, and taught
at the Visva-Bharati University, Santiniketan, the
University of Allahabad, India, and the University
of Ceylon, Peradeniya.

Being keenly interested in the Chinese
literary manuscripts from the Tun-huang caves, he
examined them on several occasions in London and
Paris. Consequently he published two works in
this area: An Anthology of Poetical Compositions
from Tun-huang, and A Study of the Twenty-Two
Dialogues on Mahāyāna Buddhism.

He is a contributor to Encyclopaedia
Britannica, Encyclopaedia of Buddhism, Dictionary
of Ming Biography, Abingdon Dictionary of Living
Religions, and many learned journals in Asia and
America. He has eight books and over forty
articles to his credit.

Professor Pachow has travelled extensively in
Asia and in Europe, and has visited many important
cultural centers in the United States.